Testing and Tuning Market Trading Systems

Algorithms in C++

Timothy Masters

Apress®

Testing and Tuning Market Trading Systems: Algorithms in C++

Timothy Masters
Ithaca, NY, USA

ISBN-13 (pbk): 978-1-4842-4172-1 ISBN-13 (electronic): 978-1-4842-4173-8
https://doi.org/10.1007/978-1-4842-4173-8

Library of Congress Control Number: 2018961186

Managing Director, Apress Media LLC: Welmoed Spahr
Acquisitions Editor: Steve Anglin
Development Editor: Matthew Moodie
Coordinating Editor: Mark Powers

Cover designed by eStudioCalamar

Distributed to the book trade worldwide by Springer Science+Business Media New York, 233 Spring Street, 6th Floor, New York, NY 10013. Phone 1-800-SPRINGER, fax (201) 348-4505, e-mail orders-ny@springer-sbm.com, or visit www.springeronline.com. Apress Media, LLC is a California LLC and the sole member (owner) is Springer Science + Business Media Finance Inc (SSBM Finance Inc). SSBM Finance Inc is a **Delaware** corporation.

For information on translations, please e-mail editorial@apress.com; for reprint, paperback, or audio rights, please email bookpermissions@springernature.com.

Apress titles may be purchased in bulk for academic, corporate, or promotional use. eBook versions and licenses are also available for most titles. For more information, reference our Print and eBook Bulk Sales web page at www.apress.com/bulk-sales.

Any source code or other supplementary material referenced by the author in this book is available to readers on GitHub via the book's product page, located at www.apress.com/9781484241721. For more detailed information, please visit www.apress.com/source-code.

Printed on acid-free paper

Table of Contents

About the Author

Timothy Masters received a PhD in mathematical statistics with a specialization in numerical computing. Since then he has continuously worked as an independent consultant for government and industry. His early research involved automated feature detection in high-altitude photographs while he developed applications for the prediction of floods and droughts, the detection of hidden missile silos, and the identification of threatening military vehicles. Later he worked with medical researchers in the development of computer algorithms for distinguishing between benign and malignant cells in needle biopsies. For the last 20 years he has focused primarily on methods for evaluating automated financial market trading systems. He has authored the following books on practical applications of predictive modeling: *Deep Belief Nets in C++ and CUDA C: Volumes 1–3* (Apress, 2018); *Assessing and Improving Prediction and Classification* (Apress, 2018), *Data Mining Algorithms in C++* (Apress, 2018); *Neural, Novel, and Hybrid Algorithms for Time Series Prediction* (Wiley, 1995); *Advanced Algorithms for Neural Networks* (Wiley, 1995); *Signal and Image Processing with Neural Networks* (Wiley, 1994); and *Practical Neural Network Recipes in C++* (Academic Press, 1993).

About the Technical Reviewer

 **Jason Whitehorn** is an experienced entrepreneur and software developer and has helped many oil and gas companies automate and enhance their oilfield solutions through field data capture, SCADA, and machine learning. Jason obtained his BS in computer science from Arkansas State University, but he traces his passion for development back many years before then, having first taught himself to program BASIC on his family's computer while still in middle school.

When he's not mentoring and helping his team at work, writing, or pursuing one of his many side projects, Jason enjoys spending time with his wife and four children and living in the Tulsa, Oklahoma, region. You can learn more about Jason at `https://jason.whitehorn.us`.

CHAPTER 1

Introduction

Before we delve into the meat (or tofu, if you prefer) of this book, we should be clear on what you will and will not find here, as well as what degree of preparation is expected of readers.

The Target Audience, and Overview of Contents

This book is intended for readers who have a modest statistics background (Statistics 101 is plenty), have some programming skill in any language (C++ with a strong bent toward traditional C is used in the examples here), and are interested in trading financial markets with a degree of mathematical rigor far beyond that of most traders. Here you will find a useful collection of algorithms, including sample code, that will help you tweak your ideas into trading systems that have above-average likelihood of profitability. But there are many things that you will *not* find in this book. We begin with an overview of the material included in this book.

What's in This Book

The following topics are covered in this book:

- If your system involves optimization of parameters, and most do, you will learn how to determine whether your optimized system has captured authentic market patterns or whether it has simply learned random noise patterns that will never again appear.

- You will learn how to modify linear regression in a way that makes it even less susceptible to overfitting than it already is and that, as a bonus, separates predictors into those that are valuable and those that are worthless. You will also learn how to modify linear regression to enable its use in moderately nonlinear situations.

1

T. Masters, *Testing and Tuning Market Trading Systems*, https://doi.org/10.1007/978-1-4842-4173-8_1

- You will discover an extremely general and powerful nonlinear optimization algorithm that is applicable to both predictive-model-based trading systems and traditional algorithmic systems.

- All trading systems assume a degree of consistency in the market being traded; if the pattern on which your system is based has occurred regularly over recent history, we must assume that this same pattern will continue into at least the near future. Some trading systems are robust against moderate changes in market patterns, while other systems are rendered worthless by even tiny changes in market patterns. You will learn how to assess the degree to which your system is robust against such changes.

- If you have designed your own proprietary indicators, you will learn how to confirm that they are reasonably stationary (a critical property for any effective indicator) or massage them into stationarity if they are not. You will also learn how to compute them so as to maximize their information content, minimize their noise, and supply them to your trading system in an effective, efficient manner so as to maximize their utility.

- Most trading system developers are familiar with walkforward testing. But not so many are aware that ordinary walkforward algorithms are often insufficient for the correct validation of trading system candidates and can produce dangerously optimistic results for subtle reasons. You will learn how to embed one walkforward algorithm inside a second layer of walkforward analysis or perhaps embed a layer of cross validation inside a walkforward analysis. This "validation-within-validation" scenario is often not only the best way to test a trading system but the only truly correct way.

- You will learn how estimate the range of possible future profits that your system can be expected to produce. If you discover that your system has almost certain future profitability but there is a high probability that this profit will be small relative to the risk incurred, you will know that your system is not yet ready to be traded.

- You will learn how to estimate the probability of catastrophic drawdown, even when your system is operating "correctly."

- You will learn about rigorous statistical testing algorithms that are resistant to the occasional large wins and losses that invalidate many "traditional" validation algorithms.

- Many trading system developers prefer to use the "spaghetti-on-the-wall" approach to trading system development. Although frequently scorned, this is actually a legitimate approach, as long as it is done intelligently. You will learn how to determine whether the "best" of numerous competing systems is truly worthwhile.

What's Not in This Book

The following topics are not covered in this book:

- This book is not an "Introduction to Statistics for Market Traders" type of book. It is assumed that the reader is already familiar with concepts such as mean and standard deviation, normal distribution, p-values from hypothesis tests, and so forth. Nothing more advanced than these concepts is required; the advanced statistical techniques presented here are built up from basic ideas that anyone who's passed Statistics 101 or even a good statistics for psychology course can handle. But if you have no idea what a standard deviation is, you will find this book rough going.

- This is also not an "Introduction to Trading Financial Markets" book. It is assumed that you know the meaning of terms such as *opening* and *closing* a trade, *long* and *short* positions, and *mean return per trade*. If you are totally new to trading financial markets, you need to study background material before tackling this book.

- You will find little or nothing in the way of actual, proven trading systems here. Those are a dime a dozen and usually worth the price. But if you have your own idea for a trading system, you will learn how to implement, test, and tweak it so as to maximize its profit potential.

- You will find no top-secret super-duper surefire indicators in this book. The few indicators presented are either common sense or widely available in the public domain. But if you have your own ideas for indicators, you will learn how to maximize their utility.

About Trading Systems

As different testing procedures are presented in this text, they will necessarily be demonstrated in the context of various trading systems. Please note the following items of interest:

- I am not endorsing any of these systems as money-makers. Rather, I am keeping the systems as simple as possible so that the focus can be on their testing, not on their practical utility. This book assumes that the reader has his or her own ideas for trading systems; the goal here is to provide advanced statistical methods for tweaking and rigorously testing existing systems.

- All the trading systems used for demonstrations assume that we are working with day bars, but this is never a requirement. Bars can be any length, from a fraction of a second to months. In fact, most demonstrations use only the open or close of each bar, so applying these algorithms to trading tick data is feasible as well. Days bars are simply most convenient, and test data is most readily available as day bars.

- Most of the demonstration systems open and close trades on the close of a bar. Naturally, in real life this is difficult or impossible; a more fair and conservative approach is to make a trade decision on the close of a bar and open or close the trade at the open of the next bar. But that would add needless confusion to the algorithms shown here. Remember, our goal is to present statistical algorithms in the most straightforward context, keeping the spotlight on the statistical test. In most cases, small modifications to the implementation do not materially change the results of rigorous statistical tests.

- In these tests, trade costs (slippage and commissions) are deliberately omitted, again to keep the focus on the statistical test without added confusion. The supplied code and accompanying description make clear how trade cost can be incorporated into the computation if desired.

Market Prices and Returns

Most equity markets cover a wide range of prices, perhaps beginning their life trading at a few dollars a share and trading today at hundreds or thousands of dollars a share after split adjustment. When we compute the return of a trade, we don't dare just subtract prices at the open and close of a trade. A $1 move from $1 to $2 is enormous, while a move from $150 to $151 is almost trivial. Thus, many people compute percent moves, dividing the price change by the starting price and multiplying by 100. This solves the scale problem, and it is intuitive. Unfortunately, it has a problem that makes it a poor method in many statistical analyses.

The problem with percent moves is that they are not symmetric. If we make 10 percent on a trade and then lose 10 percent on the next trade, we are not back where we started. If we score a move from 100 to 110 but then lose 10 percent of 110, we are at 99. This might not seem serious, but if we look at it from a different direction, we see why it can be a major problem. Suppose we have a long trade in which the market moves from 100 to 110, and our next trade moves back from 110 to 100. Our net equity change is zero. Yet we have recorded a gain of 10 percent, followed by a loss of 9.1 percent, for a net gain of almost 1 percent! If we are recording a string of trade returns for statistical analysis, these errors will add up fast, with the result that a completely worthless trading system can show an impressive net gain! This will invalidate almost any performance test.

There is a simple solution that is used by professional developers and that I will use throughout this book: convert all prices to the log of the price and compute trade returns as the difference of these logs. This solves all of the problems. For example, a trade that captures a market move from 10 to 11 is 2.39789–2.30258=0.09531, and a trade that scores a move from 100 to 110 is 4.70048–4.60517=0.09531. If a trade moves us back from 110 to 100, we lose 0.09531 for a net gain of zero. Perfect.

A nice side benefit of this method is that smallish log price changes, times 100, are nearly equal to the percent change. For example, moving from 100 to 101, a 1 percent change, compares to 100*(4.61512–4.605)=0.995. Even the 10 percent move mentioned earlier maps to 9.531 percent. For this reason, we will treat returns computed from logs as approximate percent returns.

Two Types of Automated Trading Systems

Originally, all forms of automated market trading were what might be called *algorithmic* or *rule-based*. The system developer comes up with a set of rigorously defined rules that guided the opening and closing of positions. The rules might state that if some combination of conditions becomes true, one would open a long position and hold that position until some other combination of conditions becomes true. One classic chestnut of algorithmic trading is a moving-average crossover system. One computes short-term and long-term moving averages, takes a long position if the short-term MA is above the long-term MA, and takes a short position otherwise. Training this primitive trading system is performed by finding the short-term and long-term lookbacks that provide optimal performance on a historical dataset. Algorithmic systems, many involving dozens of conditions, are still in widespread use today.

In more recent times, many developers (including myself) have formed the opinion that *model-based* systems are more powerful, despite their common disadvantage that they frequently involve blind trust in black boxes whose inner workings are largely unfathomable. In model-based automated trading we compute one or more (usually many more) *indicators* that are variables that look backward in time and measure market characteristics. These might include trend, volatility, short-term cyclic behavior, and so forth. We also compute a *target* variable that looks into the future and describes near-term market behavior. Targets might be things such as the size and direction of market movement over the next bar or few bars. A target might also be a binary flag that tells us whether the market first touches a predefined profit goal before touching a protective stop. We then train a predictive model to estimate the value of the target variable, given the values of the indicator variables. To trade this system, we present the trained model with current values of the indicators and consider the model's prediction. If the prediction is strong enough (indicating confidence), we take a market position in accord with the predicted move.

The advantage of model-based trading over rule-based algorithmic trading is that we can take advantage of the many recent developments in the field of artificial intelligence, letting sophisticated programs running on powerful computers discover trading systems that are perhaps so complex or obscure that no human could possibly hope to discover and program in explicit rules. Of course, this comes at a high price: we often have no idea exactly what "rules" the model has discovered, and we must accept the model's decisions on blind faith.

Because both styles of trading system development are in widespread use today, this text will cater to both schools of thought. Unavoidably, there are a few statistical tests presented here that are applicable to only one or the other. But an attempt is always made to design testing procedures that can be used by practitioners in either style.

The Agony of Believing the Computer

For many people, especially seasoned seat-of-the-pants traders, the most difficult part of moving toward automated trading is accepting the trade decisions of a computer when they conflict with their gut, not to mention their many years of successful trading. I'll give one specific example from my own personal experience. I had developed on contract a short-term intraday trading system. My extremely thorough, rigorous statistical testing of the system showed unequivocally that its profits were maximized when it was operated by taking numerous small profits while running the risk of occasional large losses (a very loose protective stop). This grated on the trader responsible for calling signaled trades onto the floor. He constantly bombarded me with his mantra of "Cut your losses and let your wins run." That's a truism for some trading styles but not for this particular system. He couldn't help himself; he kept overruling the computer's trade decisions. The system would call for a winning trade to be closed, but he would keep it open, hoping for an even larger gain. Or the market would move against an open position, and he would close it out for a small loss long before the system's stop was hit. He kept telling me how much money would have been lost if he had let it keep sliding instead of cutting the loss early. The fact that the computer simulation that ran in parallel made a lot of money, while his modified version made much less, had no impact on his opinion. He'd been a successful discretionary trader for many years, he knew how to trade, and no #$%^ computer was going to tell him otherwise. Our relationship never succeeded. The moral of the story: forget automated trading if you don't have the guts to believe in it.

Future Leak Is More Dangerous Than You May Think

Future leak is the illegal leakage of future knowledge into a testing procedure. It happens in the development and testing of a trading system when some aspect of future market behavior finds its way into a simulation of how a trading system will perform in real life. Since we will obviously not know the future when we are trading our system, this leakage results in optimistic performance estimates.

More than once I have been amazed at how casually otherwise serious system developers take this form of cheating. I have had intelligent, educated developers patiently explain to me that yes, they do understand that some small degree of future knowledge took part in their performance simulation. But then they go to great pains to explain how this "unavoidable" leakage is so tiny that it is insignificant and could not possibly impact their results to any material degree. Little do they know. This is why a recurring focus of this text is methods for avoiding even the tiniest touch of future leak. In my early years of system development, I was often amazed at how subtle this leakage can be.

Just to pound the point home, Figure 1-1 shows the equity curve of a nearly random Win1/Lose 1 trading system with just a 1 percent winning edge. This curve, which would be on average flat if it were truly random (worthless), is quite respectable from just this tiny edge. Future leak is far deadlier than you imagine. Take it seriously.

Figure 1-1. *Equity curve of random system with 1 percent edge*

The Percent Wins Fallacy

There is a simple mathematical formula, essential to trading system development and evaluation, that seems to be difficult for many people to accept on a gut level, even if they understand it intellectually. See Equation 1-1.

$$ExpectedReturn = Win * P(Win) - Loss * P(Loss) \qquad (1\text{-}1)$$

This formula says that the expect return on a trade (the return that we would obtain on average, if this situation were repeated many times) equals the amount we would win times the probability of winning minus the amount that we would lose times the probability that we will lose.

It's easy to accept that if we flip a fair coin, winning a dollar if we get heads and losing a dollar if we get tails, our expected return is zero; if we were to repeat the coin toss many times, over the long term our average return per coin toss is zero. It's also easy to accept that if the coin is fair and we win two dollars but lose only one dollar, we are in an enviable position.

Now think about trading a market that is a true random walk; among other properties, the changes from one bar to the next are all independent of one another and have zero mean. It is impossible to develop a trading system that has anything other than zero expectation (ignoring transaction costs, of course). But we can easily shift the expected size of wins and losses, as well as their frequencies.

For example, suppose we open a long position and set a profit target 1 point above the entry price and set a stop loss exit 9 points below the entry. Every time we experience a loss, it will be painfully large, 9 times what we win. But if we execute a large number of such trades on our hypothetical random market, we will find that we win 9 times more often than we lose. We win 9/10 of the time. By Equation 1-1, our expected return per trade is still zero. The takeaway here is that win/loss sizes and probabilities are inextricably related. If someone brags about how often their trading system wins, ask them about the size of their wins and losses. And if they brag about how huge their wins are compared to their losses, ask them how often they win. Neither exists in isolation.

CHAPTER 2

Pre-optimization Issues

Assessing and Improving Stationarity

In essence, the *stationarity* of a time series (such as market price changes, indicators, or individual trade returns) refers to the degree to which its statistical properties remain constant over time. Statisticians may cringe at such a loose definition, but that captures the practical meaning of the term. When we use market history to create a (preferably) profitable trading system, we are implicitly counting on the historical patterns that produced backtesting profitability to remain in force for at least the near-term future. If we are not willing to make that assumption, we might as well give up trading system design.

There are many aspects of this concept that are particularly relevant to automated trading of financial markets.

- Markets, and hence indicators and trade returns derived from market history, are inherently nonstationary. Their properties change constantly. The only questions are these: How bad is it? Can we deal with it? *Can we fix things to make it better?*

- There is no point in performing any rigorous traditional statistical tests for nonstationarity. Virtually any test we perform will indicate very statistically significant nonstationarity, so we need not bother; we know the answer already.

- Nonstationarity can take an infinite number of forms. Perhaps the variance is quite constant over time, while the mean wanders. Or vice versa. Or skewness may change. Or...

11

T. Masters, *Testing and Tuning Market Trading Systems*, https://doi.org/10.1007/978-1-4842-4173-8_2

- Some types of nonstationarity may be harmless to us, while others may be devastating to our trading system. One trading system may have a weakness for one type of nonstationarity, while another trading system may be hobbled by something different. As much as possible, we must consider the context when we evaluate stationarity.

- The best way to evaluate the ruggedness of a *finished* trading system is to use the progressive walkforward algorithm given on page 142.

But we are going to ignore that last point here. This chapter is dedicated to issues that we should consider *before* progressing too far into the development of a trading system. Progressive walkforward comes at the end of development, one of several final validation procedures.

Traditional statistical tests for nonstationarity are ruled out, so what should you do? You absolutely *must* carefully study plots of your indicators. You may be amazed at what you see. Their central tendency may slowly wander up and down, rendering predictive models useless at one or both extremes. Day-to-day wandering is normal, but slow wandering, or slow changes in variance, is a serious problem. If an indicator spends months or even years out in left field before returning to more "normal" behavior, a model may shut down or make false predictions for these extended periods of time. We must be on guard against this disastrous situation that can easily arise if we are not careful.

Sometimes we may not have indicators to plot. The STATN program shown in the next section is a valuable alternative. But it is important to understand the underlying problem with nonstationarity. It is extremely difficult to design an automated trading system that works consistently well year after year with no tweaking or even a complete redesign. Markets always change. The trap we can easily fall into is to design a system that appears to perform well in a backtest but whose encouraging performance is solely because of outstanding performance over a favorable segment of our backtest history. Thus, we *must* study the equity curve of our system. If it shows excellent performance for just a fraction of the time and mediocre performance elsewhere, we should ponder the situation carefully. And of course this is especially true if the excellent performance was some time ago and recent performance has deteriorated!

The key point is that when we develop a trading system under some market condition, we can expect continued good performance only as long as that market condition continues. Therefore, *we hope that market conditions change often enough during our development and testing period so that all possible market conditions are represented.*

And even if all conditions are represented, slow wandering may cause periodic extended adverse performance. Long periods of great performance, followed by long periods of poor performance, can be discouraging.

The STATN Program

For those of us who crave hard numbers, something more solid than arbitrary decisions based on eyeballing a plot, there is a good test. I have provided a sample of this algorithm in the program STATN.CPP. This version reads a market history file and checks the trend and volatility of the market across time. You can easily modify it by adding other market properties such as ADX or any custom indicators that you employ.

The principle of this program is simple yet surprisingly revealing of market anomalies. It's based on the idea that trading systems developed under certain market conditions (such as up or down trend, high or low volatility) will likely lose their profitability under other market conditions. In most situations we want to see these conditions as reflected in our indicators vary on a regular and reasonably random basis so that our developed system will have experienced as much as possible the full variety of conditions that it will encounter when put to use. Slow wandering is the essence of dangerous nonstationarity; market properties may remain in one state for an extended period and then change to a different state for another extended period, similarly impacting our indicators. This makes developing robust models difficult. Roughly speaking, stationarity equals consistency in behavior.

The program is invoked with the following command:

STATN Lookback Fractile Version Filename

Let's break this command down:

- Lookback: The number of historical bars, including the current bar, used to compute the trend and volatility of the market.

- Fractile: The fractile (0–1) of trend and volatility that serves as the above/below threshold for gap analysis.

- Version: 0 for raw indicators, 1 for differenced raw indicators, >1 for specified raw minus extended raw. See page 14 for details.

- Filename: A market history file in the format YYYYMMDD Open High Low Close.

An example using real market data will appear on page 17. First, we explore a few code snippets. See STATN.CPP for the full context.

The program passes through the market history, computing a measure of trend (the slope of the least-squares line) and volatility (average true range). It finds the quantile corresponding to the specified fractile; 0.5 would be the median. For each bar, it decides whether the current values of trend and volatility (or their modified values, as described soon) are less than the quantile versus greater than or equal to the quantile. Every time the state changes (from above to below or from below to above) it notes how many bars have passed and keeps a tally. For example, if the state changes on the next bar, the count is one. If the state changes one bar after the next bar, the count is two, and so forth. Eleven bins are defined, for bar counts of 1, 2, 4, 8, 16, 32, 64, 128, 256, 512, and greater than 512. When the program ends, it prints the bin counts, one table for the trend and one for the volatility.

The Version parameter needs a little more explanation, the justification for which will be deferred to the next section. For now, understand that if the user specifies it as 0, the trend and volatility indicators are used exactly as calculated. If it is 1, the current value of each indicator is adjusted by subtracting its value lookback bars ago, making it a classic oscillator. If it is greater than 1, the current value is adjusted by subtracting the value using a lookback of Version * Lookback, making it another sort of oscillator. These latter two versions require an actual lookback greater than the user-specified lookback, as shown in this code:

```
if (version == 0)
    full_lookback = lookback ;
else if (version == 1)
    full_lookback = 2 * lookback ;
else if (version > 1)
    full_lookback = version * lookback ;

nind = nprices - full_lookback + 1 ;   // This many indicators
```

If nprices is the number of price bars, we lose full_lookback–1 of them, getting nind values of the indicators, as shown in the last line of the previous code.

The following code block shows computation of the (possibly modified) indicators for trend. That for volatility is similar. For each pass, k is the index of the current value of the indicator. We have to begin far enough into the indicator history to encompass the full lookback.

14

```
for (i=0 ; i<nind ; i++) {
  k = full_lookback - 1 + i ;
  if (version == 0)
    trend[i] = find_slope ( lookback , close + k ) ;
  else if (version == 1)
    trend[i] = find_slope ( lookback , close + k ) –
              find_slope ( lookback , close + k - lookback ) ;
  else
    trend[i] = find_slope ( lookback , close + k ) –
              find_slope ( full_lookback , close + k ) ;
  trend_sorted[i] = trend[i] ;
  }
```

Sort the values to find the user-specified quantile and then tally the counts in each bin.

```
qsortd ( 0 , nind-1 , trend_sorted ) ;
k = (int) (fractile * (nind+1)) - 1 ;
if (k < 0)
  k = 0 ;
trend_quantile = trend_sorted[k] ;

gap_analyze ( nind , trend , trend_quantile , ngaps , gap_size , gap_count ) ;
```

Prior to calling gap_analyze(), we must do some preparation by providing it with the boundaries for the gap sizes. Feel free to change them if you want. The analysis code appears on the next page.

```
#define NGAPS 11      /* Number of gaps in analysis */

ngaps = NGAPS ;
k = 1 ;
for (i=0 ; i<ngaps-1 ; i++) {
  gap_size[i] = k ;
  k *= 2 ;
  }
```

This routine just keeps a flag, above_below, which is *True* (1) if the current value is at or above the threshold, and *False* (0) if below. For each pass through the loop, if the indicator is still on the same side of the threshold, the counter is incremented. If it switches sides, the appropriate bin is incremented, and the counter is reset. Reaching the end of the array is tantamount to flipping sides, so the last series is counted.

```
void gap_analyze (
  int n ,
  double *x ,
  double thresh ,
  int ngaps ,
  int *gap_size ,
  int *gap_count
  )
{
  int i, j, above_below, new_above_below, count ;

  for (i=0 ; i<ngaps ; i++)
    gap_count[i] = 0 ;
  count = 1 ;
  above_below = (x[0] >= thresh) ? 1 : 0 ;

  for (i=1 ; i<=n ; i++) {
    if (i == n) // Passing end of array counts as a change
      new_above_below = 1 - above_below ;
    else
      new_above_below = (x[i] >= thresh) ? 1 : 0 ;

    if (new_above_below == above_below)
      ++count ;
    else {
      for (j=0 ; j<ngaps-1 ; j++) {
        if (count <= gap_size[j])
          break ;
        }
```

```
    ++gap_count[j] ;
    count = 1 ;
    above_below = new_above_below ;
    }
   }
}
```

Improving Location Stationarity by Oscillating

A simple yet usually effective way to improve the stationarity of an indicator, at least as far as its central tendency is concerned, is to compute its value *relative to* some related "basis" value. The most common and usually most effective method is to subtract a lagged value, with the lag often (though not necessarily) being the lookback of the indicator. For example, we might compute the trend of the most recent 20 prices and subtract from this the value of this indicator 20 bars ago.

A similar but far from identical method is to compute the indicator at the current time but for two different lookbacks, one short and one long. Subtract the long-term indicator from the short-term indicator to get a more stationary modified indicator.

Both of these methods do involve a significant trade-off. It may be that the actual value of the indicator is what carries the important information. The two modifications just described discard the actual value in favor of a relative value. In my experience, this latter value usually carries *more* predictive information than the actual value, and it certainly has better stationarity in nearly all situations. But this is not universal, and this trade-off must be kept in mind.

If this trade-off is a concern, bear in mind that the first method, finding the difference between the current value and the lagged value of an indicator, is the most "powerful" in the sense that it usually induces the most stationarity while also discarding the most information about the true current value. The second method is more of a compromise. Moreover, by adjusting the long-term lookback, one can exert a great deal of control over that trade-off. Increasing the long-term lookback results in greater preservation of information about the current value, at the cost of less improvement in stationarity.

On the next page we see two tables produced by the STATN program with a lookback of 100 and a fractile of 0.5 (the median) for the S&P 100 index OEX. The top table is for trend, and the bottom is volatility. The first column is the raw indicator; the second is Version=1, the lagged difference; and the third is Version=3, giving a long-term lookback of 300 bars.

Trend with Lookback=100, Fractile=0.5

Gap	Version=0	Version=1	Version=3
1	3	1	0
2	3	1	0
4	2	2	2
8	5	2	1
16	4	3	4
32	14	2	12
64	22	14	25
128	29	54	33
256	18	15	21
512	3	1	1
>512	0	0	0

Volatility with Lookback=100, Fractile=0.5

Gap	Version=0	Version=1	Version=3
1	13	41	19
2	6	13	6
4	2	9	13
8	2	8	6
16	4	9	4
32	2	10	10
64	3	12	8
128	5	25	10
256	9	23	18
512	2	5	9
>512	6	0	1

In this *Trend* table, we see that the raw indicator has three long time periods in which the indicator remains on the same side of its median. These periods are greater than 256 consecutive bars, perhaps as long as 512 bars, over two years! The two modified versions have only one such period.

The situation is even more profound for volatility, with the raw indicator having six time periods greater than 512 bars with the volatility on the same side of its median. Modification greatly improves this situation, although with significant deterioration at the next lower level. Volatility generally has extreme nonstationarity.

Extreme Stationarity Induction

The two methods just described induce stationarity in only the central tendency of an indicator. This is important, arguably the most important quality of stationarity. If an indicator slowly wanders, staying at high values for an extended period of time and then moving to low values for long periods of time, this indicator will likely have impaired utility in a trading system. Systems based on such indicators will have a strong tendency to lose profitability, or even stop trading, for long periods of time. Of course, trade stoppage can be useful in some situations; if you have several complementary systems, it's wonderful if each alternates between trading profitably and not trading at all. Unfortunately, in real life such systems are very much the exception, not the rule.

But there are an infinite number of ways in which an indicator can be nonstationary. Central tendency (the mean) is usually the most important, and the second-most important is usually variance. If an indicator has little variation for a long period of time and then has large variation over a subsequent long period of time, this indicator will be impaired.

There is an easy way to induce stationarity in the mean, the variance, or both to an extreme but controllable degree. Simply look back at a moving window of recent values of the indicator and compute the mean (if the indicator is well behaved) or the median (if it has occasional extreme values) over this window. Subtract this from the current value to induce stationarity in the central tendency. If the window is short, the effect will be pronounced, enough to overcome nearly any degree of nonstationarity. Similarly, you can compute the standard deviation (if the indicator is well behaved) or the interquartile range (if wild values happen) over the moving window. Divide the (possible centered) current value by this quantity to induce stationarity in the variance.

No examples of this method are provided because it is a straightforward computation. Just remember that a long window will preserve a lot of information about the actual value of the indicator while providing little nonstationarity reduction. Conversely, a short window will destroy nearly all information about the actual value, making everything relative to recent history, thereby inducing tremendous stationarity.

Measuring Indicator Information with Entropy

Decades ago, Claude Shannon of Bell Labs developed a rigorous and extremely powerful approach to quantifying the amount of information that can be communicated by a message. This is relevant to trading system development, because indicators computed from recent market history can be thought of as messages from the market that convey information about the current and possible future state of the market. If we can quantify the average information in an indicator, we can get an idea of the potential value of that indicator. Even better, we can modify the indicator in ways that increase its information content. And not coincidentally, it turns out that these information-increasing modifications are exactly the same sort of modifications that are well known to improve the performance of predictive models. This is a worthy area of study.

We will take a superficial, intuitive approach to the topic of quantifying average information in an indicator. For a more detailed yet still accessible exploration of the topic, see either of my books *Data Mining Algorithms in C++* or *Assessing and Improving Prediction and Classification.*

Suppose a piece of information needs to be conveyed, and this information is the answer to a multiple-choice question. Perhaps it is a simple binary choice, such as "the market is in an upward trending state" versus "the market is in a downward trending state." Perhaps it is a bit more detailed, such as a four-possibility situation: "the market is in a strongly upward/weakly upward/weakly downward/strongly downward" state. Now add the restriction that the message must be binary, a string of one or more ones and zeros. Clearly, the answer to the first question can be given as a single binary bit, while the answer to the second question will require two bits to cover the four possible market states (00, 01, 10, 11). In general, if there are K possible answers, then we will need $\log_2(K)$ bits in the message to convey the correct answer.

A good way to quantify the value of a message is the number of bits of information that it conveys. A slightly less clear but more useful way of assigning a value to a message is the number of bits of uncertainty that are removed by receipt of the message. Suppose you enter a lottery that has a total of 1,024 tickets, one of which is yours. The identity of the winner can be encoded in $\log_2(1024)=10$ bits. Before you receive any message, you have 10 bits of uncertainty about the identity of the winner. Equivalently, each entry has a 1/1024 chance of being the winner.

A message is received that answers a simple question: you did or did not win the lottery. Let's compute the value of each of these two possible answers. If the answer is that you won the lottery, an event with probability 1/1024 has been resolved, giving that particular message a value of $\log_2(1024) = -\log_2(1/1024) = 10$ bits. If the answer is that you did not win, an event with probability 1023/1024 has been resolved, giving that particular message a value of $-\log_2(1023/1024) = 0.0014$ bits.

Most people (and computers) do not work with logs in base 2. Rather, they use natural logarithms. When this is done, the unit of information is the *nat* rather than the bit. So, in the example under discussion, the value of a *You won* answer is $-\log(1/1024) = 6.93$ nats, and the value of the disappointing answer is $-\log(1023/1024) = 0.00098$ nats.

We just computed the value of each individual answer. But we are also interested in the expected value of the message. Recall that the expected value of a discrete random variable is the sum of the products of each individual value times the probability of that value. So, the expected value of the message is the probability of a *You won* answer times its value, plus the probability of a *You did not win* answer times its value. This is $1/1024 * -\log(1/1024) + 1023/1024 * -\log(1023/1024) = 0.0077$ nats. This expected value is called the *entropy* of the message and is symbolized as H.

We can be more rigorous. Let χ be a set that enumerates every possible answer in a message stream X. Thus, χ may be {*Large up trend, Small up trend, Small down trend, Large down trend*}, for example. When we observe a value of X, we call it x, which by definition is always a member of χ. This is written as $x \in \chi$. Let $p(x)$ be the probability that x is observed. Then the entropy of X is given by Equation 2-1. In this equation, $0*\log(0)$ is defined to be zero.

$$H(X) = -\sum_{x \in \chi} p(x)\log\big(p(x)\big)$$

$(2\text{-}1)$

We state without proof that the entropy (average information content) of a message stream X is maximized when every possible answer (value of x) has equal probability, and this maximum entropy is $\log(K)$, where K is the number of possible values of x. Thus, we will be most interested in the value of $H(X)/\log(K)$ because this number will range from zero (the message stream conveys no information at all) to one (the message stream conveys the maximum possible amount of information). This ratio is called the *relative entropy* or the *proportional entropy*.

At last we can relate all this (highly abbreviated and simplified) theory to automated market trading. What we want to do is screen any indicators used in our trading system for their relative entropy. If the relative entropy turns out to be small, we should consider computing the indicator differently, perhaps taking an approach as simple as applying a nonlinear transformation to increase the relative entropy. In my own work,

I like for the relative entropy to be at least 0.5, and preferably more, although this threshold is highly arbitrary.

There are several caveats to keep in mind. First, understand that entropy is a measure of information content, but we don't know whether this information is relevant to the task at hand. An indicator may do a phenomenal job at predicting whether the market volatility will explode in the upcoming week. But if our goal is to determine whether we are to take a long position versus a short position, this information-rich indicator may be worthless for our project. Nevertheless, entropy can be thought of as an upper bound on information content, so if the entropy is small, our indicator is likely to have little value.

Second, it can happen that whatever modification we do to increase the entropy of our indicator actually impedes its performance. It may be that our original idea does a great job as an indicator, but when we apply a seemingly innocuous change that greatly increases its entropy, its utility in our trading system drops. This can happen. But please understand that these two situations, especially the second, are unusual exceptions to the rule. In the vast majority of situations, increasing the entropy of an indicator significantly improves its performance.

Computing the Relative Entropy of an Indicator

The easiest and likely best way to compute the relative entropy of an indicator from its historical values is to divide its *entire* range into bins that partition the range with equal spacing, compute the proportion of cases that fall into each bin, and use Equation 2-1 to find the entropy. Dividing this quantity by the log of the number of bins gives the relative entropy. Note that partitioning the range into bins that contain equal numbers of cases would be pointless, as this would always give a relative entropy of one. Rather, the bins must be defined by equal numerical fractions of the total range. Here is a simple subroutine to do this:

```
double entropy (
   int n ,        // Number of data values
   double *x ,    // They are here
   int nbins ,    // Number of bins, at least 2
   int *count     // Work area nbins long
   )
```

```
{
   int i, k ;
   double minval, maxval, factor, p, sum ;

   minval = maxval = x[0] ;

   for (i=1 ; i<n ; i++) {
     if (x[i] < minval)
       minval = x[i] ;
     if (x[i] > maxval)
       maxval = x[i] ;
     }

   factor = (nbins - 1.e-10) / (maxval - minval + 1.e-60) ;

   for (i=0 ; i<nbins ; i++)
     count[i] = 0 ;

   for (i=0 ; i<n ; i++) {       // Count the number of cases in each bin
     k = (int) (factor * (x[i] - minval)) ;
     ++count[k] ;
     }

   sum = 0.0 ;
   for (i=0 ; i<nbins ; i++) {  // Sum Equation 2-1
     if (count[i]) {
       p = (double) count[i] / n ;
       sum += p * log ( p ) ;
       }
     }

   return -sum / log ( (double) nbins ) ;
}
```

In the previous code, we have to do two tiny twiddles with the computation of the factor that maps data values to bins. The numerator is trivially reduced to make sure that no mapping is done to a nonexistent "bin" after the last bin. The denominator is modified to ensure that we do not divide by zero in the pathological situation of all data values being equal. The final loop just sums Equation 2-1, and we conclude by dividing the entropy by its maximum possible value to get the relative entropy.

Entropy Impacts Predictive Model Quality

The usefulness of entropy as a measure of an indicator's information content is not just theoretical fluff. Coincidentally or not, entropy correlates highly with our ability to train an effective predictive model. This is because high entropy correlates with roughly equal distribution of data values across the indicator's range, and in most situations models train most effectively when their indicators have such a distribution.

The most common problematic low-entropy situation is when there are one or more extreme outliers. Many model-training algorithms will see an outlier as saying something important and focus a lot of attention on that outlier. This reduces the attention paid to the mass of "normal" cases. Figure 2-1 illustrates a somewhat simplistic but often realistic example of the situation. This is a linear classifier dealing with two classes in what should be a problem of toy-like simplicity. The dotted line shows a linear boundary that achieves perfect classification. But that one case at the bottom left, which is an outlier for the X2 indicator, drags the boundary line in its direction, to the severe detriment of classification quality. And although this particular example features a linear classifier, even a nonlinear classifier, which can have a curved boundary, will often suffer the same degradation.

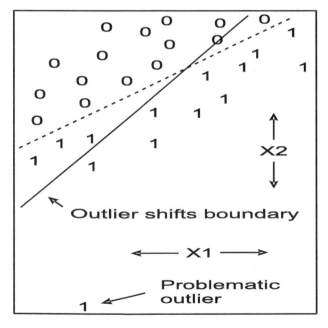

Figure 2-1. *Outliers can degrade performance*

It doesn't take outliers to produce performance degradation because of low entropy. Suppose we have a situation in which some exogenous condition, completely unrelated to the prediction/classification, causes a large fixed offset in an otherwise excellent predictor for about half of the cases. Perhaps this variable has values around 1.0 for half the cases, and there is excellent performance among these cases. Also suppose it has values around 100.0 for the other half of the cases, and it also has excellent power within this group. Not many models would be able to handle this extremely low-entropy situation. They would see the separation between the cases clustering around 1.0 and those clustering around 100.0 as the dominant factor and focus on using this cluster membership to attempt prediction/classification. The result would not be pretty.

Improving the Entropy of an Indicator

If you test an indicator and discover that it has dangerously small entropy (less than 0.5 is suspicious; less than 0.1 is serious and should be investigated and probably addressed), then your first step should be to reconsider how your idea for an indicator is being implemented. It may be that a simple revision to your computation algorithm will resolve the situation without compromising your idea. Here are some other thoughts to consider:

- If your indicator computation ever divides by a value that can become tiny, you are on thin ice.

- Your revision should be monotonically related to your original idea. In other words, if pre-revision Case A is less than pre-revision Case B, then this same ordering should remain after revision. Among other desirable properties, this ensures that if some threshold separates cases on a pre-revision basis, there exists a threshold that will perform the same separation post-revision. This is an important information-preserving quality.

- Truncation (remapping extreme values to a single limit value) is a poor way to solve the outlier problem. Among other things, it violates the prior principle just listed!

- If you have just a few rare outliers, monotonic tail-only modification is a good solution that greatly improves entropy yet has relatively small effect on indicator values. Pick a moderate percentile, perhaps something in the range of 1–10 percent for low outliers and 90–99 percent for high outliers. Cases on the "good" side of this threshold remain unchanged. Cases on the "outlier" side of this threshold are subjected to an extreme monotonic compression, such as logarithmic. This is discussed in detail on page 29.

- If only the right tail is heavy or has a positive skew (unusually large cases only), a square root or cube root transform will handle moderate skew or outliers, while a log transform should handle severe situations.

- If both tails are heavy, consider a cube root transform.

- If both tails are extremely heavy or have severe outliers, the hyperbolic tangent function (Equation 2-2 and Figure 2-2) or the logistic function (Equation 2-3 and Figure 2-3) can provide excellent results, provided that the indicator values are appropriately prescaled before applying the function. If the logistic function is used, it is good to subtract 0.5 after transformation to center it at zero, something appreciated by many training algorithms.

$$\tanh(x) = \frac{e^t - e^{-t}}{e^t + e^{-t}} \tag{2-2}$$

$$\text{logistic}(x) = \frac{1}{1 + e^{-x}} \tag{2-3}$$

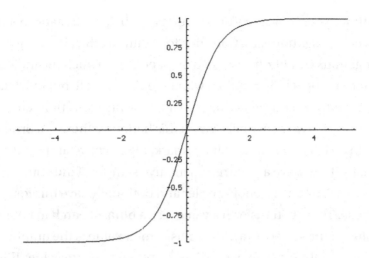

Figure 2-2. *TANH function*

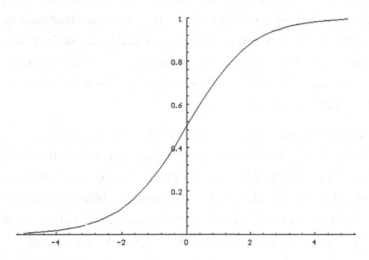

Figure 2-3. *Logistic function*

- If there is a theoretical reason why your indicator should have a distribution resembling a common statistical distribution, then transforming by applying the cumulative distribution function of that distribution can be effective. For example, many indicators (i.e., an oscillator that's the difference between two moving averages) have a nice bell curve shape that is almost normal except for modestly heavy tails, which are not severe but bad enough to be troublesome. Applying a normal cdf (normal_cdf() in STATS.CPP) will do an excellent job. Other indicators may be the ratio of two variance-like quantities, in which case an F CDF (F_CDF() in STATS.CPP) is ideal.

27

- Sometimes your indicator's distribution may be problematic in a way that is not straightforward. Consider, for example, the clumping due to an exogenous condition described on page 25, in which the indicator has a nice compact distribution, with no outliers at all, but the data is clustered into several small clumps. Or it may have this problem plus a heavy tail, or two heavy tails. When this happens, there is a brute-force approach that is clumsy but remarkably effective and general, especially if you have a large representative sample of indicator values. Sort your sample in ascending order and optionally save this for future use. Then, to transform a value, use a binary search to bound the value in the sorted array. The transformed value is the number of sorted elements less than or equal to the pre- transform value. This produces a transformed indicator that has a relative entropy very close to perfection. It works best when the sample is large, is thoroughly representative, and has few or no ties. As a nice final touch, divide this count by the total number of elements and subtract 0.5. This gives a value that ranges from –0.5 to 0.5, a range that is especially friendly to many training procedures.

- Many techniques just presented strive to produce an indicator distribution that is as uniform over its range as possible. But sometimes this is not ideal, despite it having maximum entropy. This happens when extreme values of the indicator do have special significance but such extreme values impede or even prevent correct training of a predictive model. In such cases all you want to do is tame the tails without eliminating them. If you have employed a transformation that produces a distribution that is nearly uniform but you want extreme original values to map to values that are extreme enough to be outstanding yet not so extreme as to be problematic, there is a simple fix: transform to a normal distribution. This distribution has a bell curve shape in which most cases cluster in the interior, but there are modest extremes in both tails. To do so, first apply whatever transform maps the indicator to a nearly uniform distribution. Then transform a second time, using the inverse normal cumulative distribution function. This can be done by calling the function inverse_normal_cdf() in STATS.CPP. The resulting indicator will still have extremes but not enough to degrade model training.

Monotonic Tail-Only Cleaning

Sometimes you are generally happy with your indicator's distribution, except for the fact that it occasionally has a wild outlier that needs taming to produce decent entropy. Or perhaps the target in a predictive-model trading system has occasional extremes that hobble your training algorithm, but you don't want to meddle too much with target values for fear of excessively distorting performance figures. Such situations call for a transformation that impacts only the most extreme values while leaving the majority of cases untouched. Here is a great way to handle this.

This transformation takes place in two steps. The first step identifies the data values that mark the low and high tails, and the second step modifies the tails (only). The version shown here processes both tails and does so in identical manners. Readers should have no trouble modifying it to process just one tail or to process the lower and upper tails differently.

The subroutine is called as shown next. The user provides a work vector because we have to sort the raw data to locate the tails. The caller specifies the fraction (generally small, perhaps 0.01 to 0.1) of *each* tail that will be compressed monotonically, preserving order relationships while strongly pulling in outliers. The variable cover is the fraction of cases that remain unchanged. We copy the raw data to a work area and sort it.

```
void clean_tails (
   int n ,                // Number of cases
   double *raw ,          // They are here
   double *work ,         // Work area n long
   double tail_frac       // Fraction of each tail to be cleaned (0-0.5)
   )
{
   int i, istart, istop, best_start, best_stop ;
   double cover, range, best, limit, scale, minval, maxval ;

   cover = 1.0 - 2.0 * tail_frac ;  // Internal fraction preserved

   for (i=0 ; i<n ; i++)
      work[i] = raw[i] ;

   qsortd ( 0 , n-1 , work ) ; // Sort data ascending
```

A good way to identify the tails is to examine every possible contiguous set of cases in the sorted array that has the specified coverage (contains the required number of "interior" cases). Find the set whose range (maximum value minus minimum value) is smallest. Then it is reasonable to label those cases that lie outside this minimal-range interior set to be the tails. This interior set will be identified as running from istart through istop.

```
istart = 0 ;                           // Start search at the beginning
istop = (int) (cover * (n+1)) - 1 ;    // This gives desired coverage
if (istop >= n)                        // Happens if careless user has tail=0
   istop = n - 1 ;
```

We run this interior set through every possible position, from leftmost to rightmost. For each trial set of endpoints, find the range and keep track of which position has the narrowest range.

```
best = 1.e60 ;                         // Will be minimum span
best_start = best_stop = 0 ;           // Not needed; shuts up LINT

while (istop < n) {                    // Test every possible position
   range = work[istop] - work[istart] ;  // This is what we minimize
   if (range < best) {
      best = range ;
      best_start = istart ;
      best_stop = istop ;
      }
   ++istart ;
   ++istop ;
   }
```

At this point we have located the narrowest interior set. Get its lower and upper values and insure against a careless caller.

```
minval = work[best_start] ;    // Value at start of interior interval
maxval = work[best_stop] ;     // And end
if (maxval <= minval) {        // Rare pathological situation
   maxval *= 1.0 + 1.e-10 ;
   minval *= 1.0 - 1.e-10 ;
   }
```

The final step is to modify the tails (and only the tails). We keep the process immune to changes in scaling of the data by employing maxval–minval as a scaling constant. The limit variable controls the degree to which the transformed tail values can lie outside the interior range. Employing the factor of (1.0–cover) is my own heuristic that seems reasonable to me. Feel free to disagree and change it if you want.

Readers should examine this code and confirm that limit does indeed define the departure limit of the transformed value, that values at the minimum and maximum (and in between!) remain unchanged, and that the transformation is monotonic (order preserving).

```
limit = (maxval - minval) * (1.0 - cover) ;
scale = -1.0 / (maxval - minval) ;

for (i=0 ; i<n ; i++) {
  if (raw[i] < minval)            // Left tail
    raw[i] = minval - limit * (1.0 - exp ( scale * (minval - raw[i]) ) ) ;
  else if (raw[i] > maxval)       // Right tail
    raw[i] = maxval + limit * (1.0 - exp ( scale * (raw[i] - maxval) ) ) ;
  }
}
```

The ENTROPY Program

The file ENTROPY.CPP contains a complete program that demonstrates the computation of entropy for a variety of indicators computed from a market price history file. Two of these indicators are the *Trend* and *Volatility* indicators from the STATN program described on page 13. Also, the *Version* parameter here is the same as in the STATN program, although it is not as interesting in the context of entropy as in stationarity.

The program is invoked with the following command:

ENTROPY Lookback Nbins Version Filename

Let's break this command down:

- Lookback: The number of historical bars, including the current bar, used to compute the indicators from the market price history.

- Nbins: The number of bins used to compute entropy. For a market history of at least several thousand records, around 20 or so bins is good, although in practice the number is not overly critical. If varying the number of bins by a small amount produces large changes in computed entropy, there's something fishy about the data or whatever custom indicator has been designed by the reader. *Plot a histogram!*

- Version: 0 for raw indicators, 1 for differenced raw indicators, >1 for specified raw minus extended raw. See page 14 for details.

- Filename: A market history file in the format YYYYMMDD Open High Low Close.

The following indicators are computed, and their minimum, maximum, median, and relative entropy are printed.

- *Trend* is the (log) price change per bar as defined by a least-squares fit.

- *Volatility* is the average true range computed according to the standard definition.

- *Expansion* is a deliberately poorly designed indicator that demonstrates how *not* to define an indicator and how low entropy can reveal the problem. The range of closing prices (maximum close minus minimum close) is computed for the most recent prices covering half of the specified lookback distance. Then the same quantity is computed, but at a lag of half the lookback. The *Expansion* indicator is the recent range divided by the older range, with the denominator increased slightly to prevent division by zero. This indicator reveals whether a crude measure of volatility (the price range) is increasing, decreasing, or remaining about the same.

- *RawJump* measures how the most recent closing price compares to the most recent exponentially smoothed closing price. This quantity reveals whether the market has taken a sudden jump up or down or remained about the same. It has occasional outliers on both tails and hence has poor entropy.

- *CleanedJump* is *RawJump* after the monotonic tail smoothing described on page 29 has been applied to the outer 5 percent of each tail.

When the ENTROPY program is run on the S&P 500 market history using a lookback of 20 bars and 20 bins for entropy, the relative entropy values in the first column are computed. When the lookback is dropped to seven bars, we get the results shown in the second column.

Trend	0.580	0.483
Volatility	0.639	0.559
Expansion	0.461	0.000
RawJump	0.484	0.395
CleanedJump	0.958	0.952

Especially for the shorter lookback, the *Trend* and *Volatility* indicators have marginally acceptable relative entropy. They could use a little tweaking; something gentle would likely do. The *Expansion* indicator, deliberately poorly designed by using an unstable ratio, becomes worthless at a lookback of seven bars. And take special note of the fact that the relative entropy of the *RawJump* indicator goes from poor to excellent by nothing more than cleaning the outer 5 percent tails, touching nothing else.

CHAPTER 3

Optimization Issues

Regularizing a Linear Model

If I could leave readers of this book with only one thought, it would be this: *the strength of your indicators is vastly more important than the strength of the predictive model that uses them to signal trades.* Some of the best, most stable and profitable trading systems I've seen over the years use a simple linear or nearly linear model with high-quality indicators as inputs. I've also seen far too many people feed marginal indicators to some modern, highly sophisticated nonlinear model in the vain hope that the model will miraculously overcome the *garbage-in, garbage-out* rule. It doesn't happen. When I am developing a new trading system, I turn to a linear model first and advance to a nonlinear model only if I see a clear advantage.

There are many advantages to using a linear model for a predictive-model-based trading system, as opposed to a complex nonlinear model.

- Linear models are less likely, often *much* less likely to overfit the training data. As a result, *training bias* is minimized. This subject is treated in more detail in the section that begins on page 121.

- Linear models are easier to understand than many or most nonlinear models. Understanding how indicator values relate to trade decisions can be an extremely valuable property of prediction models.

- Linear models are usually faster to train than nonlinear models. In Chapter 7 we will explore powerful testing algorithms that require frequent retraining, so fast training is a major advantage.

© Timothy Masters 2018
T. Masters, *Testing and Tuning Market Trading Systems*, https://doi.org/10.1007/978-1-4842-4173-8_3

- It is easy to convert a linear model to a nonlinear model in a way that does not seriously damage the properties just listed. This will be discussed on page 67.

- With only a moderate increase in algorithmic complexity, it is easy to penalize linear models for excessive complexity/power, an important and often neglected part of correct training called *regularization*.

Overview of the Regularized Model

As will be discussed in detail in the section that begins on page 121, a common and serious problem in the design and training of predictive models arises when the model mistakenly conflates random noise with authentic, repeatable patterns. This is called *overfitting*. Because by definition noise does not repeat, an overfit model will underperform when it is put to use.

Ordinary linear models are less likely to overfit than most nonlinear models, especially those that are extremely complex and powerful. But even ordinary linear models can overfit the training data, usually because too many predictors are employed. There are at least two common and moderately effective ways to handle the problem of overfitting because of an excessive number of predictors.

- *Reduce the number of predictors*: The most common method for doing this is *forward stepwise selection*. Select the single most effective predictor. Then select the one predictor that adds the most predictive power, given the presence of the first predictor. Then select a third, and so forth. A serious problem with this approach is that finding that first solo predictor can be difficult to do well. In most applications, it is the interaction of several predictors that provides the power; no single predictor does well. In fact, it may be that A and B together do a fabulous job while either alone is worthless. But if C happens to do a modest job, C may be picked first, with the result that neither A nor B ever enter the competition, and this excellent combination is lost. There are other often superior variations, such as reverse selection or subset retention. These are discussed in detail in my book *Data Mining Algorithms in C++*. However, each method has its own problems.

- *Shrink the coefficients in the linear regression equation toward zero,* away from their "optimal" least-squares values. This can be extremely useful because it lets us keep all relevant predictors and their joint relationship information, while reducing their ability to learn random noise along with more prominent authentic patterns. But this is not a trivial undertaking.

The goal of effective model design and training, linear or nonlinear, is to perform one or (usually) both of these two fixes. There are numerous ways of doing this, and most of them involve imposing a penalty on the complexity of the model, a process called *regularization*. What distinguishes the various approaches are the definition of complexity and the nature of the associated penalty. The method shown here, when applied to linear models, is particularly powerful because it can do either or both of the fixes at the user's discretion, and it does so in a way that is easy to understand and fast to train. Moreover, there exists a simple cross-validation scheme that lets us optimize the complexity-reduction hyperparameter. It's truly beautiful.

First we must lay out some notation. Without loss of generality, all subsequent developments will assume that all predictors *x have been standardized to have zero mean and unit variance*. This tremendously simplifies the relevant equations as well as the associated computer code. Trivial algebraic manipulation can recover the coefficients for the raw variables if they are needed.

N - The number of cases.

K - The number of predictor variables.

x_{ij} - The value of predictor j for case i.

$\boldsymbol{x}_i$ - The predictor vector (K long) for case i. This is a column vector, and it is a convenient notation for representing the set of x_{ij} for all j.

y_i - The target variable for case i.

β - The K coefficients in the linear model expressed in Equation 3-1. This is a column vector.

β_0 - The scalar constant in the linear model expressed in Equation 3-1.

α - A constant ranging from 0 to 1 that controls the *type* of regularization.

λ - A non-negative constant that controls the *degree* of regularization.

The basic linear model says that the expected value of the target variable is equal to a weighted combination of the predictors, plus a constant. This is shown in vector form in Equation 3-1.

$$\hat{y} = \beta_0 + x^{\mathrm{T}}\beta \tag{3-1}$$

We've already assumed that the predictors have been standardized to have zero mean and unit variance. When this is the case, β_0 equals the mean of the target. (Derivation of this easy result is shown in many standard statistics texts.) We can gain even more simplicity in development and programming if we assume that *the target variable has also been standardized*. We thereby know that $\beta_0 = 0$, so it can be ignored in all subsequent work. In this case, we are predicting the standardized value of the target. To get the predicted value of the raw target, just unstandardize: multiply by the standard deviation and add the mean. And even with this additional assumption, the coefficients and β_0 for all raw values are easily obtained with basic algebra.

The traditional way to find optimal values for the beta weights is to compute those values that minimize the mean squared error, the mean squared difference between each predicted value $\hat{y}_i$, and the true target value y_i. But in our regularized version, we add a penalty term to the error, with the penalty being a function of the set of beta weights. This is shown in Equation 3-2. In this equation, the multiplier of 2 could be absorbed into either λ or $P_\alpha()$, but it is shown this way to clarify some intermediate derivations that we will not present here, as our focus will be on the equations essential to programming the model. For full details, see the excellent paper "Regularization Paths for Generalized Linear Models via Coordinate Descent" by Friedman, Hastie, and Tibshirani (*Journal of Statistical Software*, Jan 2010). Note that λ controls the impact of the penalty term, and if λ = 0, we have the ordinary least squares solution. The subscript of *α* is applied to the penalty function *P* to clarify the fact that it controls the nature of the penalty. Also note that Equation 3-2 is double the error in that paper, which has no practical consequences.

$$RegErr = \frac{1}{N} \sum_{i=1}^{N} \left(y_i - x^{\mathrm{T}}\beta \right)^2 + 2\lambda P_\alpha(\beta) \tag{3-2}$$

The penalty function P_α is a weighted sum of the two-norm (sum of squares) and the one-norm (sum of absolute values) of the weight vector, with the relative weighting determined by the α parameter. This is shown in Equation 3-3.

$$P_\alpha(\beta) = \sum_{j=1}^{K}\left[\frac{(1-\alpha)}{2}\beta_j^2 + \alpha|\beta_j|\right]$$

(3-3)

The value of α, which can range from zero to one, has a profound effect on the nature of the penalty function. The two extreme values have common names that are well known to many developers. When $\alpha = 0$, we have *ridge regression*, and when $\alpha = 1$, we have the *lasso*. The difference between these two extreme models is best illustrated by considering what happens when there are sets of highly correlated predictors present. Ridge regression will tend to assign approximately equal weights to *all* predictors in a correlated set, drawing roughly equal contributions from all of them. In fact, if there is a set of m perfectly correlated (identical after normalization) predictors, ridge regression will assign a beta weight to each that is equal to $1/m$ times the weight that would have been assigned to one of them in the absence of the others.

The lasso ($\alpha = 1$) responds in the opposite way to sets of highly correlated variables. Instead of assigning small, similar weights to all of them, it will tend to pick the one that is most useful to the model, assign a relatively large weight to it, and assign a weight of zero to the other members of the correlated set, essentially removing them from the model.

One potential problem with $\alpha = 1$ is that if there happens to be two or more predictors that are perfectly correlated, the lasso loses its mind trying to figure out which one is best, as they are all equally useful. The training algorithm becomes numerically unstable. For this reason, unless you are positive that there are no such degeneracies in the data, if you want to use a lasso model, you should set α to a value that is very close to one but not quite there. This model will be nearly identical to a true lasso but will not suffer instability from perfect or near perfect correlation.

In most financial trading development in which there are a large number of predictors thrown at the model in a "spaghetti-on-the-wall" approach, it would usually be best to set α to a value between zero and one to be in the best of all worlds. For any fixed λ, the number of zero coefficients (variables excluded from the model) increases monotonically as α goes from zero to one. All variables are included when $\alpha = 0$, and then they tend to drop out (their beta weights go to zero) one by one for larger values of α. In this way, the developer can set the value of α to favor a desired degree of sparsity.

There are three things that readers should remember in comparing the model described here to ordinary linear regression:

- When we penalize the model this way, the solution we get is no longer a least-squares solution. The computed beta weights will produce a mean squared error that exceeds that from ordinary linear regression. In most practical applications, this is a good thing because it produces better generalization. That's the whole point of this approach! However, on the surface this may seem counterintuitive, as if we are deliberately crippling the model. But that's exactly what we are doing to make it less able to erroneously learn random noise.

- We should be especially happy about how this model handles strongly correlated predictors. Ordinary linear regression often has a horrific response to this situation, blowing up some coefficients to enormous positive values and then compensating by blowing up other coefficients to enormous negative values, pitting one correlated variable against the other in a delicately balanced relationship.

- This regularized model usually finds a subset, often a small subset, of the candidate predictors, just as is the case with ordinary stepwise inclusion. But its method for doing so is very different and vastly superior to stepwise inclusion. The latter takes an ordered all-or-nothing approach; once a variable is included, it stays forever. But the regularized linear model operates gradually, slowly converging on the ideal subset of predictors. Variables may come and go as their value in the presence of other variables waxes and wanes. This makes it much more likely that the final subset will be truly optimal.

Beta Adjustment with Guaranteed Convergence

There is a straightforward formula by which, given training data, along with the hyperparameters λ and α, we can efficiently compute an adjusted beta weight that reduces the error criterion shown in Equation 3-2. Under all realistic conditions this error criterion has a single local minimum that is also the global minimum. Thus, simple rotation among the weights is guaranteed to converge, usually quite quickly, even for large problems. In this section, we present this adjustment formula, omitting many details of its derivation that can be found in the previously cited paper. We will soon see how to use this formula to implement an efficient and stable training algorithm.

First, define the *residual* of the model as its prediction error, as shown in Equation 3-4.

$$r_i = y_i - \hat{y}_i \qquad (3\text{-}4)$$

Define for each predictor *j* a term that I call *argument*ⱼ, as shown in Equation 3-5. This is the slow part of the computation, as it requires summing products over all cases. Define the soft-thresholding operator $S()$, as shown in Equation 3-6. Then the new value of β_j which reduces the error criterion, is given by Equation 3-7.

$$argument_j = \frac{1}{N}\sum_{i=1}^{N} x_{ij} r_i + \beta_j \qquad (3\text{-}5)$$

$$S(z,g) = \begin{vmatrix} z-g & \text{if } z>0, g<z \\ z+g & \text{if } z<0, g<-z \\ 0 & \text{otherwise} \end{vmatrix} \qquad (3\text{-}6)$$

$$\hat{\beta}_j = \frac{S\left(argument_j, \lambda\alpha\right)}{1+\lambda(1-\alpha)} \qquad (3\text{-}7)$$

Differential Case Weighting

In some applications (though not often in market-trading applications), it can be useful to rate some cases as more important than others and thereby guide the training algorithm to focus more on reducing the error of important cases. The beta update formula shown in the prior section is easily modified to implement this capability.

Let the *N* case weights be denoted w_i, where these weights sum to one. The argument to the soft-thresholding operator is given by Equation 3-8, and the updated beta weight is given by Equation 3-9.

$$argument_j = \sum_{i=1}^{N} w_i x_{ij}\left(r_i + \beta_j x_{ij}\right) \qquad (3\text{-}8)$$

$$\hat{\beta}_j = \frac{S\left(argument_j, \lambda\alpha\right)}{\sum\limits_{i=1}^{N} w_i x_{ij}^2 + \lambda(1-\alpha)} \qquad (3\text{-}9)$$

Interested readers would do well to undertake a simple exercise. Suppose all weights are equal to $1/N$, so there is no differential weighting. Work through the fact that Equation 3-8 reduces to Equation 3-5, and Equation 3-9 reduces to Equation 3-7. If you don't see it right away (spoiler alert!), remember that the predictors have been standardized to unit variance. Thus, for each j, the sum over all cases of x_{ij} squared equals N.

Rapid Computation with Covariance Updates

If there are a lot more cases (N) than predictors (K), which is the usual situation in market trading, there is an alternative formula for computing the beta weight updates that is much faster than the "naive" Equations 3-5 and 3-8. The fundamental formula is given by Equation 3-10.

$$argument_j = Yinner_j - \sum_{k=1}^{K} Xinner_{jk}\beta_k + Xss_j\beta_j \qquad (3\text{-}10)$$

If no differential case weighting is used, $Xss_j = 1$ for all j, $Yinner_j$ is given by Equation 3-11, and $Xinner_{jk}$ is given by Equation 3-12. Derivation of these expressions is given in the paper cited earlier.

$$Yinner_j = \frac{1}{N}\sum_{i=1}^{N} x_{ij} y_i \qquad (3\text{-}11)$$

$$Xinner_{jk} = \frac{1}{N}\sum_{i=1}^{N} x_{ij} x_{ik} \qquad (3\text{-}12)$$

If we use differential weighting, we need Equations 3-13, 3-14, and 3-15. These derivations are not given in the cited paper, but they are easily obtained by beginning with their Equation 10 and following the nonweighted steps, remembering that the predictors are standardized.

$$Xss_j = \sum_{i=1}^{N} w_i x_{ij}^2 \qquad (3\text{-}13)$$

$$Yinner_j = \sum_{i=1}^{N} w_i x_{ij} y_i \qquad (3\text{-}14)$$

$$Xinner_{jk} = \sum_{i=1}^{N} w_i x_{ij} x_{ik} \qquad (3\text{-}15)$$

Note that Equations 3-13 through 3-15 depend on only the training data and weights, so they can be computed just once at the start of training. And Equation 3-10, which must be evaluated for each iteration, involves summing only K terms, not N. When K<<N, the time savings is huge.

Preparatory Code

We begin the presentation of code with some fragments that illustrate key parts of how we prepare for training the model. Complete source code for the entire CoordinateDescent class that encapsulates this model and all of its training algorithms is in the file CDMODEL.CPP.

The programmer would first call the constructor, as shown next. We'll skip its code here because it is concerned only with memory allocation and other simple housekeeping. Ignore the nl parameter for now; this will be discussed later. The other parameters are self-explanatory.

```
CoordinateDescent::CoordinateDescent (
   int nv ,      // Number of predictor variables
   int nc ,      // Number of cases we will be training
   int wtd ,     // Will we be using case weights?  1=Yes, 0=No
   int cu ,      // Use fast covariance updates rather than slow naive method
   int nl        // Number of lambdas we will be using in training
   )
```

After we have constructed a CoordinateDescent object, we must call a member function to input the training data and compute some things in preparation.

```
void CoordinateDescent::get_data (
   int istart ,    // Starting index in full database for getting nc cases of training set
   int n ,         // Number of cases in full database (we wrap back to the start if needed)
   double *xx ,  // Full database (n rows, nvars columns)
   double *yy ,  // Predicted variable vector, n long
   double *ww  // Case weights (n long) or NULL if no weighting
   )
```

In this call, we can specify a starting index in the dataset (for the predictors, target, and optional weights). The number of cases specified in the constructor call (nc) will be taken from xx, yy, and ww (if used) starting at index istart. If the end of the data is reached before nc cases are obtained, it wraps around to the beginning of the dataset. We'll see later how this wrapping is useful.

The get_data() routine begins by saving the predictors and target in private arrays and standardizing them by subtracting the mean and dividing by the standard deviation. These straightforward actions are not shown here. If differential weighting is to be used, the weights are scaled to sum to one (so the user need not worry about this), and XSSvec is computed using Equation 3-13. This weight-related code is as follows:

```
if (w != NULL) {
  sum = 0.0 ;
  for (icase=0 ; icase<ncases ; icase++) {
    k = (icase + istart) % n ;    // Wrap to start if needed
    w[icase] = ww[k] ;
    sum += w[icase] ;
    }
  for (icase=0 ; icase<ncases ; icase++)
    w[icase] /= sum ;

  for (ivar=0 ; ivar<nvars ; ivar++) {
    xptr = x + ivar ;
    sum = 0.0 ;
    for (icase=0 ; icase<ncases ; icase++)    // Equation 3-13
      sum += w[icase] * xptr[icase*nvars] * xptr[icase*nvars] ;
    XSSvec[ivar] = sum ;
    }
  }
```

If we are using the fast covariance-update method, which is the sensible course whenever there are more cases than predictors, we have to compute Yinner and Xinner as described in the prior section. Note that Xinner is a symmetric matrix, but we save the entire matrix anyway. This is wasteful of very cheap memory, but the simpler addressing saves very expensive time.

In the code that follows, we process one variable at a time. Addressing is simplified by using the pointer xptr to get the offset to the current variable in the first case. Thereafter, we can get this variable by just jumping down one case.

```
for (ivar=0 ; ivar<nvars ; ivar++) {
  xptr = x + ivar ;
  sum = 0.0 ;          // Do Yinner
  if (w != NULL) {    // Weighted cases
    for (icase=0 ; icase<ncases ; icase++)
      sum += w[icase] * xptr[icase*nvars] * y[icase] ;    // Equation 3-14
    Yinner[ivar] = sum ;
    }
  else {
    for (icase=0 ; icase<ncases ; icase++)
      sum += xptr[icase*nvars] * y[icase] ;                // Equation 3-11
    Yinner[ivar] = sum / ncases ;
    }

  // Do Xinner
  if (w != NULL) { // Weighted
    for (jvar=0 ; jvar<nvars ; jvar++) {
      if (jvar == ivar)
        Xinner[ivar*nvars+jvar] = XSSvec[ivar] ; // Already computed, so use it
      else if (jvar < ivar)                        // Matrix is symmetric, so just copy
        Xinner[ivar*nvars+jvar] = Xinner[jvar*nvars+ivar] ;
      else {
        sum = 0.0 ;
        for (icase=0 ; icase<ncases ; icase++)
          sum += w[icase] * xptr[icase*nvars] * x[icase*nvars+jvar] ; // Eq (3-15)
        Xinner[ivar*nvars+jvar] = sum ;
        }
      }
    } // If w

  else { // Unweighted
    for (jvar=0 ; jvar<nvars ; jvar++) {
      if (jvar == ivar)
        Xinner[ivar*nvars+jvar] = 1.0 ;       // Recall that X is standardized
      else if (jvar < ivar)                        // Matrix is symmetric, so just copy
        Xinner[ivar*nvars+jvar] = Xinner[jvar*nvars+ivar] ;
```

```
    else {
      sum = 0.0 ;
      for (icase=0 ; icase<ncases ; icase++)
        sum += xptr[icase*nvars] * x[icase*nvars+jvar] ;    // Equation 3-12
      Xinner[ivar*nvars+jvar] = sum / ncases ;
      }
    }
  } // // Else not weighted
} // For ivar
```

Outline of the Beta Optimization Process

In the prior few sections, we saw how, for any chosen beta weight, we can compute a
revised value that reduces the error criterion toward the unique global minimum. So
at the most naive level we could just rotate through the weights, adjusting each in turn
until satisfactory convergence is obtained. But we can do it more intelligently, taking
advantage of the fact that once a beta weight has become zero, it has a tendency to
remain zero on subsequent iterations. The outline of the training algorithm is shown
here, and explanations follow. More detailed code appears later.

```
do_active_only = 0 ;                  // Begin with a complete pass
for (iter=0 ; iter<maxits ; iter++) {  // Main iteration loop; maxits is for safety only
  active_set_changed = 0 ;            // Did any betas go to/from 0.0?

  for (ivar=0 ; ivar<nvars ; ivar++) {  // Descend on this beta
    if (do_active_only  &&  beta[ivar] == 0.0)
      continue ;

    [ Compute correction ]
    if (correction != 0.0) {            // Did this beta change?
      if ((beta[ivar]==0.0 && new_beta != 0.0) || (beta[ivar] != 0.0 && new_beta==0.0))
        active_set_changed = 1 ;
      }

    } // For all variables; a complete pass

  converged = [ Convergence test ] ;
```

```
   if (do_active_only) {              // Are we iterating on the active set only?
      if (converged)                  // If we converged
         do_active_only = 0 ;         // We now do a complete pass
      }
   else {                             // We just did a complete pass (all variables)
      if (converged  &&  ! active_set_changed)
         break ;
      do_active_only = 1 ;            // We now do an active-only pass
      }
   } // Outer loop iterations
```

The essential idea of this training algorithm is that we can save a lot of computational effort by focusing most of our effort on only those beta weights that are nonzero, called the *active* set. Roughly stated, we pass through all predictors, adjusting each beta weight. After this pass, it will often be the case that some of the betas, perhaps many of them, are zero. So we do additional passes, adjusting only those that are nonzero (the active set), until convergence is obtained. When we converge, we do a pass through all predictors, just in case the revised beta weights caused one or more betas to change to or from zero. If no such change occurs and we pass the convergence test, we are done. Otherwise, we go back to rotating through only the active set.

We start with do_active_only *False* so that all predictors are adjusted. The main iteration loop is limited by maxits for safety, although in practice this limit will never be hit. We use active_set_changed to flag whether any beta weight changed to or from zero.

The ivar loop makes a single pass through all predictors. If we are to do the active set only and this beta is zero, skip it. Otherwise, we compute a corrected beta. If beta changed, we see whether the change was to or from zero, and if so, we note this by setting the active_set_changed flag.

After we have made a pass through the predictors, we perform a convergence test. If we have been checking the active set only and if we have converged, we reset do_active_only so that the next time we check all predictors.

If, on the other hand, our last pass was a complete check of all predictors, convergence was obtained, and the active set did not change, we are all done. Otherwise, we set the do_active_only flag so that we go back to focusing on only the active set.

This fancy algorithm that focuses on the active set is advantageous only if there are a significant number of zero beta weights. However, this is often the case in applications in which this model is used. Moreover, there is little or no penalty in situations in which few or none of the betas are zero, so we might as well use the fancy version.

Code for Beta Optimization

The prior section presented an outline of the beta optimization algorithm, with details omitted so that the essential logic of the procedure would be clear. In this section, we work through the entire optimization code in detail. It is called as follows:

```
void CoordinateDescent::core_train (
    double alpha ,          // User-specified alpha (0-1) (0 problem for descending lambda)
    double lambda ,         // Can be user-specified, but usually from lambda_train()
    int maxits ,            // Maximum iterations, for safety only
    double eps ,            // Convergence criterion, typically 1.e-5 or so
    int fast_test ,         // Convergence via max beta change vs explained variance?
    int warm_start          // Start from existing beta, rather than zero?
    )
```

The alpha (α) and lambda (λ) parameters have been seen many times already. We use maxits simply to limit the number of iterations to prevent unexpected hangs. In practice, it would be set very large. The eps parameter controls how accurate the result must be before convergence is signaled. The fast_test parameter controls which of two convergence tests (described later) is used. Finally, warm_start allows training to begin from the current values of the beta weights, as opposed to starting from zero (the default). The routine begins with some initialization.

```
    S_threshold = alpha * lambda ;    // Threshold for the soft-thresholding S() of Eq (3-6)
    do_active_only = 0 ;              // Begin with a complete pass
    prior_crit = 1.0e60 ;            // For convergence test

    if (warm_start) {                 // Pick up with current betas?
      if (! covar_updates) {    // If not using covar updates, must recompute residuals
        for (icase=0 ; icase<ncases ; icase++) {
          xptr = x + icase * nvars ;
          sum = 0.0 ;
```

```
      for (ivar=0 ; ivar<nvars ; ivar++)
        sum += beta[ivar] * xptr[ivar] ;
      resid[icase] = y[icase] - sum ;
        }
      }
    }

  else {                            // Not warm start, so initial betas are all zero
    for (i=0 ; i<nvars ; i++)
      beta[i] = 0.0 ;
    for (i=0 ; i<ncases ; i++)      // Initial residuals are just the Y variable
      resid[i] = y[i] ;
    }
```

The most notable aspect of the previous initialization code is that if we are doing a warm start and we are not using the fast covariance-update method, then we must recompute the residuals. Recall that the naive update method of Equations 3-7 and 3-9 requires the residuals. Of course, if we are starting with all beta weights at zero, then all predictions are also zero, and the residuals are just the targets.

As iterations progress, we will be computing the fraction of explained target variance for the user's edification. For this we will need the mean square of the target, weighted appropriately if the user has chosen to weight cases by importance. The following code computes this quantity:

```
  if (w != NULL) {          // We need weighted squares to evaluate explained variance
    YmeanSquare = 0.0 ;
    for (i=0 ; i<ncases ; i++)
      YmeanSquare += w[i] * y[i] * y[i] ;
    }
  else
    YmeanSquare = 1.0 ;   // The target has been normalized to unit variance
```

We now begin the main outer loop, which iterates until convergence is obtained. The iteration limit maxits should be set very large (thousands or more) so that it does not cause premature exit; it is "hang insurance" only. We reset the flag that will indicate if the active set changed, and we will use max_change to keep track of the maximum beta change for a convergence test.

```
for (iter=0 ; iter<maxits ; iter++) {

    active_set_changed = 0 ;      // Did any betas go to/from 0.0?
    max_change = 0.0 ;            // For fast convergence test
```

The loop that makes a single pass through all predictors begins now. If we are to process only the active set (nonzero betas) and this beta is zero, skip it. Equation 3-9 for the weighted case and Equation 3-7 for the unweighted case will need update_factor in the denominator, so compute it now. Recall that XSSvec[] was computed by Equation 3-13.

```
    for (ivar=0 ; ivar<nvars ; ivar++) {  // Descend on this beta

        if (do_active_only  &&  beta[ivar] == 0.0)
            continue ;

        // Denominator in update
        if (w != NULL)       // Weighted?
            Xss = XSSvec[ivar] ;
        else
            Xss = 1 ;        // X was standardized
        update_factor = Xss + lambda * (1.0 - alpha) ;
```

We compute the argument to the soft-thresholding function. There are three possibilities. Either we are using the fast covariance-update method, we are using the naive method with differential case weighting, or we are using the naive method with equal weighting. We don't have to split the covariance-update method into with-and-without-weights here because any weighting was taken care of in the computation of Xss, Xinner, and Yinner already, as shown on page 42.

```
        if (covar_updates) {   // Any sensible user will specify this unless ncases < nvars
            sum = 0.0 ;
            for (kvar=0 ; kvar<nvars ; kvar++)
                sum += Xinner[ivar*nvars+kvar] * beta[kvar] ;
            residual_sum = Yinner[ivar] - sum ;
            argument = residual_sum + Xss * beta[ivar] ;   // Equation 3-10
            }
```

```
else if (w != NULL) {        // Use slow naive formula (okay if ncases < nvars)
   argument = 0.0 ;
   xptr = x + ivar ;     // Point to column of this variable
   for (icase=0 ; icase<ncases ; icase++)   // Equation 3-8
      argument += w[icase] *
                  xptr[icase*nvars] * (resid[icase] + beta[ivar] * xptr[icase*nvars]) ;
   }

else {                        // Use slow naive formula (okay if ncases < nvars)
   residual_sum = 0.0 ;
   xptr = x + ivar ;        // Point to column of this variable
   for (icase=0 ; icase<ncases ; icase++)
      residual_sum += xptr[icase*nvars] * resid[icase] ;  // X_ij * RESID_i
   residual_sum /= ncases ;
   argument = residual_sum + beta[ivar] ;   // Equation 3-5
   }
```

We just computed the argument to the soft-thresholding function, Equation 3-6. Apply this function and compute the new value for this beta using either Equation 3-7 or Equation 3-9. Not long ago we computed update_factor to be the denominator in these equations.

```
if (argument > 0.0  &&  S_threshold < argument)
   new_beta = (argument - S_threshold) / update_factor ;
else if (argument < 0.0  &&  S_threshold < -argument)
   new_beta = (argument + S_threshold) / update_factor ;
else
   new_beta = 0.0 ;
```

The amount of correction is the difference between the new beta and the old value. Keep track of the maximum change in this pass, as we may be using it for a convergence test. If we are using the slow naive update method, we will also use this correction to quickly recompute the residuals, which are needed for the naive method.

```
      correction = new_beta - beta[ivar] ;
      if (fabs(correction) > max_change)
         max_change = fabs(correction) ;  // Used for fast convergence test

      if (correction != 0.0) {                    // Did this beta change?
         if (! covar_updates) {                   // Must we update the residual vector?
            xptr = x + ivar ;                      // Point to column of this variable
            for (icase=0 ; icase<ncases ; icase++)    // Update residual per this new beta
               resid[icase] -= correction * xptr[icase*nvars] ;
            }
         if ((beta[ivar]==0.0 && new_beta!=0.0) || (beta[ivar]!=0.0 && new_beta==0.0))
            active_set_changed = 1 ;
         beta[ivar] = new_beta ;
         }
      } // For all variables; a complete pass
```

We have completed a pass through the betas, either all of them or just the active set, according to do_active_only. We now do the convergence test, either the fast, simple version or the much slower version. The fast test is based on only the maximum (across all predictors) change in beta. But the slow test is more complex.

If we were using the fast covariance update method, we did not need residuals for the beta updates, so we didn't take the (huge!) time to compute them. But we need the residuals for the slow convergence test, so we must compute them if we haven't so far. Compute the (possibly weighted) mean squared error using the residuals.

```
   if (fast_test) {          // Quick and simple test
      if (max_change < eps)
         converged = 1 ;
      else
         converged = 0 ;
      }

   else {   // Slow test (change in explained variance) which requires residual
      if (covar_updates) {   // We have until now avoided computing residuals
         for (icase=0 ; icase<ncases ; icase++) {
            xptr = x + icase * nvars ;
            sum = 0.0 ;
```

```
    for (ivar=0 ; ivar<nvars ; ivar++)
      sum += beta[ivar] * xptr[ivar] ; // Cumulate predicted value
    resid[icase] = y[icase] - sum ;   // Residual = true - predicted
    }
  }

  sum = 0.0 ;      // Will cumulate squared error for convergence test
  if (w != NULL) { // Are the errors of each case weighted differently?
    for (icase=0 ; icase<ncases ; icase++)
      sum += w[icase] * resid[icase] * resid[icase] ;
    crit = sum ;
    }
  else {
    for (i=0 ; i<ncases ; i++)
      sum += resid[i] * resid[i] ;
    crit = sum / ncases ;          // MSE component of optimization criterion
    }
```

A fundamental quality measure of a model is the fraction of the target variance that is explained by the model. This is computed by subtracting the mean squared error just computed from the mean square (variance) of the target to get the quantity of variance that is explained. Divide this by the target mean square to get the fraction of the target variance that is explained by the model. This is used strictly for optional user edification; it plays no role in the optimization algorithm.

Compute the regularization penalty using Equation 3-3 on page 39 and then add this penalty to the mean squared error to get the criterion that we are minimizing, as shown in Equation 3-2 on page 38.

This "slow" convergence criterion is based on the change from one iteration to the next in the optimization criterion. If the change is small (where "small" is defined by the user's specified eps), then we are deemed to have converged.

```
  explained_variance = (YmeanSquare - crit) / YmeanSquare ;

  penalty = 0.0 ;
  for (i=0 ; i<nvars ; i++)
    penalty += 0.5 * (1.0 - alpha) * beta[i] * beta[i]  +  alpha * fabs (beta[i]) ;
  penalty *= 2.0 * lambda ;  // Regularization component of optimization criterion
```

```
    crit += penalty ;              // This is what we are minimizing

    if (prior_crit - crit < eps)
      converged = 1 ;
    else
      converged = 0 ;

    prior_crit = crit ;
    }
```

We can now finish the outer loop with the control logic described in the prior section, alternating between active-set-only and full predictor passes.

```
    if (do_active_only) {          // Are we iterating on the active set only?
      if (converged)               // If we converged
        do_active_only = 0 ;       // We now do a complete pass
      }

    else {                         // We just did a complete pass (all variables)
      if (converged  &&  ! active_set_changed)
        break ;
      do_active_only = 1 ;         // We now do an active-only pass
      }

  } // Outer loop iterations
```

We are essentially done. For the user's edification we compute and save the fraction of target variance explained by the model. If we did the fast convergence test and covariance updates, we must compute the residual to get the explained variance. Those two options do not require regular residual computation, so we don't currently have the residual.

```
  if (fast_test && covar_updates) { // Residuals have not been maintained?
    for (icase=0 ; icase<ncases ; icase++) {
      xptr = x + icase * nvars ;
      sum = 0.0 ;
      for (ivar=0 ; ivar<nvars ; ivar++)
        sum += beta[ivar] * xptr[ivar] ;
      resid[icase] = y[icase] - sum ;
      }
    }
```

```
sum = 0.0 ;
if (w != NULL) {   // Error term of each case weighted differentially?
  for (i=0 ; i<ncases ; i++)
    sum += w[i] * resid[i] * resid[i] ;
  crit = sum ;
  }
else {
  for (i=0 ; i<ncases ; i++)
    sum += resid[i] * resid[i] ;
  crit = sum / ncases ;              // MSE component of optimization criterion
  }

explained = (YmeanSquare - crit) / YmeanSquare ;
```

Descending a Lambda Path

As is usually the case with models that have hyperparameters, choosing an effective value for the regularization strength lambda (λ) may not be straightforward. In the next section, we will explore a good way to automate the choice of a good value. In this section, we present a tool that will be called by that automated routine and that can also be used to aid in manually selecting a good lambda.

Consider that if lambda is huge, the penalty for any nonzero beta will be so large that all beta weights will be forced to zero. (This may not be the case if alpha is exactly zero, so from now on we will assume $\alpha > 0$.) This model obviously has zero explained variance. Conversely, if $\lambda = 0$, then we have ordinary linear regression, which has the minimum possible mean squared error or maximum possible explained variance. So, we can start at a large lambda, train the model, slightly decrease lambda and train again, and so forth, until lambda is tiny, almost zero. We will generally see the number of nonzero betas steadily increase, along with the explained variance. Even for the same number of nonzero betas, the explained variance will increase as lambda decreases. If we print a chart showing the number of nonzero betas and the explained variance as a function of lambda, we may be able to make an intelligent choice for lambda.

There is an interesting fringe benefit of this approach, even if we know in advance the lambda we want to use. This approach increases the already quite good stability of the training algorithm without much cost in terms of speed. In fact, it can happen that we can train *faster* this way. What we do is start with a large lambda that gives us just one or very few active predictors. That simple model will train quickly. Then, when we slightly decrease lambda, instead of starting all over again, we do a warm start, beginning iterations with the existing betas. So, each time we recommence training with a slightly smaller lambda, we are starting from betas that are already very close to correct. Thus, convergence will be obtained rapidly.

It's easy to find a good starting lambda for the descent, the smallest lambda such that all betas are zero. The entire process begins with all betas at zero. Look at Equation 3-7, along with the two prior equations for the argument and the soft-thresholding operator. For the differentially weighted situation, look at their analogs in the following section. Recall that when all betas are zero, the residual equals the target, y. It should be apparent from the definition of the soft-thresholding function that β_j will remain at zero if Equation 3-16 in the unweighted situation or Equation 3-17 in the differentially weighted situation is true.

$$\text{AbsoluteValue}\left[\frac{1}{N}\sum_{i=1}^{N}x_{ij}y_i\right] < \lambda\alpha \tag{3-16}$$

$$\text{AbsoluteValue}\left[\sum_{i=1}^{N}w_i x_{ij}y_i\right] < \lambda\alpha \tag{3-17}$$

Dividing both sides of these equations by alpha gives the threshold lambda for any predictor, and if we find the maximum such lambda across all predictors, we have our starting lambda. Here is code for doing this:

```
double CoordinateDescent::get_lambda_thresh ( double alpha )
{
  int ivar, icase ;
  double thresh, sum, *xptr ;

  thresh = 0.0 ;
  for (ivar=0 ; ivar<nvars ; ivar++) {
    xptr = x + ivar ;
    sum = 0.0 ;
    if (w != NULL) {
      for (icase=0 ; icase<ncases ; icase++)        // Left side of Equation 3-17
        sum += w[icase] * xptr[icase*nvars] * y[icase] ;
    }
```

```
  else {
    for (icase=0 ; icase<ncases ; icase++)          // Left side of Equation 3-16
      sum += xptr[icase*nvars] * y[icase] ;
    sum /= ncases ;
    }
  sum = fabs(sum) ;
  if (sum > thresh)          // We must cover all predictors
    thresh = sum ;
  }

  return thresh / (alpha + 1.e-60) ;   // Solve for lambda; protect from division by zero
}
```

Descending on lambda is straightforward. One thing to note is that we save the beta weights for every trial lambda, as we may want to access them later. Also, if the caller sets the print_steps flag, this routine will open a text file and append results for easy examination by the user.

We use get_lambda_thresh() to find the smallest lambda that ensures all betas remain at zero and decrease it slightly to get our starting lambda. We arbitrarily set the minimum lambda to be 0.001 times that quantity. The number of trial lambdas was specified in the constructor call. Here is the code:

```
void CoordinateDescent::lambda_train (
    double alpha ,              // User-specified alpha, (0,1) (Greater than 0)
    int maxits ,                // Maximum iterations, for safety only
    double eps ,                // Convergence criterion, typically 1.e-5 or so
    int fast_test ,             // Convergence via max beta change vs explained variance?
    double max_lambda ,         // Starting lambda, or negative for automatic computation
    int print_steps             // Print lambda/explained table?
    )
{
    int ivar, ilambda, n_active ;
    double lambda, min_lambda, lambda_factor ;
    FILE *fp_results ;
```

```
if (print_steps) {
  fopen_s ( &fp_results , "CDtest.LOG" , "at" ) ;
  fprintf ( fp_results , "\n\nDescending lambda training..." ) ;
  fclose ( fp_results ) ;
  }

if (n_lambda <= 1)       // Nonsensical parameter from caller
  ireturn ;

/*
  Compute the minimum lambda for which all beta weights remain at zero
  This (slightly decreased) will be the lambda from which we start our descent.
*/

if (max_lambda <= 0.0)
  max_lambda = 0.999 * get_lambda_thresh ( alpha ) ;
min_lambda = 0.001 * max_lambda ;
lambda_factor = exp ( log ( min_lambda / max_lambda ) / (n_lambda-1) ) ;

/*
  Repeatedly train with decreasing lambdas
*/

if (print_steps) {
  fopen_s ( &fp_results , "CDtest.LOG" , "at" ) ;
  fprintf ( fp_results , "\nLambda  n_active  Explained" ) ;
  }

lambda = max_lambda ;
for (ilambda=0 ; ilambda<n_lambda ; ilambda++) {

  lambdas[ilambda] = lambda ;   // Save in case we want to use later
  core_train ( alpha , lambda , maxits , eps , fast_test , ilambda ) ;
  for (ivar=0 ; ivar<nvars ; ivar++)       // Save these in case we want them later
    lambda_beta[ilambda*nvars+ivar] = beta[ivar] ;

  if (print_steps) {
    n_active = 0 ;      // Count active predictors for user's edification
```

```
      for (ivar=0 ; ivar<nvars ; ivar++) {
        if (fabs(beta[ivar]) > 0.0)
          ++n_active ;
        }
      fprintf ( fp_results , "\n%8.4lf %4d %12.4lf", lambda, n_active, explained ) ;
      }

    lambda *= lambda_factor ;
    }

  if (print_steps)
    fclose ( fp_results ) ;
}
```

Optimizing Lambda with Cross Validation

One of the most popular, if not the most popular, method for optimizing a model's hyperparameter(s) is cross validation, so that's what we will do here. The principle is simple. For each fold we call lambda_train() to test a descending set of lambdas, saving the beta coefficients for each trial lambda. We then compute the out-of-sample explained variance for each trial lambda and cumulate this quantity. When all folds are done, we examine the pooled OOS performance and choose whichever lambda gave the best OOS performance. There are a few things to watch out for, though, so we will break down this code into separate segments, explaining each. Here is the calling parameter list:

```
double cv_train (
  int n ,                    // Number of cases in full database
  int nvars ,                // Number of variables (columns in database)
  int nfolds ,               // Number of folds
  double *xx ,               // Full database (n rows, nvars columns)
  double *yy ,               // Predicted variable vector, n long
  double *ww ,               // Optional weights, n long, or NULL if no weighting
  double *lambdas ,          // Returns lambdas tested by lambda_train()
  double *lambda_OOS ,       // Returns OOS explained for each of above lambdas
  int covar_updates ,        // Does user want (usually faster) covariance update method?
  int n_lambda ,             // This many lambdas tested by lambda_train() (at least 2)
```

```
double alpha ,          // User-specified alpha, (0,1) (greater than 0)
int maxits ,            // Maximum iterations, for safety only
double eps ,            // Convergence criterion, typically 1.e-5 or so
int fast_test           // Convergence via max beta change vs explained variance?
)
```

Note that this is not a member of the CoordinateDescent class; it is a stand-alone routine. Most of the parameters are self-explanatory and have been seen many times before. The last four parameters and covar_updates are just passed to the core training routine. We do have to supply two vectors n_lambdas long: lambdas will return the tested lambda values, and lambda_OOS will return the OOS explained variance fraction corresponding to each tested lambda. We should specify n_lambdas as large as feasible for thorough testing; 50 is not unreasonable. Numerous lambdas do not appreciably slow training, because warm starts are used, meaning that each time lambda is decreased, the beta optimization begins at the prior optimal values. This is very fast. Finally, the number of folds should also be as large as feasible for best accuracy; five would be a bare minimum, ten is reasonable, and even more is better if computer time allows.

We begin with some initializations. Naturally we will want to use the same set of descending lambdas for each fold, so we use the entire dataset to find the threshold. If the cases are weighted, we copy the normalized weights for use in OOS scoring. The first training fold will begin at the first case, and we have not yet done any OOS cases. We will cumulate the fraction of variance explained in lambda_OOS, so initialize this vector to zero for each trial lambda. We will cumulate the (possibly weighted) target sum of squares in YsumSquares.

```
cd = new CoordinateDescent ( nvars , n , (ww != NULL) , covar_updates , n_lambda ) ;
cd->get_data ( 0 , n , xx , yy , ww ) ;               // Fetch the training set for this fold
max_lambda = cd->get_lambda_thresh ( alpha ) ;
if (ww != NULL) {
  for (icase=0 ; icase<n ; icase++)
    work[icase] = cd->w[icase] ;
  }
delete cd ;

i_IS = 0 ;       // Training data starts at this index in complete database
n_done = 0 ;   // Number of cases treated as OOS so far
```

```
for (ilambda=0 ; ilambda<n_lambda ; ilambda++)
  lambda_OOS[ilambda] = 0.0 ;  // Will cumulate across folds here

YsumSquares = 0.0 ;    // Will cumulate to compute explained fraction
```

The fold loop begins here. The number of OOS cases is the number remaining to be done divided by the number of remaining folds. The remaining cases are in-sample, and the OOS set starts past the IS set.

```
for (ifold=0 ; ifold<nfolds ; ifold++) {

  n_OOS = (n - n_done) / (nfolds - ifold) ;   // Number of cases in OOS  (test set)
  n_IS = n - n_OOS ;                          // Number IS (training set)
  i_OOS = (i_IS + n_IS) % n ;                 // OOS starts at this index
```

We now train with this in-sample set, descending on lambda. This set begins at index i_IS, and if the end of the dataset is reached, it will cycle back to the beginning.

```
cd = new CoordinateDescent ( nvars , n_IS , (ww != NULL) , covar_updates ,
                             n_lam bda ) ;
cd->get_data ( i_IS , n , xx , yy , ww ) ;               // Fetch the training set for this fold
cd->lambda_train ( alpha , maxits , eps , fast_test , max_lambda , 0 ) ;
```

Training is done, so we evaluate performance on the OOS set. Here is the code; a step-by-step explanation is on the next page:

```
for (ilambda=0 ; ilambda<n_lambda ; ilambda++) {
  lambdas[ilambda] = cd->lambdas[ilambda] ;  // This will be the same for all folds
  coefs = cd->lambda_beta + ilambda * nvars ;
  sum = 0.0 ;
  for (icase=0 ; icase<n_OOS ; icase++) {
    k = (icase + i_OOS) % n ;
    pred = 0.0 ;
    for (ivar=0 ; ivar<nvars ; ivar++)
      pred += coefs[ivar] * (xx[k*nvars+ivar] - cd->Xmeans[ivar]) / cd->Xscales[ivar] ;
    Ynormalized = (yy[k] - cd->Ymean) / cd->Yscale ;
    diff = Ynormalized - pred ;
```

```
      if (ww != NULL) {
        if (ilambda == 0)
          YsumSquares += work[k] * Ynormalized * Ynormalized ;
        sum += work[k] * diff * diff ;
        }
      else {
        if (ilambda == 0)
          YsumSquares += Ynormalized * Ynormalized ;
        sum += diff * diff ;
        }
      }
    lambda_OOS[ilambda] += sum ;    // Cumulate for this fold
    } // For ilambda

  delete cd ;
  n_done += n_OOS ;                 // Cumulate OOS cases just processed
  i_IS = (i_IS + n_OOS) % n ;       // Next IS starts at this index

  } // For ifold
```

The code on the prior page processes the OOS set for a single fold. The training routine saved beta weights for every trial lambda along the way as the efficient lambda descent algorithm progressed. So, we loop through the lambdas, getting the betas for each lambda into coefs. We will loop through all OOS cases, cumulating the sum of squared errors in sum.

We cycle through the dataset, looping back to the beginning when the end is reached, so k is the index of the OOS case about to be tested. The OOS case (target and all predictors) must be normalized in the same way that the training data was normalized, using the same mean and standard deviation.

The error for this case, diff, is the true value minus the predicted value. We cumulate the squared error, multiplying it by the user-specified case weight if differential weighting is employed. We simultaneously cumulate the sum of squared normalized targets. This has to be done only once, as it would of course be the same for all trial lambdas. When the case loop is done, we add the error sum to the sum for the lambda being tested. This vector will cumulate sums across all folds. After the lambda loop is done, we delete the CoordinateDescent object for this fold and advance to the next fold.

All that's left to do is compute the OOS explained variance fraction for each lambda and return the best-performing lambda to the caller. The target sum of squares minus the error sum of squares gives the explained sum of squares. Dividing this by the target SS gives the fraction of explained variance.

```
best = -1.e60 ;
for (ilambda=0 ; ilambda<n_lambda ; ilambda++) {
  lambda_OOS[ilambda] = (YsumSquares - lambda_OOS[ilambda]) / YsumSquares ;
  if (lambda_OOS[ilambda] > best) {
    best = lambda_OOS[ilambda] ;
    ibest = ilambda ;
    }
  }

return lambdas[ibest] ;
}
```

The CD_MA Program

The file CD_MA.CPP contains a program that reads a market price file, computes a large number of indicators based on moving-average oscillators, and uses the CoordinateDescent regularized linear model to find an optimal subset of the indicators for predicting the (log) price change to the next day. One year of market data at the end of the history file is held out for use as a test set.

The program is invoked with the following command:

CD_MA Lookback_inc N_long N_short Alpha Filename

Let's break this command down:

- Lookback_inc: The long-term lookback will begin with this number of bars (including the current bar) looking back. Subsequent long-term lookbacks will be incremented by this amount. For example, if this is specified to be 3, the long-term lookbacks will be 3, 6, 9, ...

- N_long: This many long-term lookbacks will be employed. The maximum long-term lookback will be Lookback_inc * N_long.

- N_short: This many short-term lookbacks will be employed. They are the current long-term lookback times i and then divided by N_short+1, for i from 1 through N_short, truncated down to an integer. Note that when the current long-term lookback is less than N_short+1, there will be multiple equal values of the short-term lookback, resulting in perfectly correlated predictors. The total number of indicators is N_long * N_short.

- Alpha: The desired alpha to control the type of regularization. If specified less than or equal to zero, lambda will be set to zero, producing ordinary linear regression (no regularization). It must never be greater than or equal to one.

- Filename: A market history file in format YYYYMMDD Open High Low Close.

Two tables will be printed. The first shows the computations involved in selecting the optimal lambda. The left column in this table lists the trial lambdas. The right column shows the corresponding out-of-sample fraction of explained variance.

The second table lists the beta coefficients. Each row corresponds to a long-term lookback, with the lookback printed at the start of each row. Each column corresponds to a short-term lookback. These lookbacks are not printed because they change with each row. They can be easily computed with the formula on the prior page. Coefficients that are exactly zero, usually but not always because the training algorithm removed them from the model, are shown with dashes.

Figure 3-1 shows the table of beta coefficients produced for OEX when lambda=0, no regularization. This is practically identical to ordinary linear regression. Figure 3-2 shows the result when alpha=0.1, and Figure 3-3 is for alpha=0.9. A discussion follows.

```
Betas, with in-sample explained variance = 1.63114 percent
Row label is long-term lookback; Columns run from smallest to largest short-term lookback
  2    0.0061    0.0000    ----     ----     ----     ----      ----     ----     ----     ----
  4   -0.0308    0.0000    ----     ----     ----    -0.0206    0.0000   ----    -0.0038    ----
  6   -0.0288    0.0000    ----    -0.0285   -0.0000  -0.0263   ----    -0.0453   0.0000   -0.0121
  8    0.0833    0.0000   -0.0103  -0.0000   -0.0105  -0.0220   0.0032   ----     0.0146   -0.0631
 10    0.0541    0.0000   -0.0016  -0.0029   -0.0128   0.0054   0.0095  -0.0302   0.0044   -0.0410
 12    0.0496    0.0054    0.0041  -0.0045    0.0106   0.0132  -0.0151   0.0099  -0.0080    0.0240
 14    0.0019    0.0059    0.0057   0.0123    0.0165  -0.0045   0.0179   0.0452  -0.1955    0.2897
 16   -0.1248   -0.0072   -0.0193   0.0008   -0.0106   0.0046   0.0133  -0.1388  -0.0493    0.1353
 18    0.1013    0.0054   -0.0023   0.0220    0.0115   0.0088  -0.0676   0.0204   0.1233    0.1864
 20   -0.1785   -0.0238   -0.0189  -0.0151   -0.0021   0.0107   0.0178  -0.0100   0.1043   -0.0383
 22   -0.0175   -0.0287   -0.0092  -0.0175    0.0010   0.0103  -0.0118   0.0729  -0.0325   -0.0146
 24    0.0090   -0.0283   -0.0118  -0.0208   -0.0053  -0.0739  -0.3926   0.1944   0.2326   -0.1855
 26    0.2769    0.0005    0.0144   0.0152   -0.0369   0.0832   0.0589  -0.0115  -0.0176    0.0564
 28   -0.0269    0.0075    0.0092   0.0388    0.0355  -0.2901   0.2165   0.2661   0.1255   -0.1889
 30   -0.2978   -0.0386   -0.0308  -0.0105   -0.0661   0.0491  -0.0449  -0.0635   0.0867    0.2027
 32   -0.0107   -0.0431   -0.0396  -0.0784    0.0096  -0.1708   0.0847  -0.0621  -0.1054   -0.0524
 34    0.4224    0.0089    0.0079   0.0274   -0.2471   0.2707  -0.0039   0.1318   0.2195    0.2206
 36   -0.4997   -0.0485   -0.0574  -0.1041   -0.0042  -0.0799  -0.0676  -0.1122  -0.0011    0.1153
 38    0.3700   -0.0124   -0.0223  -0.0575   -0.1103   0.0706   0.0272   0.0908  -0.4496    0.1118
 40    0.2054   -0.0012    0.0042  -0.0177   -0.0280  -0.0425  -0.1598   0.1604   0.1042    0.0732
 42   -0.0052   -0.0012   -0.0363  -0.1843    0.1693  -0.0294  -0.0426   0.1137  -0.2644   -0.0119
 44    0.1669    0.0183    0.0128  -0.0052   -0.0470   0.0176  -0.2574   0.2893   0.0125   -0.1128
 46    0.0405    0.0231    0.0179  -0.0005   -0.0415  -0.1400   0.1164   0.1240  -0.1500    0.2505
 48   -0.0690    0.0175   -0.0206  -0.0696    0.0414  -0.0237   0.0766  -0.1785   0.2429   -0.2635
 50    0.0980    0.0304   -0.0125   0.0131   -0.0154   0.0645  -0.2300   0.2507  -0.0217    0.1157
 52   -0.1647    0.0090   -0.0107  -0.0304   -0.0519  -0.1839   0.2244  -0.1247  -0.1811    0.1219
 54    0.2273    0.0361    0.0186  -0.0057    0.0109  -0.0228  -0.1013   0.1544   0.0592   -0.2475
 56    0.0607    0.0449   -0.1307   0.1484   -0.0864   0.1445   0.1251  -0.0869   0.0866    0.0172
 58   -0.2383    0.0185   -0.1555   0.0962   -0.0325  -0.1288   0.1588  -0.1356   0.1328    0.1148
 60    0.0112    0.0164   -0.0050  -0.0606    0.0308  -0.0328  -0.1347  -0.0263  -0.0251   -0.0022

OOS total return = 0.05855 (6.030 percent)
```

Figure 3-1. *Lambda=0 (no regularization)*

```
Betas, with in-sample explained variance = 0.38293 percent
Row label is long-term lookback; Columns run from smallest to largest short-term lookback
  2    ----     ----     ----     ----     ----     ----      ----     ----     ----     ----
  4    ----     ----     ----     ----     ----    -0.0031   -0.0031  -0.0031   ----     ----
  6   -0.0009   -0.0009  -0.0009  -0.0023   -0.0023   ----      ----     ----     ----     ----
  8   -0.0039   -0.0039  -0.0021  -0.0021    ----     ----      ----     ----     ----     ----
 10   -0.0056   -0.0056  -0.0023   ----      ----     ----      ----     ----     ----     ----
 12   -0.0011    ----     ----     ----      ----     ----      ----     ----     ----     ----
 14    ----     ----     ----     ----      ----     ----      ----     ----     ----     ----
 16    ----     ----     ----     ----      ----     ----      ----     ----     ----     ----
 18    ----     ----     ----     ----      ----     ----      ----     ----     ----     ----
 20    ----     ----     ----     ----      ----     ----      ----     ----     ----     ----
 22    ----     ----     ----     ----      ----     ----      ----     ----     ----     ----
 24    ----     ----     ----     ----      ----     ----      ----     ----     ----     ----
 26    ----     ----     ----     ----      ----     ----      ----     ----     ----     ----
 28    ----     ----     ----     ----      ----     ----      ----     ----     ----     ----
 30    ----     ----     ----     ----      ----     ----      ----     ----     ----     ----
 32    ----     ----     ----     ----      ----     ----      ----     ----     ----     ----
 34    ----     ----     ----     ----      ----     ----      ----     ----     ----     ----
 36    ----     ----     ----     ----      ----     ----      ----     ----     ----     ----
 38    ----     ----     ----     ----      ----     ----      ----     ----     ----     ----
 40    ----     ----     ----     ----      ----     ----      ----     ----     ----     ----
 42    ----     ----     ----     ----      ----     ----      ----     ----     ----     ----
 44    ----     ----     ----     ----      ----     ----      ----     ----     ----     ----
 46    ----     ----     ----     ----      ----     ----      ----     ----     ----     ----
 48    ----     ----     ----     ----      ----     ----      ----     ----     ----     ----
 50    ----     ----     ----     ----      ----     ----      ----     ----     ----     ----
 52    ----     ----     ----     ----      ----     ----      ----     ----     ----     ----
 54    ----     ----     ----     ----      ----     ----      ----     ----     ----     ----
 56    ----     ----     ----     ----      ----     ----      ----     ----     ----     ----
 58    ----     ----     ----     ----      ----     ----      ----     ----     ----     ----
 60    ----     ----     ----     ----      ----     ----      ----     ----     ----     ----

OOS total return = 0.09887 (10.392 percent)
```

Figure 3-2. *Alpha=0.1*

```
Betas, with in-sample explained variance = 0.37841 percent
Row label is long-term lookback; Columns run from smallest to largest short-term lookback
 2   -----   -----   -----   -----   -----   -----   -----   -----   -----   -----
 4  -0.0010 -0.0014 -0.0017 -0.0015 -0.0010 -0.0027 -0.0028 -0.0027  -----   -----
 6   -----   -----   -----   -----   -----   -----   -----   -----   -----   -----
 8   -----   -----  -0.0145 -0.0143  -----   -----   -----   -----   -----   -----
10   -----   -----   -----   -----   -----   -----   -----   -----   -----   -----
12   -----   -----   -----   -----   -----   -----   -----   -----   -----   -----
14   -----   -----   -----   -----   -----   -----   -----   -----   -----   -----
16   -----   -----   -----   -----   -----   -----   -----   -----   -----   -----
18   -----   -----   -----   -----   -----   -----   -----   -----   -----   -----
20   -----   -----   -----   -----   -----   -----   -----   -----   -----   -----
22   -----   -----   -----   -----   -----   -----   -----   -----   -----   -----
24   -----   -----   -----   -----   -----   -----   -----   -----   -----   -----
26   -----   -----   -----   -----   -----   -----   -----   -----   -----   -----
28   -----   -----   -----   -----   -----   -----   -----   -----   -----   -----
30   -----   -----   -----   -----   -----   -----   -----   -----   -----   -----
32   -----   -----   -----   -----   -----   -----   -----   -----   -----   -----
34   -----   -----   -----   -----   -----   -----   -----   -----   -----   -----
36   -----   -----   -----   -----   -----   -----   -----   -----   -----   -----
38   -----   -----   -----   -----   -----   -----   -----   -----   -----   -----
40   -----   -----   -----   -----   -----   -----   -----   -----   -----   -----
42   -----   -----   -----   -----   -----   -----   -----   -----   -----   -----
44   -----   -----   -----   -----   -----   -----   -----   -----   -----   -----
46   -----   -----   -----   -----   -----   -----   -----   -----   -----   -----
48   -----   -----   -----   -----   -----   -----   -----   -----   -----   -----
50   -----   -----   -----   -----   -----   -----   -----   -----   -----   -----
52   -----   -----   -----   -----   -----   -----   -----   -----   -----   -----
54   -----   -----   -----   -----   -----   -----   -----   -----   -----   -----
56   -----   -----   -----   -----   -----   -----   -----   -----   -----   -----
58   -----   -----   -----   -----   -----   -----   -----   -----   -----   -----
60   -----   -----   -----   -----   -----   -----   -----   -----   -----   -----

OOS total return = 0.06655 (6.882 percent)
```

Figure 3-3. *Alpha=0.9*

This run used the S&P 100 index OEX as its market history. The lookback increment was 2, with 30 long-term lookbacks and 10 short-term lookbacks.

- Recall from the discussion on the first page of this section that for long-term lookbacks less than the number of short-term lookbacks plus 1, some short-term lookbacks must be duplicated, meaning that some indicators are exact copies of others.

- This duplication makes ordinary linear regression impossible, as some weights would be undefined. Special techniques such as singular value decomposition would be needed. The algorithm here for lambda=0 handles this fine, even effectively eliminating a few of the duplicates. But the vast majority of indicators take part in the model.

- Because when lambda=0 there is no regularization, it is a fully least-squares fit. This means that the in-sample fraction of explained variance should be the maximum possible, and indeed we see that this is the case, with 1.63 percent of the target variance explained.

- Because of the vast number of indicators taking part (no regularization), we would expect to see poor OOS performance. We do, with this scoring the worst of the three tests.

- When we apply regularization with alpha=0.1 (nearly ridge regression), the in-sample explained variance drops, but the OOS performance soars to the best.

- With alpha=0.1, we see that the duplicated indicators receive equal beta coefficients, as expected.

- With alpha=0.9 (nearly a lasso), the model minimizes the number of indicators retained in an attempt to make the model as simple as possible, even at the cost of performance. We see this happen, and even the chosen indicators change. OOS performance plunges, meaning that the model was forced to drop some useful indicators.

- The regularized models have all negative coefficients, meaning that this trading system is a mean reversion system, not a trend follower!

Making a Linear Model Nonlinear

As much as a linear model is often to be preferred to a nonlinear model, sometimes two or more of our indicators have an unavoidable nonlinear interaction in their relationship to the target. Be aware that an indicator simply having a nonlinear relationship with the target, on its own, is not usually a problem. We can just transform the indicator in such a way that its relationship with the target becomes largely linear. This is always a good thing to at least attempt. Of course, it can also happen that we merely suspect a solo nonlinear relationship, but we cannot prove it enough to be able to sensibly transform the indicator. But the vast majority of the time, what kills a linear model is when indicators interact with one another in a nonlinear fashion in regard to their joint relationship with a target. In such cases, we have no choice but to abandon a strictly linear model.

But all is not lost. The advantages of a linear model, especially of the regularized sort (simple understanding of how it works, fast training, lower likelihood of overfitting), are so great that it is worthwhile to transform indicators and their interaction in a moderately nonlinear fashion and apply these new values to the regularized linear model. We almost never want to apply such extreme measures that the trade decision boundaries wander all over the place, twisting and turning to catch every errant training case. But there is an easy way to apply modest nonlinear transformations that allow us to use a regularized linear model in a gently nonlinear manner.

Naturally, we could supplement the model's predictors with one or more nonlinear functions of one or more original predictors. And if we have a theoretical reason for choosing some particular function(s), we should certainly do so. But that situation is rare. The most common and effective general procedure is to use low-degree polynomials, with two special twists that I'll discuss soon. The general idea is this: we choose a low degree, typically two and rarely three. Also, choose a subset of the predictors on which we want to allow nonlinear interactions. This may be the entire set of predictors, although things blow up fast as we include more predictors. Then supplement the original predictors with every possible combination of them up through the chosen degree.

For example, suppose we have three predictors for which we want to allow nonlinearity. Call them A, B, and C. Also suppose we want to allow up to second degree, the most common choice. Then the predictors we send to the model are A, B, C, A^2, B^2, C^2, AB, AC, BC. If we decide to move up to third degree, the additional predictors are A^3, B^3, C^3, A^2B, A^2C, B^2C, AB^2 AC^2, BC^2, ABC. It should be painfully obvious that increasing the number of predictors in the nonlinear set, or increasing the degree of the polynomial, produces an explosive growth in the number of new predictors.

There are two things that should be done when polynomial expansion is employed. Neither of these is mathematically required, but both are important if we are to guard against hardware floating-point inaccuracies, as well as improve the speed and stability of most model-training algorithms. First, we must ensure that the transformed indicators have a natural range of approximately minus one to one. If this is done, all polynomial transformed values have this same natural range. If our raw indicators do not have this range, at least approximately, we should find their true natural range, *Min* to *Max*, either from theoretical considerations or from examination of a large representative set. Then the range-adjusted value of X is $2 * (X - Min) / (Max - Min) - 1$.

The other action we should take is needed only if we go to third degree (or, heaven forbid, higher). The problem is that even with range adjustment, X and X^3 can have enough correlation to slightly impede some training algorithms. It's rarely serious, and the technique about to be described may be considered overkill by some, but it's a cheap investment with a nice return. Instead of using X^3, use $0.5 * (5 X^3 - 3 X)$. This is still a cubic polynomial with a range of minus one to one, and it will allow the same effective nonlinearity as X^3, but it will typically have much less correlation with X and hence will be handled more effectively by many training algorithms. You have nothing to lose and potentially much to gain.

Going beyond third degree is nearly always pointless. If you have that much nonlinearity, just use a nonlinear model. But if for some reason you insist, look up *Legendre polynomials* and use them for the higher-degree terms.

Differential Evolution: A Universal Nonlinear Optimizer

Whether your trading system is based on a nonlinear predictive model or is a traditional algorithmic (rule-based) system, you want a fast and stable method for optimizing your chosen performance criterion. In most scenarios, a major trade-off is involved in the selection of an optimization algorithm. It is common for a function of multiple variables to have several (perhaps many!) local optima. The fastest optimizers are hill climbers, rapidly rising to the top of the nearest hill, whether that particular hill happens to be the grand best or not. Optimizers that are more likely to find the best hilltop among many are much slower than simple hill climbers. So, what to do?

Fortunately, there is an algorithm that is a good compromise between the two extremes. It has a relatively high likelihood of finding the best, or at least nearly the best, hilltop among many, yet it is also quite fast. This algorithm is a special sort of genetic or evolutionary optimization called *differential evolution*. I will not provide any references here because the Internet is filled with examples and discussions. Instead, I will focus on a highly tweaked variation of this algorithm that I have used in my own work for many years and that I have found to be a reliable performer.

Like all evolutionary algorithms, it begins with a population of individuals, each individual being a completely specified parameter set for the trading system. It then iterates through the population, combining qualities of different members of the population in a way that has a good probability of producing individuals that are superior to the parents.

Unlike most plant and animal reproduction, differential evolution requires four individuals to produce a child. One of these, called *Parent 1*, is chosen deterministically. The other three, *Parent2*, *Differential1*, and *Differential2*, are randomly selected. The difference between the two differentials determines a direction, and *Parent2* is perturbed in this direction. The new child is created by selecting some parameters from *Parent1* and the others from the perturbed *Parent2*. This is illustrated in Figure 3-4 and Figure 3-5.

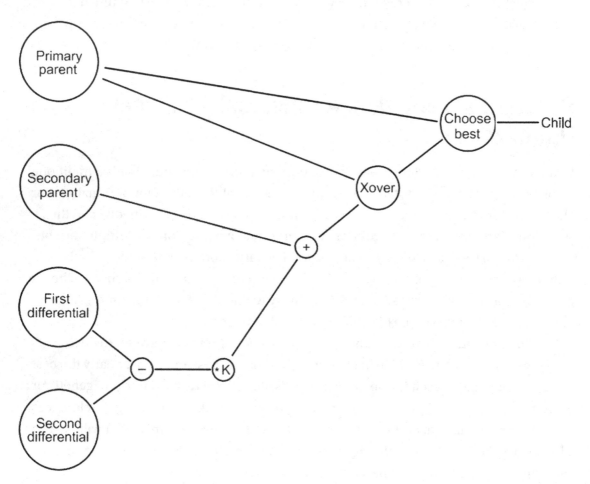

Figure 3-4. *One step of differential evolution*

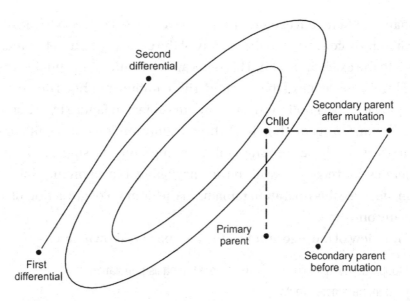

Figure 3-5. *Differential child generation*

Figure 3-4 shows that the first and second differentials are subtracted and their difference multiplied by a constant, usually smaller than one. This shrunken difference is added to the secondary parent, and the sum is merged with the primary parent in a random crossover operation. The performance of this child is compared to the performance of the primary parent, and the superior individual is retained for the next generation.

This is shown graphically in Figure 3-5 for two variables. The difference between the two differentials determines a direction, and the secondary parent is perturbed in this direction. This operation is called *mutation* in this illustration, though this is not a universal term. Then the horizontal variable is taken from the primary parent, and the vertical variable is taken from the mutated secondary parent.

This scheme has an important property: it scales perturbations to the natural scales of the parameters. Suppose the performance function has a narrow ridge in some direction, a common situation. Then the population will gravitate to this same layout. Individuals (complete parameter sets) will be spread widely in the direction of the ridge and compressed in the perpendicular direction. As a result, differential differences, which control the degree of perturbation of the secondary parent, will be large along the ridge and small across the ridge, exactly what we want.

Unfortunately, differential evolution shares a weakness common to most stochastic procedures: it quickly converges to the vicinity of the global optimum but then never quite makes it to the exact optimum. This is because it is inherently unable to take advantage of local knowledge of the function. Hill-climbing methods do an excellent job of converging to a local optimum, but they are subject to failure by missing the global optimum. So, my method is a hybrid, mainly implementing differential evolution but occasionally performing a hill-climbing step on a single individual. This greatly accelerates convergence, while having negligible impact on the globality of the algorithm, because this operation remains in the domain of attraction of a *single* individual at any one time.

A rough overview of the algorithm on the next page is shown here.

```
for (ind=0 ; ind<popsize+overinit ; ind++) { // Generate the basis population
  Generate a random parameter vector
  value = performance of this random vector

  If this individual fails to meet a minimum requirement {
    --ind ;       // Skip it entirely
    continue ;
    }

  if (ind >= popsize) {  // If we finished population, now doing overinit
    Find the worst individual in population (popsize individuals)
    if (value > worst)
      Replace the worst with this new individual
    } // If doing overinit
  } // For all individuals (population and overinit)

for (generation=1 ; ; generation++) {

  for (ind=0 ; ind<popsize ; ind++) {  // Generate all children
    parent1 = individual 'ind'

    Generate three different random indices for parent2 and the two differentials:
      parent2, diff1, diff2
```

```
for all variables j {   // This is the mutation and crossover step
   with small probability
      trial[j] = parent2[j] + constant * (diff1[j] - diff2[j]) ;
   else
      trial[j] = parent1[j] ;
   }
value = performance of trial parameter set

if (value > parent1's performance)
   replace parent1 with trial parameter set

Optionally pick one variable in one individual (favoring the best so far)
and find the optimal value of that variable

} // Create all children in this generation
} // For all generations
```

Return the best individual in the final population

The first step is to generate an initial population, which is done by the first loop in this pseudocode. The user specifies the number of individuals in the population, popsize. The traditional algorithm does not include overinitialization, the testing of overinit additional individuals. I have found that setting overinit to approximately popsize produces a substantially superior initial population with faster convergence and better global representation at relatively little additional cost.

This population generation loop creates a random individual (complete set of trading-system parameters) and computes its performance. If this individual fails any user-specified requirement, such as a minimum number of trades, it is rejected, and we try again.

When we have generated popsize individuals and are into overinitialization, for each new candidate we search the existing population for the poorest-performing individual. If the new candidate is superior to the worst individual in the population, the new candidate replaces the worst. This steadily improves the quality of the population, and it also makes it more likely that we will have one or more individuals in the domain of attraction of the global optimum.

We then come to the evolutionary part of the code. There are two nested loops. The outer loop processes generations, and within each generation we employ each individual in the current population as the primary parent. The secondary parent and the two differential individuals are chosen randomly, and of course these four individuals must be different.

Mutation (perturbing the secondary parent by the shrunken difference between the differentials) and crossover (randomly replacing some variables in the primary parent with the corresponding mutated variables) are done in the same loop for efficiency. We loop through all variables to create a trial individual. For each, we roll the dice and with generally small probability we set that variable equal to the mutated value. Otherwise, we copy the variable from the primary parent.

We compute the performance of this trial individual. If it is superior to the primary parent, it goes into the population for the next generation. Otherwise, the primary parent goes into the next generation.

Last, we optionally perform a step that does not appear in the traditional algorithm but that I have found to be useful in speeding convergence while having little or no impact on the ability of the algorithm to find the global optimum in the presence of multiple inferior local optima. We pick one individual in the population, with some favoritism shown to the currently best individual, and we also pick one variable. We use a hill-climbing algorithm to find the value of this variable that optimizes the performance of this individual. This gives us the best of both worlds (stochastic optimization versus hill-climbing) because it lets the algorithm accurately converge to the exact optimum much faster than a purely stochastic algorithm could, while it does not interfere with the ability of differential evolution to find the global optimum. This is because when it is done, it happens to just one individual, which keeps this individual within the domain of attraction of its local optimum while not touching the other individuals in the population that may have their own domains of attraction. Thus, the domains of attraction are kept separated, enabling the globally best to eventually dominate.

After all generations are complete, we choose the best individual in the final population and return it to the user.

The algorithm just shown is abbreviated for clarity. My implementation is much more complex because over the years I have refined it in many ways to tweak its performance, especially in the context of optimizing trading systems. Beginning on the next page we will work through the entire subroutine, listing and commenting on each section separately. This code can be found in the file DIFF_EV.CPP. Note that this file also includes some other code unrelated to differential evolution but that is efficient to perform at the same time. We will ignore this code here and cover it in detail on page 91.

The DIFF_EV.CPP Routine for Differential Evolution

The differential evolution subroutine is called with the following parameter list:

```
int diff_ev (
   double (*criter) ( double * , int ) ,  // Crit function maximized
   int nvars ,                            // Number of variables (trading system parameters)
   int nints ,                            // Number of first variables that are integers
   int popsize ,                          // Population size
   int overinit ,                         // Overinitialization for initial population
   int mintrades ,                        // Minimum number of trades for candidate system
   int max_evals ,                        // For safety, max number of failed initial performance evals
   int max_bad_gen ,                      // Max number of contiguous gens with no improvement
   double mutate_dev ,                    // Deviation for differential mutation
   double pcross ,                        // Probability of crossover
   double pclimb ,                        // Probability of taking a hill-climbing step, can be zero
   double *low_bounds ,                   // Lower bounds for parameters
   double *high_bounds ,                  // And upper
   double *params ,                       // Returns nvars best parameters, plus criterion at end
   int print_progress                     // Print progress to screen?
   )
```

The caller-supplied criter() function computes the trading system's performance criterion, which will be maximized. It takes a vector of the trading system's optimizable parameters. The integer that is also supplied is, in my implementation, the user-specified minimum number of trades. Readers should find it easy to add other variables that might be involved in setting minimum requirements for generated trading systems.

The parameters may be integers or real numbers; they are handled differently internally, as will be seen. All integer parameters must come first in the parameter array, and nints specifies the number of integers.

The user can set overinit to zero to use the traditional version of the algorithm. However, I have found it advantageous to set it equal to something in the vicinity of popsize. This tends to speed convergence and increase the probability of finding the true global maximum. But note that the point of diminishing returns is reached rapidly. It soon happens that the worst individual in the steadily improving population is usually superior to most overinitialized individuals, making continued overinitialization a waste.

The user specifies in mintrd the minimum number of trades required. As will be seen in the code presentation, the specified quantity may be automatically reduced if the optimizer has extreme difficulty finding systems that meet this requirement. Thus, the user should check the number of trades obtained by the optimal system to confirm that it is satisfactory. Eliminating this automatic reduction is easy if the programmer want, but I have found it useful.

The max_evals parameter is a safety measure. If the trading system is so inherently poor that most trial parameters produce rejected systems, it can take an inordinate amount of time to generate the initial population. To prevent this, set max_evals to a large but reasonable value. This should not be thought of as a convergence test; in practice, this limit should *never* be encountered.

Convergence is defined by the max_bad_gen parameter. If this many *consecutive* generations pass with no improvement in the best individual, convergence is obtained, and the algorithm stops. This should usually be quite large, perhaps 50 or even more, as it can happen that things go badly because of bad luck for a while before suddenly taking off again.

A *crossover* happens when a mutated parameter is substituted for the corresponding parameter in the primary parent, and the probability of this happening is given by pcross. This should usually be small, perhaps 0.1 to 0.5 at most.

The probability of a hill-climbing step is given by pclimb. This can be zero to strictly avoid hill climbing, keeping true to the traditional version of differential evolution. It could be set to a tiny positive value, such as 0.00001, in which case the current best individual (and no others) will occasionally be subjected to hill climbing. This greatly enhances end-stage accurate convergence to the maximum. Finally, it could be set to a somewhat larger but still smallish value, such as 0.2. This way, in addition to tweaking the best individual, it will occasionally randomly tweak other individuals. Setting it to larger values is usually not very beneficial, as hill climbing is an expensive operation, especially for real parameters, and the payoff from doing it more than occasionally is usually not sufficient to justify the increased cost. Also, if hill climbing is done too often, detection of the true global maximum can be somewhat impeded, although this is not usually a problem.

The caller must specify lower and upper bounds for the parameters, using the low_ bounds and high_bounds vectors, respectively.

The params vector, which must be nvars+1 long, returns the optimal parameters. The last item in this array is the value of the criterion function for this optimal parameter set.

If print_progress is input nonzero, frequent progress reports will be printed to the console screen.

Only three work arrays are allocated: one to hold the "current" population, one to hold the population being created, and one short array to keep track of the grand best individual. We use failures to count how many times a randomly generated individual for the initial population is rejected, usually because the trading system had too few trades. It will be used to reduce the minimum trade requirement, as we'll see soon. And for safety, n_evals counts the total number of times we evaluate a randomly generated individual for creating the initial population. This allows an emergency escape to avoid hanging the computer. The first popsize individuals fill the pop1 array, and overinitializations go in pop2[0].

```
dim = nvars + 1 ;  // Each individual is nvars variables plus criterion
pop1 = (double *) malloc ( dim * popsize * sizeof(double)) ;
pop2 = (double *) malloc ( dim * popsize * sizeof(double)) ;
best = (double *) malloc ( dim * sizeof(double)) ;

failures = 0 ;      // Counts consecutive failures
n_evals = 0 ;       // Counts evaluations for catastrophe escape

for (ind=0 ; ind<popsize+overinit ; ind++) {
   if (ind < popsize)               // If we are in pop1
      popptr = pop1 + ind * dim ;   // Point to the slot in pop1
   else                             // Use first slot in pop2 for work
      popptr = pop2 ;               // Point to first slot in pop2
```

We now generate a random individual and put it in popptr. The first nints parameters are integers, and the rest are real. Both types are generated by uniformly selecting values within the specified range of each. However, integers and reals are handled slightly differently. The function unifrand() generates a uniform random number in the range 0–1.

```
for (i=0 ; i<nvars ; i++) {      // For all variables (parameters)

  if (i < nints) {                // Is this an integer?
    popptr[i] = low_bounds[i]+(int)(unifrand() * (high_bounds[i]-low_bounds[i] + 1.0));
    if (popptr[i] > high_bounds[i]) // Virtually impossible, but be safe
      popptr[i] = high_bounds[i] ;
    }
```

```
    else                              // real
      popptr[i] = low_bounds[i] + (unifrand () * (high_bounds[i] - low_bounds[i])) ;
    } // For all parameters
```

Evaluate the performance of the trading system for this individual, the parameter set in popptr. Save this performance in the last slot in popptr, immediately past the parameters. Recall that each slot is nvars+1 long. Count the number of performance evaluations while building the initial population so that we can use it as an emergency exit to avoid being stuck in a seemingly (or actually!) endless loop. Finally, initialize the grand best, worst, and average performances to the first individual tested. That memcpy() copies the parameters and performance of this individual to the short array where we keep track of the all-time best to ultimately return to the user.

```
    value = criter ( popptr , mintrades ) ;
    popptr[nvars] = value ;        // Also save criterion after variables
    ++n_evals ;                    // Count evaluations for emergency escape

    if (ind == 0) {
      grand_best = worstf = avgf = value ;
      memcpy ( best , pop1 , dim * sizeof(double) ) ; // Best so far is first!
      }
```

The next block of code handles rejected individuals. Note that this code uses a threshold of zero for rejecting a parameter set, such as for showing a loss or failing to meet the minimum trade count requirement. If you want to use a different performance criterion, one for which this threshold is not appropriate, you should either modify this code or, better still, transform your performance criterion. For example, if you want to maximize profit factor, for which the appropriate threshold would be one instead of zero, you could define your performance as the log of the profit factor.

In the reject-handling code shown next, we first check to see if we have such a terrible trading system that the number of evaluations needed to generate the initial population has gotten out of control, in which case we take an emergency exit. If not, we count the number of such failures. If it has reached a large number (500 is hard-coded here; feel free to change it), we reset the failure counter and reduce the minimum trade requirement, as in my experience this is the most common cause of failure unless mintrades has been set very small. In any case, failure of this individual causes it to be skipped, while success resets the failure counter. Thus, it takes a *lot* of failure to trigger reduction of the minimum trade count. Things have to be very bad before this drastic action is taken.

```
if (value <= 0.0) {            // If this individual is totally worthless
  if (n_evals > max_evals)  // Safety escape should ideally never happen
    goto FINISHED ;
  --ind ;                      // Skip it entirely
  if (++failures >= 500) {     // This many in a row
    failures = 0 ;
    mintrades = mintrades * 9 / 10 ;
    if (mintrades < 1)
      mintrades = 1 ;
    }
  continue ;
  }
else
  failures = 0 ;
```

We maintain the best, worst, and average performances. The latter two are strictly for progress reports, and if the user will not be updated on progress, the worst and average computation can be omitted.

```
if (value > grand_best) {  // Best ever
  memcpy ( best , popptr , dim * sizeof(double) ) ;
  grand_best = value ;
  }

if (value < worstf)
  worstf = value ;

avgf += value ;
```

If we have completed finding popsize individuals, we are into overinitialization. Search the existing population for the worst individual. If this new overinitialization individual is superior to the worst, replace the worst with it, which improves the gene pool. Recall that the performance is stored just past the parameters, so it is at index [nvars]. Once again, we maintain the average performance only for user updates; it plays no role in the optimization algorithm.

```
if (ind >= popsize) {            // If we finished pop1, now doing overinit
  avgf = 0.0 ;
  minptr = NULL ;                // Not needed.  Shuts up 'use before define'
  for (i=0 ; i<popsize ; i++) {  // Search pop1 for the worst
    dtemp = (pop1+i*dim)[nvars] ;
    avgf += dtemp ;
    if ((i == 0)  ||  (dtemp < worstf)) {
      minptr = pop1 + i * dim ;
      worstf = dtemp ;
      }
    } // Searching pop1 for worst
  if (value > worstf) {          // If this is better than the worst, replace worst with it
    memcpy ( minptr , popptr , dim * sizeof(double) ) ;
    avgf += value - worstf ;  // Account for the substitution
    }
  } // If doing overinit

} // For all individuals (population and overinit)
```

At this point we have completely generated the starting population. Locate the best performer, because we will occasionally do a little hill climbing on it (unless the user forbids this, a generally bad move). Then set the points to the old (source) and new (destination) generations and zero the convergence counter. We will use n_tweaked to control hill climbing.

```
ibest = n_tweaked = 0 ;
value = pop1[nvars] ;
for (ind=1 ; ind<popsize ; ind++) {
  popptr = pop1 + ind * dim ;      // Point to the slot in pop1
  if (popptr[nvars] > value) {
    value = popptr[nvars] ;
    ibest = ind ;
    }
  }

old_gen = pop1 ;         // This is the old, parent generation
new_gen = pop2 ;         // The children will be produced here
bad_generations = 0 ;    // Counts contiguous generations with no improvement of best
```

We have nested loops, with generations being the outer loop and individuals within a generation the inner loop. Keep track of the average and worst only for optional user updates. The variable improved flags if the best individual improved at any point in the generation. This is used to signal convergence. The primary parent, parent1, comes from the source population, and the child we will create will go to the destination population.

```
for (generation=1 ; ; generation++) {

   worstf = 1.e60 ;
   avgf = 0.0 ;
   improved = 0 ;                      // Will flag if we improved in this generation

   for (ind=0 ; ind<popsize ; ind++) {    // Generate all children for this generation

      parent1 = old_gen + ind * dim ;     // Pure (and tested) parent
      dest_ptr = new_gen + ind * dim ;    // Winner goes here for next gen
```

We randomly select the secondary parent and the two differentials. These must be different from the primary parent and from one another.

```
   do { i = (int) (unifrand() * popsize) ; }
     while ( i >= popsize || i == ind ) ;

   do { j = (int) (unifrand() * popsize) ; }
     while ( j >= popsize || j == ind || j == i ) ;

   do { k = (int) (unifrand() * popsize) ; }
     while ( k >= popsize || k == ind || k == i || k == j ) ;

   parent2 = old_gen + i * dim ;   // Parent to mutate
   diff1 = old_gen + j * dim ;     // First differential vector
   diff2 = old_gen + k * dim ;     // Second differential vector
```

The following code takes care of mutation and crossover to create a new child. We'll loop through every parameter, randomly deciding for each whether to mutate and do crossover. If we get to the last parameter and have not done this yet, we do it to the last to ensure that there is at least one change. We randomly choose a starting parameter so that when we get to the end we will not always be at the same place for the final action. The mutation can easily push parameters outside their legal range. Fix this as needed. The ensure_legal() routine will be discussed later.

```
do { j = (int) (unifrand() * nvars) ; }
  while ( j >= nvars ) ;  // Pick a starting parameter

used_mutated_parameter = 0 ;        // We must act at least once; we haven't yet

for (i=nvars-1 ; i>=0 ; i--) {
  if ((i == 0 && ! used_mutated_parameter) || (unifrand() < pcross)) {
    dest_ptr[j] = parent2[j] + mutate_dev * (diff1[j] - diff2[j]) ;
    used_mutated_parameter = 1 ;
    }  // We mutated this variable
  else   // We did not mutate this variable, so copy old value
    dest_ptr[j] = parent1[j] ;
  j = (j + 1) % nvars ;   // Rotate through all variables
  }

ensure_legal ( nvars , nints , low_bounds , high_bounds , dest_ptr ) ;
```

Evaluate the performance of this newly created child. If it is superior to the primary parent, put it into the destination population. Otherwise, copy the primary parent into the destination population. Keep track of the all-time best individual, which will eventually be returned to the caller. Flag via improved that we had an improvement this generation so that we are not ready to quit yet. The variable n_tweaked will be used in conjunction with hill climbing soon.

```
value = criter ( dest_ptr , mintrades ) ;

if (value > parent1[nvars]) {        // If the child is better than parent1
  dest_ptr[nvars] = value ;        // Get the child's value (The vars are already there)
  if (value > grand_best) {        // And update best so far
    grand_best = value ;
    memcpy ( best , dest_ptr , dim * sizeof(double) ) ;
    ibest = ind ;
    n_tweaked = 0 ;
    improved = 1 ;                // Flag that the best improved in this generation
    }
  }
```

```
else {                              // Else copy parent1 and its value
  memcpy ( dest_ptr , parent1 , dim * sizeof(double) ) ;
  value = parent1[nvars] ;
  }
```

We now embark on the optional (but very useful) hill-climbing step. The following code is the logic for deciding if and what to hill climb. We'll discuss it on the next page.

```
if (pclimb > 0.0  &&
        ((ind == ibest  &&  n_tweaked < nvars) || (unifrand() < pclimb))) {
  if (ind == ibest) {               // Once each generation tweak the best
    ++n_tweaked ;                   // But quit if done all vars
    k = generation % nvars ;        // Cycle through all vars
    }
  else {                            // Randomly choose an individual
    k = (int) (unifrand() * nvars) ;  // Which var to optimize
    if (k >= nvars)                 // Safety only
      k = nvars - 1 ;
    }
```

If the user specifies pclimb=0, then hill climbing (called *tweaking* here) will never be done. Assuming that we can do it, two conditions are checked, either of which will allow a single climbing operation on this individual, which may be the newly created child or may be a copy of the primary parent. If the individual is the best so far and not all of its variables have been tweaked, we tweak it. Recall that n_tweaked was reset to zero every time the grand best changed. If this is the best, we count this tweaking and choose the variable according to the generation. It is common for the best individual to remain the same for multiple generations in a row, and this choice of parameter causes the tweaking to rotate among parameters, avoiding duplication.

If that first test fails (either this is not the best individual or all of its parameters have been tweaked already), then we roll the dice and randomly decide whether to tweak a randomly chosen parameter in this individual.

Integer and real parameters are tweaked differently, with the former being much simpler and faster. Here is half of the integer code:

```
if (k < nints) {          // Is this an integer?
  ivar = ibase = (int) dest_ptr[k] ;
  ilow = (int) low_bounds[k] ;
  ihigh = (int) high_bounds [k] ;
  success = 0 ;
  while (++ivar <= ihigh) {
    dest_ptr[k] = ivar ;
    test_val = criter ( dest_ptr , mintrades ) ;
    if (test_val > value) {
      value = test_val ;
      ibase = ivar ;
      success = 1 ;
      }
    else {
      dest_ptr[k] = ibase ;
      break ;
      }
    }
```

We preserve in ibase the current value of this parameter so we can restore it if no improvement is found. We'll vary ivar in the vicinity of the current value to seek improvement. A full global search over its entire legal range would usually be a waste of time. The variable success flags if we found any improvement. We move the parameter upward until it hits its upper limit or performance fails to improve. (The possibility of flat performance followed by improvement is ignored here to keep the search fast.) As long as we are improving, we keep updating ibase and the improved value. When performance fails to improve, which may happen on the first test, we set the parameter to ibase and stop advancing.

If we did not find success by increasing the parameter, we try decreasing it instead. This algorithm is essentially identical to the upward-search algorithm, so there is no point in discussing it here.

```
if (! success) {
  ivar = ibase ;
  while (--ivar >= ilow) {
    dest_ptr[k] = ivar ;
    test_val = criter ( dest_ptr , mintrades ) ;
    if (test_val > value) {
      value = test_val ;
      ibase = ivar ;
      success = 1 ;
      }
    else {
      dest_ptr[k] = ibase ;
      break ;
      }
    } // While searching downward
  } // If the upward search did not succeed
} // If k < nints (this parameter is an integer)
```

The code for handling real parameters is a bit more complex. We begin, as shown on the next page, by copying information needed for performance computation to static variables, all of which begin with local_. This technique allows the parameter optimization routines to be general purpose, calling a criterion function that references only the parameters being optimized.

```
else {                         // This is a real parameter
  local_criter = criter ;
  local_ivar = k ;              // Pass it to criterion routine
  local_base = dest_ptr[k] ;    // Preserve orig var
  local_x = dest_ptr ;
  local_nvars = nvars ;
  local_nints = nints ;
  local_low_bounds = low_bounds ;
  local_high_bounds = high_bounds ;
  old_value = value ;
```

Optimization is done in two steps. First, we call a rough global search routine glob_max()
(source code in GLOB_MAX.CPP) that tests a handful of discrete points in a range and finds
the one having maximum function value. If the value is increasing at an endpoint, it advances
until a peak is found. Then this maximum is refined using Brent's algorithm in brentmax()
(source code in BRENTMAX.CPP). This, unfortunately, can be an expensive operation. But
the return is often substantial, especially when differential evolution has gotten us close to
the global maximum and all we need is accurate maximization of the best individual.

We commence the rough global search in the near vicinity of the current value of the
parameter:

```
lower = local_base - 0.1 * (high_bounds[k] - low_bounds[k]) ;
upper = local_base + 0.1 * (high_bounds[k] - low_bounds[k]) ;

if (lower < low_bounds[k]) {
  lower = low_bounds[k] ;
  upper = low_bounds[k] + 0.2 * (high_bounds[k] - low_bounds[k]) ;
  }

if (upper > high_bounds[k]) {
  upper = high_bounds[k] ;
  lower = high_bounds[k] - 0.2 * (high_bounds[k] - low_bounds[k]) ;
  }

k = glob_max ( lower , upper , 7 , 0 , c_func ,
          &x1 , &y1 , &x2 , &y2 , &x3 , &y3 ) ;
```

At this point we have a trio of points such that the center point has maximum
function value. Refine this and call ensure_legal()to ensure that the parameters are
within their legal bounds. This will likely be the case, or at least very close, because the
criterion function applies a huge penalty when the legal bounds are exceeded, and the
maximization routine will respond vigorously to this penalty. If the performance has
been improved, even after forcing legality, which will nearly always be the case, save the
superior parameter and update the grand best. Finally, update the worst and average
performance, strictly for user updates (not a part of the algorithm).

```
brentmax ( 5 , 1.e-8 , 0.0001 , c_func , &x1 , &x2 , &x3 , y2 ) ;
dest_ptr[local_ivar] = x2 ;  // Optimized var value
ensure_legal ( nvars , nints , low_bounds , high_bounds , dest_ptr ) ;
value = criter ( dest_ptr , mintrades ) ;
```

```
      if (value > old_value) {
        dest_ptr[nvars] = value ;
        }
      else {
        dest_ptr[local_ivar] = local_base ;      // Restore original value
        value = old_value ;
        }
      if (value > grand_best) {      // Update best so far
        grand_best = value ;
        memcpy ( best , dest_ptr , dim * sizeof(double) ) ;
        ibest = ind ;
        n_tweaked = 0 ;
        improved = 1 ;   // Flag that the best improved in this generation
        }
      } // If optimizing real parameter
    } // If doing hill-climbing step

  if (value < worstf)
    worstf = value ;

  avgf += value ;

  } // Create all children in this generation
```

We are practically done. If this generation saw no improvement in the best individual, increment the convergence counter and quit if we reached the user-specified count. But if we did get improvement, reset the counter. Then reverse the roles of pop1 and pop2 for the source and destination generation populations. The little remaining code is just cleanup work, omitted here.

```
if (! improved) {
  ++bad_generations ;
  if (bad_generations > max_bad_gen)
    goto FINISHED ;
  }
else
  bad_generations = 0 ;
```

```
    if (old_gen == pop1) {
      old_gen = pop2 ;
      new_gen = pop1 ;
      }
    else {
      old_gen = pop1 ;
      new_gen = pop2 ;
      }

    } // For all generations
```

The routine for ensuring legality simply checks each parameter against its user-specified limit, computes a stiff penalty for being outside the limit (used only for real-parameter tweaking), and enforces the limit. For integers, we treat positive and negative values separately to ensure correct truncation. Recall that mutation will generally cause integer parameters to obtain non-integer values, so we fix that here as a first step.

```
static double ensure_legal ( int nvars , int nints , double *low_bounds , double
*high_bounds , double *params )
{
  int i, j, varnum, ilow, ihigh ;
  double rlow, rhigh, penalty, dtemp ;

  penalty = 0.0 ;

  for (i=0 ; i<nvars ; i++) {

    if (i < nints) {                // Is this an integer parameter?
      if (params[i] >= 0)
        params[i] = (int) (params[i] + 0.5) ;
      else if (params[i] < 0)
        params[i] = -(int) (0.5 - params[i]) ;
      }

    if (params[i] > high_bounds[i]) {
      penalty += 1.e10 * (params[i] - high_bounds[i]) ;
      params[i] = high_bounds[i] ;
      }
```

```
  if (params[i] < low_bounds[i]) {
    penalty += 1.e10 * (low_bounds[i] - params[i]) ;
    params[i] = low_bounds[i] ;
     }
   }

 return penalty ;
}
```

The routine called by glob_max() and brentmax() is a simple function of the single parameter being optimized. The appropriate parameter is set to the trial value, and ensure_legal() is called to enforce legality and compute a possible penalty for being outside the bounds. Then the performance computation routine is called to compute the trading system's performance, and the penalty, if any, is subtracted from the performance.

```
static double c_func ( double param )
{
  double penalty ;

  local_x[local_ivar] = param ;
  penalty = ensure_legal ( local_nvars , local_nints , local_low_bounds ,
                           local_high_bounds , local_x ) ;
  return local_criter ( local_x , mintrades ) - penalty ;
}
```

A complete program to demonstrate this algorithm, DEV_MA.CPP, will be presented on page 112.

CHAPTER 4

Post-optimization Issues

Cheap Bias Estimates

On page 121 we'll present a detailed examination of training bias, and on page 286 we'll see a powerful way to deal with this serious problem. But for the moment, we'll provide a rough overview of training bias and show how, if one has trained a trading system using differential evolution or some similar stochastic algorithm, we can get a rough but useful estimate of training bias as an inexpensive by-product of parameter optimization.

As we embark on developing a trading system, we have in our possession a set of historical data on which we will optimize our system. This is usually called the *in-sample* or *IS* data. When the system is tested or put to use on a different set of data, that data is called the *out-of-sample* or *OOS* data. We virtually always expect that the IS performance will be superior to the OOS performance. This can be because of several factors, the most important of which is that the inevitable noise present in our IS data will, to some small or large degree, be mistaken by our training algorithm for legitimate patterns. When (by definition) identical noise does not appear in the OOS data, performance will suffer.

A key aspect of responsible trading system development is estimation of *training bias*, the degree to which IS performance exceeds OOS performance. Later we'll see some sophisticated ways of doing so with decent accuracy. But when we have tested a large number of random parameter combinations as a preliminary population for a stochastic optimization procedure, we can use those parameter sets and associated bar-by-bar returns to quickly generate an estimate of training bias that, while far from the accuracy obtainable with more sophisticated methods, is often good enough for a rough preliminary estimate. This gives us an early idea of whether we are on the right track, and it may save us more work in a direction that leads to a dead end.

T. Masters, *Testing and Tuning Market Trading Systems*, https://doi.org/10.1007/978-1-4842-4173-8_4

The StocBias Class

The file STOC_BIAS.CPP contains code for a class that lets us intercept preliminary population generation and use this data to roughly estimate training bias. To do so, we need access to the bar-by-bar returns of every trial trading system during generation of the initial population.

It is vital that the trial parameter estimates be generated either randomly or by a deterministic grid search. They must not be generated from any sort of intelligent guided search. Thus, we will examine all of the legitimate cases used in constructing the initial population for differential evolution, but we must not use any of the cases that are created by mutation and crossover.

The motivation for the algorithm is this: suppose we were to choose some bar in advance that will serve as a single OOS bar. As we process every trial parameter set, we will find the parameter set from among all trials that maximizes the total return of all *other* bars—all bars except the one we have chosen in advance to be an OOS bar. We might call this the IS set. Our chosen OOS bar will play no role in selecting the best-performing parameter set because it is ignored during calculation of the IS return. After we have examined all parameter sets that went into the creation of the initial population, the IS per-bar return of our best parameter set, minus the return of our single OOS bar, will be a crude but honest estimate of the training bias.

If we did this for just a single chosen OOS bar, our training bias estimate would be too subject to random variation to be useful. But it is easy to do this essentially simultaneously for every bar and then combine the individual returns. For any parameter set, we just compute the total return of all bars. If we subtract the return of any single bar from the total, the difference is the IS return for that parameter set, and the bar we remove is the corresponding OOS return. As we process trial parameter sets, we keep track of, for each bar separately, the maximum IS return and the OOS return corresponding to that superior IS return so we can subtract later.

The primary limitation is that for this to give a really good estimate of training bias, we would need to find the truly optimal parameter set for each IS set, and there are as many IS sets as there are bars in the historical data. This is obviously impractical. Because we are basing our "optimum" on nothing more than randomly selected trial parameter sets, we cannot expect great accuracy. In fact, unless the trial population is large, perhaps several thousand at least, our bias estimate will be worthless. But by using large over-initialization in the differential evolution, we can accomplish this and provide a great starting population to boot!

The class declaration is as follows:

```
class StocBias {
public:
  StocBias::StocBias ( int ncases ) ;
  StocBias::~StocBias () ;

  int ok ;        // Flags if memory allocation went well

  void collect ( int collect_data ) ;
  void process () ;
  void compute ( double *IS_mean , double *OOS_mean , double *bias ) ;
  double *expose_returns () ;

private:
  int nreturns ;           // Number of returns
  int collecting ;         // Are we currently collecting data?
  int got_first_case ;     // Have we processed the first case (set of returns)?
  double *returns ;        // Returns for currently processed case
  double *IS_best ;        // In-sample best total return
  double *OOS ;            // Corresponding out-of-sample return
} ;
```

The constructor for our StocBias class allocates memory and initializes a few flags. The collecting flag signals whether we are collecting and processing cases. This must be turned on (nonzero) when we are building the initial population and turned off during optimization. I have omitted code that verifies successful memory allocation and sets the ok flag.

```
StocBias::StocBias (
  int nc
  )
{
  nreturns = nc ;
  collecting = 0 ;
  got_first_case = 0 ;

  IS_best = (double *) malloc ( nreturns * sizeof(double) ) ;
  OOS = (double *) malloc ( nreturns * sizeof(double) ) ;
  returns = (double *) malloc ( nreturns * sizeof(double) ) ;
}
```

The following trivial routine is called (with collect_data=1) when we want to begin collecting trial parameter sets and returns, and it is called again (with collect_data=0) when we are finished collecting:

```
void StocBias::collect ( int collect_data )
{
  collecting = collect_data ;
}
```

We could let returns be public, but C++ purists would like it to remain private and expose it to the criterion routine, so that's what I do here:

```
double *StocBias::expose_returns ()
{
  return returns ;
}
```

Every time the parameter evaluation routine is called, that routine is responsible for placing the bar-by-bar returns in this returns and then calling process().

```
void StocBias::process ()
{
  int i ;
  double total , this_x ;

  if (! collecting)
    return ;

  total = 0.0 ;
  for (i=0 ; i<nreturns ; i++)
    total += returns[i] ;

  // Initialize if this is the first call
  if (! got_first_case) {
    got_first_case = 1 ;
    for (i=0 ; i<nreturns ; i++) {
      this_x = returns[i] ;
      IS_best[i] = total - this_x ;
      OOS[i] = this_x ;
      }
    }
```

```
// Keep track of best if this is a subsequent call
else {
  for (i=0 ; i<nreturns ; i++) {
    this_x = returns[i] ;
    if (total - this_x > IS_best[i]) {
      IS_best[i] = total - this_x ;
      OOS[i] = this_x ;
      }
    }
  }
}
```

The process() routine begins by summing the returns of all bars to get a total return for this trial parameter set. If this is the first call (got_first_case is false), we initialize by setting the "best-so-far" IS returns in IS_best[] to be the IS returns, and we also initialize the corresponding OOS returns. Recall that the IS return for any OOS bar is the sum of all returns except that for the OOS bar. This is easily obtained by subtracting the OOS bar's return from the total of all returns.

If this is a subsequent call, the procedure is similar, except that instead of initializing IS_best[], we update it if this IS return is greater than the running best. If we do this update, we must also update the corresponding OOS return.

All that remains is trivial computation of final results. The values we return are based on the total return across the market history. Each element of IS_best[] is the sum of nreturns−1 bar returns, so we divide the sum by this quantity to make the sum commensurate with the sum of OOS returns.

```
void StocBias::compute (
  double *IS_return ,
  double *OOS_return ,
  double *bias
  )
{
  int i ;

  *IS_return = *OOS_return = 0.0 ;
```

```
for (i=0 ; i<nreturns ; i++) {
   *IS_return += IS_best[i] ;
   *OOS_return += OOS[i] ;
   }

*IS_return /= (nreturns - 1) ;    // Each IS_best is the sum of nreturns-1 returns
*bias = *IS_return - *OOS_return ;
}
```

What do we do with the bias after we've computed it? In isolation it's of limited value. Plus, we must remember that this is a crude estimate. Still, it's useful to subtract the bias from the total return of the trading system obtained from the optimal parameter set produced by the differential evolution or other optimization algorithm. If removal of the approximate training bias produces a less-than-excellent estimate of how the parameter set will perform out of sample, we should pause and reconsider our trading system.

It can be important to compare the IS_return computed here with the optimal value produced by the optimization routine. Naturally it will virtually always be less; the optimization algorithm would be pretty poor otherwise! But ideally it will be fairly close. If we find that our IS_return is much smaller than the optimal return, we should conclude that we have employed too few trial parameter sets, and hence our bias estimate will be exceptionally poor.

A complete example of this routine in the context of an actual trading system will appear in the discussion of the DEV_MA program on page 112.

Cheap Parameter Relationships

In the prior section, we saw how the initial population from a stochastic optimization routine like differential evolution could be borrowed to provide a quick-and-dirty estimate of training bias. In this section, we will see how the final population, after optimization is complete, can be used to quickly generate some interesting measures of how the parameters relate to one another. As with the cheap training bias, these are rough estimates and can sometimes be wildly inaccurate. However, more often than not, they will prove interesting and useful, especially if a large population is used and optimization continues until stability is obtained. Moreover, as part of this presentation, we will point out how the algorithm can be modified to produce much more reliable estimates, though at a cost of more computation time.

Some of the mathematics in this development is beyond the scope of this book and will be presented as stated fact, with the reader having to trust in the process. Moreover, many claims are simplified for this presentation, though never to the point of being rendered incorrect. On the other hand, there is nothing really esoteric here; all of these results are standard material, widely available in standard statistical references. With these caveats in mind...

The *Hessian* of a function of several variables is the matrix of second partial derivatives of the function with respect to the variables. In other words, the i,j element of the Hessian matrix is the partial derivative of the function with respect to the i'th and j'th variables. Suppose the function is the negative log likelihood of a probability density; the variables are the parameters of the probability density function, and we have computed the Hessian at the maximum likelihood estimates of the parameters. Then for a broad class of probability density functions, including the venerable normal distribution, the estimated standard error of a parameter estimate is the square root of the corresponding diagonal of the inverse of the Hessian matrix. In fact, the inverse of the Hessian is the covariance matrix of the parameter estimates.

Before any statisticians start screaming, let me emphasize that the performance maximum of a trading system is a very different animal from the log likelihood of a statistical distribution, so it is a bit of a stretch to treat them similarly. On the other hand, the general behavior of an optimized trading system near its maximum (or any multivariate function, for that matter) follows the same principles. The inverse of its Hessian in the vicinity of the optimum describes the directional rates of change of the level curves of parameters. As long as we don't talk about standard errors of estimates, but rather keep everything relative, we can glean a lot of information about the relationships among parameters with some relatively simple techniques.

Complete source code for this algorithm is in the file PARAMCOR.CPP, and the DEV_MA.CPP program that will be presented on page 112 will illustrate it in the context of an actual trading system. We now work through the code one section at a time. The routine is called as follows:

```
int paramcor (
   int ncases ,      // Number of cases
   int nparams ,     // Number of parameters
   double *data      // Ncases (rows) by nparams+1 input of trial pts and f vals
   )
```

The structure of the data matrix is identical to that in the DIFF_EV.CPP program. Each individual (complete parameter set along with performance metric) occupies a single row, with the parameters first and the performance at the end. This means paramcor() can be called with the final population after optimization is complete. It would make no sense to call it with the initial population, as we did when estimating training bias. This is because we want the entire population to be near the global optimum, and in fact we want that optimum to be part of the population.

A fast and easy way to compute the Hessian matrix, which is what we will do here, is to fit a least-squares quadratic function in the vicinity of the optimum and then compute the Hessian directly. We need the number of parameters in this fit:

```
if (nparams < 2)
   return 1 ;

ncoefs = nparams                        // First-order terms
     + nparams * (nparams + 1) / 2    // Second-order terms
     + 1 ;                            // Constant
```

Before proceeding, it is important to emphasize that there are at least two alternative methods for computing the Hessian, both of which are more work but are likely superior in terms of accuracy. Readers who find value in the techniques described in this section would do well to explore these alternative methods, each of which has its own advantages and disadvantages. Here is a brief comparison of them:

- The method used here is a cheap by-product of differential evolution. We do not need to repeatedly evaluate the performance for various parameter sets because we already have a population in hand, most of whose members are relatively near the optimum. The use of a least-squares fit tends to smooth out noise. The big disadvantage of this method is that trial parameter sets that are far from the optimum can throw an annoying monkey wrench into calculations. This method works best when we have a very large population and we optimize until convergence is solid.

- We can take a large number of random samples in the vicinity of the optimal parameter set, evaluate the performance of each, and do a least-squares fit just as in the first method. This has the significant advantage that wild parameter sets will not appear and interfere with computations. But it does require numerous performance evaluations, which can complicate code and add significant computation time if a large number of evaluations are done. More important, choosing an appropriate degree of random variation is not a trivial undertaking, while differential evolution tends to gravitate to appropriate values.

- We can use standard numerical methods, perturbing each parameter and numerically computing the partial derivatives directly. Again, finding an appropriate perturbation can be difficult, and misjudgment can have a profound effect on accuracy. But if done carefully, this would almost certainly be a good approach.

Here we deal with an annoyingly heuristic decision. To limit the population to only those parameter sets that are close to the optimum, we keep only a fraction of the final population, those with the smallest Euclidean distance from the optimum. How many cases do we keep? My own heuristic is to keep 50 percent more cases than there are coefficients to be estimated. If this is too small, we may not get enough variation to allow accurate computation of every interaction coefficient. If it is too large, we may suffer contamination from wild parameter sets, so far from the optimum that we are prevented from getting accurate local behavior. But in my own experience this factor is reasonably reliable, especially if the population is large (at least several hundred). If the population is many hundreds, it would likely be beneficial to increase this factor to increase the likelihood of being able to model all parameter interactions.

```
nc_kept = (int) (1.5 * ncoefs) ;  // Keep this many individuals

if (nc_kept > ncases) {
   return 1 ;
   }
```

We need a lot of work areas allocated. We'll use the SingularValueDecomp object for doing the least-square quadratic fit. Its source code can be found in SVDCMP.CPP. Readers unfamiliar with this technique will find it easy to locate more information on singular value decomposition, a standard and reliable least-squares fitting method. We also open a log file to which the information from this algorithm will be written for the user.

```
sptr = new SingularValueDecomp ( nc_kept , ncoefs , 0 ) ;
coefs = (double *) malloc ( ncoefs * sizeof(double) ) ;
hessian = (double *) malloc ( nparams * nparams * sizeof(double) ) ;
evals = (double *) malloc ( nparams * sizeof(double) ) ;
evect = (double *) malloc ( nparams * nparams * sizeof(double) ) ;
work1 = (double *) malloc ( nparams * sizeof(double) ) ;
dwork = (double *) malloc ( ncases * sizeof(double) ) ;
iwork = (int *) malloc ( ncases * sizeof(int) ) ;
fopen_s ( &fp , "PARAMCOR.LOG" , "wt" ) ;
```

We locate the best individual in the population and get a pointer to it.

```
for (i=0 ; i<ncases ; i++) {
  pptr = data + i * (nparams+1) ;
  if (i==0 || pptr[nparams] > best_val) {
    ibest = i ;
    best_val = pptr[nparams] ;
    }
  }

bestptr = data + ibest * (nparams+1) ;    // This is the best individual
```

We will want to work with a subset of the population made up of only those individuals that are closest to the optimal parameter set. This lets us focus on local information without being confused by performance variation far from the optimum. To do this, compute the Euclidean distance between the optimum and every member of the population. Sort these distances, simultaneously moving their indices so we end up with the indices of the sorted individuals. One implication of using Euclidean distance is that *we must define the trading system's parameters in such a way that they are at least roughly commensurate.* Otherwise, some parameters may receive excess or insufficient weight in computing distances. Later, we will see still another reason why this is important. Source code for the subroutine qsortdsi() is in QSORTD.CPP.

```
for (i=0 ; i<ncases ; i++) {
  pptr = data + i * (nparams+1) ;
  sum = 0.0 ;
```

```
for (j=0 ; j<nparams ; j++) {
  diff = pptr[j] - bestptr[j] ;
  sum += diff * diff ;
  }
dwork[i] = sum ;
iwork[i] = i ;
}

qsortdsi ( 0 , ncases-1 , dwork , iwork ) ; // Closest to most distant
```

Here is where we use singular value decomposition to compute the coefficients of a least-squares fit quadratic surface to the performance curve. This is a quadratic equation that provides minimum-squared-error estimates of the performance as a function of the coefficients, at least in the neighborhood of the optimum. To aid numerical stability, we subtract the coefficients and parameter value of the best individual from each other individual, thus centering the computation around the best parameter set. This is not mathematically necessary; if it were not done, any differences would just be absorbed into the constant offset. However, it does provide a quick-and-easy way to somewhat improve numerical stability. Comments at the beginning of the source code file SVDCMP.CPP provide some explanation of what's going on here, and more details can be easily found online or in many standard regression textbooks.

```
aptr = sptr->a ;                            // Design matrix goes here
best = data + ibest * (nparams+1) ;         // Best individual, parameters and value

for (i=0 ; i<nc_kept ; i++) {               // Keep only the nearby subset of population
  pptr = data + iwork[i] * (nparams+1) ;
  for (j=0 ; j<nparams ; j++) {
    d = pptr[j] - best[j] ;                 // This optional centering slightly aids stability
    *aptr++ = d ;                           // First-order terms
    for (k=j ; k<nparams ; k++) {
      d2 = pptr[k] - best[k] ;
      *aptr++ = d * d2 ;                    // Second-order terms
      }
    }
```

```
  *aptr++ = 1.0 ;                                // Constant term
  sptr->b[i] = best[nparams] - pptr[nparams] ;   // RHS is function values, also centered
  }

sptr->svdcmp () ;
sptr->backsub ( 1.e-10 , coefs ) ;               // Computes optimal weights
```

At this point we have the quadratic function coefficients in coefs. The constant of 1.e–10 is heuristic and not terribly important. It just controls the extent to which the coefficients will be computed in case of near singularity, which would be almost impossible to obtain in this application. We omit here the tedious code for printing the coefficients in case the user is interested.

Something subtle but vitally important should be noted in the code just shown: *we flipped the sign of the performance*. This converts the problem from one of maximization to one of minimization, akin to minimizing the negative log likelihood of a statistical distribution. This is not necessary; the results we need would follow just as well without the sign reversal. Not only is it nice to conform to traditional usage, but this will also give us positive numbers on the diagonal, which when printed are easier to read and more user-friendly.

Computing the Hessian matrix from the quadratic fit is trivial, just differentiating each term once for each parameter. Of course, this means we compute second derivatives for the diagonal terms, in which the same parameter appears twice. Linear terms vanish when differentiated twice. The matrix is symmetric, so we just copy one term to the other.

```
cptr = coefs ;
for (j=0 ; j<nparams ; j++) {
  ++cptr ;   // Skip the linear term
  for (k=j ; k<nparams ; k++) {
    hessian[j*nparams+k] = *cptr ;
    if (k == j)                          // If this is a diagonal element
      hessian[j*nparams+k] *= 2.0 ;      // Second partial is twice coef
    else                                 // If off-diagonal
      hessian[k*nparams+j] = *cptr ;     // Copy the symmetric element
    ++cptr ;
    }
  }
```

This is a good place for a short digression on what can go wrong and why apparent problems may not actually be as serious as they appear. Some problems can be informative in their own right. Recall that because we flipped the sign of the performance measure, we are now minimizing our function. The implication is that if we are at a true local (and ideally global!) minimum, the second derivatives of the function with respect to each parameter (the diagonal of the Hessian matrix) would be strictly positive. But what if one or more diagonals is zero or, heaven forbid, negative?

The short answer is that subsequent calculations are severely compromised. Remember that our fundamental assumption is that we are at a minimum (our performance is at a maximum). Everything that we will venture to conclude about parameter relationships hinges on the validity of this assumption. Here are some more thoughts on this issue:

- Any parameter whose diagonal element is not positive must be ignored in subsequent calculations. At least in regard to the least-squares fit to the data, this parameter is not at its optimal value.

- "Local" is a subjective description. A parameter may indeed be at a local optimum in a narrow vicinity of its location, but this local optimum may not be global.

- The parameter may indeed be globally optimal, but the least-squares fit is extended over such a distance that it no longer represents the local behavior of the function. In other words, it's the least-squares fit that's the problem, as it's being asked to approximate highly nonquadratic behavior.

- Perhaps most important, *nonpositive diagonals are a red flag that the parameterization of the trading system is unstable.* Typically, this indicates that instead of the performance curve being a nice smooth function of each parameter, it bounces up and down wildly. A small change in a parameter may move the performance violently, or perhaps move it up, then down after a little more move, and then back up again, multiple times. This happens when the trading system, instead of reliably capitalizing on repeatable patterns, more or less randomly catches big wins and then big losses, back and forth as a parameter varies throughout its range. This is poor behavior.

- A corollary of the prior statement is that "local" behavior should extend as far beyond locality as possible. If the performance curve behaves one way near its optimum but then quickly changes to different behavior just a little distance away, it's a dangerous system. We want to see, for each parameter, a broad peak of performance near the optimal value, with a smooth, steady drop-off as we move further from the optimal value.

The upshot of the prior points is that if we find that one or more diagonals are nonpositive, we should not curse the algorithm and automatically consider switching to numerical differentiation as an alternative to the least-squares-fit method, which has nice noise-cancellation properties. Instead, we should look long and hard at our trading system and especially plot sensitivity curves as will be discussed on page 108.

Okay, enough said, so we move on to what to do about negative diagonals. It's simple: just make any diagonal element, along with its row and column, zero. This will remove it from all subsequent computation.

```
for (j=0 ; j<nparams ; j++) {
  if (hessian[j*nparams+j] < 1.e-10) {
    for (k=j ; k<nparams ; k++)
      hessian[j*nparams+k] = hessian[k*nparams+j] = 0.0 ;
    }
  }
```

It's also the case that we are at a local minimum (remember that we flipped the sign of the performance) if and only if the Hessian matrix is positive semidefinite. But it's possible for wild parameter values to cause a quadratic fit whose Hessian does not have this property. We encourage this if necessary by limiting off-diagonal elements, although weird correlation patterns may still produce negative eigenvalues.

```
for (j=0 ; j<nparams-1 ; j++) {
  d = hessian[j*nparams+j] ;        // One diagonal
  for (k=j+1 ; k<nparams ; k++) {
    d2 = hessian[k*nparams+k] ;    // Another diagonal
    limit = 0.99999 * sqrt ( d * d2 ) ;
    if (hessian[j*nparams+k] > limit) {
      hessian[j*nparams+k] = limit ;
      hessian[k*nparams+j] = limit ;
      }
```

```
    if (hessian[j*nparams+k] < -limit) {
      hessian[j*nparams+k] = -limit ;
      hessian[k*nparams+j] = -limit ;
      }
    }
  }
```

The Hessian matrix will not be invertible with usual methods if any diagonal has been zeroed, and we will soon need the eigenvalues and vectors of it anyway, so we compute them and use them to compute the generalized inverse of the Hessian. We put the inverse back in the Hessian matrix to avoid yet another memory allocation. The source code for evec_rs() is in EVER_RS.CPP.

```
evec_rs ( hessian , nparams , 1 , evect , evals , work1 ) ;

for (j=0 ; j<nparams ; j++) {
  for (k=j ; k<nparams ; k++) {
    sum = 0.0 ;
    for (i=0 ; i<nparams ; i++) {
      if (evals[i] > 1.e-8)
        sum += evect[j*nparams+i] * evect[k*nparams+i] / evals[i] ;
      }
    hessian[j*nparams+k] = hessian[k*nparams+j] = sum ;    // Generalized inverse
    }
  }
```

We are finally ready to print some truly useful information. We begin with the relative variation of each parameter. If we were working with the negative log likelihood of a distribution, these values would be the estimated standard errors of maximum-likelihood estimators of the parameters. But because we are far from that scenario, we rescale so that the largest-variation parameter has a value of 1.0. These are the relative amount each parameter can vary while having minimal impact on the performance of the trading system. Larger values mean that the system is relatively impervious to variation in the parameter. Compute the scaling and then print them across the line. For an example of this output, please take a quick look at page 118.

```
for (i=0 ; i<nparams ; i++) {          // Scale so largest variation is 1.0
  if (hessian[i*nparams+i] > 0.0)
    d = sqrt ( hessian[i*nparams+i] ) ;
  else
    d = 0.0 ;
  if (i == 0  ||  d > rscale)
    rscale = d ;
  }

strcpy_s ( msg , " " ) ;
for (i=0 ; i<nparams ; i++) {
  sprintf_s ( msg2, "    Param %d", i+1 ) ;
  strcat_s ( msg , msg2 ) ;
  }
fprintf ( fp , "\n%s", msg ) ;

strcpy_s ( msg , " Variation-->" ) ;
for (i=0 ; i<nparams ; i++) {
  if (hessian[i*nparams+i] > 0.0)
    d = sqrt ( hessian[i*nparams+i] ) / rscale ;
  else
    d = 0.0 ;
  sprintf_s ( msg2 , " %12.3lf", d ) ;
  strcat_s ( msg , msg2 ) ;
  }
fprintf ( fp , "\n%s", msg ) ;
```

We can now compute and print the parameter correlations by scaling the covariances by the standard deviations.

```
for (i=0 ; i<nparams ; i++) {
  sprintf_s ( msg, " %12d", i+1 ) ;
  if (hessian[i*nparams+i] > 0.0)
    d = sqrt ( hessian[i*nparams+i] ) ;        // 'Standard deviation' of one parameter
  else
    d = 0.0 ;
```

```
for (k=0 ; k<nparams ; k++) {
  if (hessian[k*nparams+k] > 0.0)
    d2 = sqrt ( hessian[k*nparams+k] ) ;   // 'Standard deviation' of the other
  else
    d2 = 0.0 ;
  if (d * d2 > 0.0) {
    corr = hessian[i*nparams+k] / (d * d2) ;
    if (corr > 1.0)                           // Keep them sensible
      corr = 1.0 ;
    if (corr < -1.0)
      corr = -1.0 ;
    sprintf_s ( msg2 , " %12.3lf", corr ) ;
    }
  else
    strcpy_s ( msg2 , "      -----" ) ;        // If either diagonal is zero, corr is undefined
  strcat_s ( msg , msg2 ) ;
  }
fprintf ( fp , "\n%s", msg ) ;
}
```

Again, if you would like to see a sample printout of this, please see page 118.

We come now to what I find to be the most interesting and informative output. The eigenvectors of the Hessian matrix define the dominant axes of the level-curve ellipses of the trading system's performance as a function of the parameters. In particular, the eigenvector corresponding to the largest eigenvalue is the direction in which parameter change causes the most change in performance, the direction of maximum sensitivity. The eigenvector corresponding to the smallest eigenvalue is the direction that causes the least change in performance, the direction of minimum sensitivity.

We find these two extreme eigenvalues. Unless we have at least two positive eigenvalues, there is no point in continuing. Of course, some users might want to proceed if there is just one, but if things are so bad that there is only one positive eigenvalue, the trading system is so unstable that this whole process is probably pointless anyway.

```
for (k=nparams-1 ; k>0 ; k--) { // Find the smallest positive eigenvalue
  if (evals[k] > 0.0)
    break ;
  }

if (! k)
  goto FINISH ;
```

For easier interpretability, I choose to scale the directions so that the larest element in each direction vector is 1.0. Compute the scaling factors and then print the output.

```
fprintf ( fp, "\n         Max      Min\n" ) ;

lscale = rscale = 0.0 ;  // Scale so largest element is 1.0.  Purely heuristic.

for (i=0 ; i<nparams ; i++) {
  if (fabs ( evect[i*nparams] ) > lscale)
    lscale = fabs ( evect[i*nparams] ) ;
  if (fabs ( evect[i*nparams+k] ) > rscale)
    rscale = fabs ( evect[i*nparams+k] ) ;
  }

for (i=0 ; i<nparams ; i++) {
  sprintf_s ( msg, "    Param %d %10.3lf %10.3lf",
    i+1, evect[i*nparams] / lscale, evect[i*nparams+k] / rscale) ;
  fprintf ( fp , "\n%s", msg ) ;
  }
```

A sample of this output in the context of a real trading system appears on page 119.

Parameter Sensitivity Curves

Prior sections presented fast-and-easy methods for estimating training bias and for discovering relationships between parameters. These are both rough methods, susceptible to significant error, and their information is not vital to responsible trading system development. Nonetheless, I like to include these capabilities in my development systems because they add virtually no computational overhead and their results are almost always interesting. But please understand that the topic of this section is critical and must be considered minimal due diligence for any trading system developer.

Numbers are great for presenting information, but nothing beats a picture. In particular, we should examine plots of trading system performance as parameters vary around their computed optimal values. We want to see a smooth curve, especially near the optimal value. Bouncing at more distant values is of no great concern, but in the vicinity of the optimal value we want smooth behavior. If the optimal value is at a narrow peak, our trading system will be unstable; when market conditions inevitably evolve as time passes, the once-optimal value will tumble over the edge of the cliff and no longer be anywhere near optimal. Also, if we have distinct multiple peaks near the optimal value, this is a sign that the system is probably obtaining its lofty performance by virtue of luckily latching onto a few good trades and/or avoiding a few bad trades. Small shifts in a parameter alternately gain and lose these special trades, meaning that luck has played an inordinate role in the system backtest.

On the other hand, if we see that the trading system's performance slowly and smoothly tapers down from the optimum value as parameters move away from their trained values, we know that the system responds gently to perturbation, likely has good immunity to changes in luck, and will probably remain stable for some time into the future.

Computing these sensitivity curves is almost trivially simple, but we'll examine the code anyway. If possible, in practice it's best to display these as smooth curves on a computer screen. But to keep things simple, here I use the clumsy but serviceable approach of printing histograms to a text file. It's not the most elegant approach, but it's easy, and it does the job.

Code for the routine we are about to see is in SENSITIV.CPP. The subroutine is called as follows:

```
int sensitivity (
   double (*criter) ( double * , int ) , // Crit function maximized
   int nvars ,                    // Number of variables
   int nints ,                    // Number of first variables that are integers
   int npoints ,                  // Number of points at which to evaluate performance
   int nres ,                     // Number of resolved points across plot
   int mintrades ,                // Minimum number of trades
   double *best ,                 // Optimal parameters
   double *low_bounds ,           // Lower bounds for parameters
   double *high_bounds            // And upper
   )
```

The criterion function is the same one we saw for differential evolution, taking the vector of trial parameters and the required minimum number of trades. We have nvars parameters, the first nint of which are integers. Each parameter will be evaluated at npoints values equally spaced across its low_bound to high_bound range. The horizontal histogram will have nres discrete values ranging from zero to the maximum performance value. Negative performances are plotted as if they are zero. We also need the best vector of optimal parameter values.

We allocate memory and open the text file to which results will be written. Then we commence the main loop that processes each parameter. The first step in this loop is to set all parameters to their optimal values so that only one parameter at a time is perturbed from its optimum.

```
vals = (double *) malloc ( npoints * sizeof(double) ) ;
params = (double *) malloc ( nvars * sizeof(double) ) ;

fopen_s ( &fp , "SENS.LOG" , "wt" ) ;

for (ivar=0 ; ivar<nvars ; ivar++) {

   for (i=0 ; i<nvars ; i++)
     params[i] = best[i] ;
```

Integer and real parameters are processed separately, with integers being slightly more complicated. Here is that section of code. Integer values should be exactly represented in the floating-point parameter vector, but we take out cheap insurance that anomalies do not cause problems.

```
if (ivar < nints) {

   fprintf ( fp , "\n\nSensitivity curve for integer parameter %d (optimum=%d)\n",
           ivar+1, (int) (best[ivar] + 1.e-10) ) ;

   label_frac = (high_bounds[ivar] - low_bounds[ivar] + 0.99999999) / (npoints - 1) ;
   for (ipoint=0 ; ipoint<npoints ; ipoint++) {
     ival = (int) (low_bounds[ivar] + ipoint * label_frac) ;
     params[ivar] = ival ;
     vals[ipoint] = criter ( params , mintrades ) ;
     if (ipoint == 0  ||  vals[ipoint] > maxval)
       maxval = vals[ipoint] ;
     }
```

```
hist_frac = (nres + 0.9999999) / maxval ;
for (ipoint=0 ; ipoint<npoints ; ipoint++) {
  ival = (int) (low_bounds[ivar] + ipoint * label_frac) ;
  fprintf ( fp , "\n%6d|", ival ) ;
  k = (int) (vals[ipoint] * hist_frac) ;
  for (i=0 ; i<k ; i++)
    fprintf ( fp , "*" ) ;
  }
}
```

In the previous code, it's a little tricky ensuring that we test and print integer values that are as equally spaced as possible. We compute label_frac as the increment in parameter value attributed to each step to the next point. If you don't understand that computation, test the formula at the boundary values. After the maximum performance among the tested points is found, the histogram scaling is computed as hist_frac. We then pass through the saved performance values, compute the number of characters to print, and do it.

Real parameters are slightly easier because we don't have to worry about testing strictly integer values. Here is that code. No explanation should be needed because it is a simplified version of the integer code just shown.

```
else {

  fprintf ( fp , "\n\nSensitivity curve for real parameter %d (optimum=%.4lf)\n", ivar+1,
          best[ivar] ) ;

  label_frac = (high_bounds[ivar] - low_bounds[ivar]) / (npoints - 1) ;
  for (ipoint=0 ; ipoint<npoints ; ipoint++) {
    rval = low_bounds[ivar] + ipoint * label_frac ;
    params[ivar] = rval ;
    vals[ipoint] = criter ( params , mintrades ) ;
    if (ipoint == 0  ||  vals[ipoint] > maxval)
      maxval = vals[ipoint] ;
    }

  hist_frac = (nres + 0.9999999) / maxval ;
  for (ipoint=0 ; ipoint<npoints ; ipoint++) {
    rval = low_bounds[ivar] + ipoint * label_frac ;
    fprintf ( fp , "\n%10.3lf|", rval ) ;
```

```
    k = (int) (vals[ipoint] * hist_frac) ;
    for (i=0 ; i<k ; i++)
      fprintf ( fp , "*" ) ;
    }
  }
}
```

In the next section, we'll see an example of parameter sensitivity plotting in the context of a real application.

Putting It All Together Trading OEX

We now present a program that combines differential evolution, cheap training bias estimation, cheap computation of parameter relationships, and plotting parameter sensitivity curves. Source code for this program is in DEV_MA.CPP. The trading algorithm is a four-parameter thresholded moving-average crossover system. Readers should have no trouble replacing this system with their own trading system.

The Trading System

Normally I don't pay much attention to the trading systems used in the examples in this book, instead focusing on the technique under discussion. But in this case the trading system is so intimately connected to the techniques that it's important for the user to understand it. This is especially true here because the parameter relationships computed in PARAMCOR.CPP are most meaningful when the parameters are commensurately scaled, so make sure to do so if you implement a system.

The philosophy of the system is to compute a short-term and a long-term moving average of log prices. If the short-term MA exceeds the long-term MA by at least a specified long threshold, a long position is taken for the next day. If the short-term MA is less than the long-term MA by at least a specified short threshold, a short position is taken. Otherwise, we remain neutral. Thus, there are four parameters: the two lookbacks and the two thresholds. The evaluation routine is called as follows:

```
double test_system (
  int ncases ,              // Number of prices in history
  int max_lookback ,        // Max lookback that will ever be used
  double *x ,               // Log prices
```

```
int long_term ,          // Long-term lookback
double short_pct ,       // Short-term lookback is this / 100 times long_term, 0-100
double short_thresh ,    // Short threshold times 10000
double long_thresh ,     // Long threshold times 10000
int *ntrades ,           // Returns number of trades
double *returns          // If non-NULL returns ncases-max_lookback bar returns
)
```

Only one optimizable parameter is an integer, the long-term lookback. The short-term lookback is specified as the percent of the long-term lookback. The short and long thresholds are specified as 10,000 times the actual threshold. This is because in practice the optimal thresholds will be very small, and using this multiplier brings the thresholds up to a range commensurate with the other two parameters. If we worked with the actual thresholds, the PARAMCOR.CPP algorithms would be rendered nearly worthless because of the huge disparity in scaling. Everything else would be fine, though.

The last parameter, returns, can be input NULL if desired. But if non-null, the individual bar returns are placed there. This information is needed by the cheap bias estimating routine in STOC_BIAS.CPP.

The first step is to convert the specified commensurately scaled parameters to the values that are meaningful here. Readers, if you substitute your own trading system for this one, be sure to pay attention to this commensurate scaling requirement! Also initialize the total return cumulator, the trade counter, and the index for returns if used.

```
short_term = (int) (0.01 * short_pct * long_term) ;
if (short_term < 1)
   short_term = 1 ;
if (short_term >= long_term)
   short_term = long_term - 1 ;
short_thresh /= 10000.0 ;
long_thresh /= 10000.0 ;

sum = 0.0 ;              // Cumulate performance for this trial
*ntrades = 0 ;
k = 0 ;                 // Will index returns
```

The main loop that traverses the market history is here. Note that regardless of long_ term, we always start trading at the same bar for conformity. This is important. Compute the short-term moving average.

```
for (i=max_lookback-1 ; i<ncases-1 ; i++) {   // Sum performance across history
   short_mean = 0.0 ;                          // Cumulates short-term lookback sum
   for (j=i ; j>i-short_term ; j--)
      short_mean += x[j] ;
```

We then compute the long-term moving average, taking care that we take advantage of the summation already done for the short-term MA.

```
long_mean = short_mean ;        // Cumulates long-term lookback sum
while (j>i-long_term)
   long_mean += x[j--] ;

short_mean /= short_term ;
long_mean /= long_term ;
```

Compare the short-term/long-term MA difference to the thresholds and compute the next-bar return accordingly. Note that I chose to define the difference in terms of a ratio rather than a difference. I prefer this sort of normalization despite its asymmetry, but please feel free to disagree, especially since we are working with log prices. In practice, the difference is minimal anyway.

```
change = short_mean / long_mean - 1.0 ;      // Fractional diff in MA of log prices

if (change > long_thresh) {                   // Long position
   ret = x[i+1] - x[i] ;
   ++(*ntrades) ;
   }

else if (change < -short_thresh) {            // Short position
   ret = x[i] - x[i+1] ;
   ++(*ntrades) ;
   }

else
   ret = 0.0 ;
```

```
      sum += ret ;

   if (returns != NULL)
      returns[k++] = ret ;

   } // For i, summing performance for this trial

   return sum ;
}
```

Linking Criterion Routines

It would be bad programming style to embed the parameterization of a trading system into the differential evolution routine or any other general-use routine. It's bad enough that I embed the mintrades parameter, but since this is a trading-system application and this is a common parameter, I felt justified in doing so. But the remaining parameters, which can change significantly with different trading systems, must be supplied as a real vector. So, we need a way to map the generic criterion routine to the ultimate performance evaluator, as well as pass nuisance parameters. The standard method I have always used is to let the nuisance parameters be statics and use a criterion wrapper. In particular, I make static declarations at the top of the program and set them before they are needed. The wrapper is also shown here:

```
static int local_n ;
static int local_max_lookback ;
static double *local_prices ;

double criter ( double *params , int mintrades )
{
   int long_term, ntrades ;
   double short_pct, short_thresh, long_thresh, ret_val ;

   long_term = (int) (params[0] + 1.e-10) ;    // This addition likely not needed
   short_pct = params[1] ;
   short_thresh = params[2] ;
   long_thresh = params[3] ;
```

```
ret_val = test_system ( local_n , local_max_lookback , local_prices , long_term ,
                        short_pct , short_thresh , long_thresh , &ntrades ,
                        (stoc_bias != NULL) ? stoc_bias->expose_returns() : NULL ) ;

if (stoc_bias != NULL  &&  ret_val > 0.0)
  stoc_bias->process () ;

if (ntrades >= mintrades)
  return ret_val ;
else
  return -1.e20 ;
}
```

The code on the prior page nicely demonstrates a clean way of using a generic wrapper that insulates a toolbox routine like diff_ev() from differences among trading systems as well as nuisance parameters like price history and trade starting bars. We just have to make sure that the local_ statics are set to their correct values before the criter() routine is called. This wrapper also takes care of checking that the minimum trades requirement is met, and it handles the StocBias processing (page 92).

We'll skip presentation of the banal market-reading code; see DEV_MA.CPP for details. After the market is read, we initialize the statics that pass nuisance parameters, we set the bounds for the four optimizable parameters, and we set a minimum trade count. Create the StocBias object, optimize using differential evolution, and compute the bias, which we can subtract from the optimal performance to get the estimated true performance. Finally, we do the sensitivity tests.

```
local_n = nprices ;
local_max_lookback = max_lookback ;
local_prices = prices ;

low_bounds[0] = 2 ;
low_bounds[1] = 0.01 ;
low_bounds[2] = 0.0 ;
low_bounds[3] = 0.0 ;

high_bounds[0] = max_lookback ;
high_bounds[1] = 99.0 ;
high_bounds[2] = max_thresh ;  // These are 10000 times actual threshold
high_bounds[3] = max_thresh ;
```

116

```
mintrades = 20 ;

stoc_bias = new StocBias ( nprices - max_lookback ) ;   // This many returns

diff_ev ( criter , 4 , 1 , 100 , 10000 , mintrades , 10000000 , 300 , 0.2 , 0.2 , 0.3 ,
        low_bounds , high_bounds , params , 1 , stoc_bias ) ;

stoc_bias->compute ( &IS_mean , &OOS_mean , &bias ) ;
delete stoc_bias ;
stoc_bias = NULL ;   // Needed so criter() does not process returns in sensitivity()
sensitivity ( criter , 4 , 1 , 30 , 80 , mintrades , params , low_bounds , high_bounds ) ;
```

Application to Trading OEX

I ran the DEV_MA program using OEX, the S&P 100 index, from its inception through the middle of 2017. Figure 4-1 shows the main output from the program. We see that the total log return is 2.671, and the optimal parameters (long lookback, short lookback as percent of long lookback, 10,000 times short threshold, 10,000 times long threshold) are also shown. The remaining four lines of numbers are from the StocBias operations, with the expected return of 2.3489 being the optimized return of 2.6710 minus the bias of 0.3221.

```
Best performance = 2.6710  Variables follow...
   79.0000
   88.4591
   17.0877
   0.5328

Very rough estimates from differential evolution initialization...
   In-sample mean = 2.2410
   Out-of-sample mean = 1.9189
   Bias = 0.3221
   Expected = 2.3489
```

Figure 4-1. *Main output of DEV_MA for OEX*

Figure 4-2 shows the output generated by the PARAMCOR.CPP algorithms (page 96). Examine the *Variation* row. At one extreme we see that the short-term lookback and the short threshold have the least impact on performance in the vicinity of their optimal values, and the long-term lookback has only slightly less impact. The outstanding parameter is the long threshold, which has extreme sensitivity. Even tiny changes in its value have extreme impact on performance.

Estimated parameter variation and correlations

Variation very roughly indicates how much the parameter can change
RELATIVE to the others without having a huge impact on performance.

A strong positive correlation between A and B means that an increase
in parameter A can be somewhat offset by an increase in parameter B.

A strong negative correlation between A and B means that an increase
in parameter A can be somewhat offset by a decrease in parameter B.

	Param 1	Param 2	Param 3	Param 4
Variation-->	0.653	0.972	1.000	0.069
1	1.000	-0.441	-0.359	0.246
2	-0.441	1.000	-0.679	0.075
3	-0.359	-0.679	1.000	-0.299
4	0.246	0.075	-0.299	1.000

Directions of maximum and minimum sensitivity
Moving in the direction of maximum sensitivity causes the most change in performance.
Moving in the direction of minimum sensitivity causes the least change in performance.

	Max	Min
Param 1	0.124	0.031
Param 2	0.090	-0.971
Param 3	0.068	1.000
Param 4	-1.000	-0.015

Figure 4-2. *PARAMCOR output of DEV_MA for OEX*

The correlation of –0.679 between the short lookback and the short threshold indicates that changes in one can be somewhat offset by opposing changes in the other. I have no explanation for this unexpected phenomenon.

These observations are born out by the direction of maximum sensitivity, which is almost totally dominated by the long threshold. The fact that the dominant weight is –1 instead of 1 is irrelevant; this is a direction, and it may point either way.

The direction of minimal impact is a bit more interesting, and it substantiates the correlation noted earlier. We see that moving the parameters—such that the short-term lookback as a percent of the long-term lookback goes in one direction and the short threshold goes almost as much in the opposite direction—is the direction of parameter change that, of all possible parameter changes, produces the least impact on the performance. Fascinating.

Figure 4-3 through Figure 4-6 show the sensitivity curves for the four parameters. Note that especially for the two threshold parameters, the *Variation* reported earlier, in which Parameter 3 has minimum sensitivity and Parameter 4 has maximum sensitivity, agrees clearly with the plots.

```
Sensitivity curve for integer parameter 1 (optimum=79)

  2|**************************************
  5|*****
  8|*********
 12|***************
 15|**************************************
 19|*************************************************
 22|****************************
 25|****************************************************
 29|*********
 32|**************************
 36|*************************************************
 39|*****************************
 42|*****************************************************
 46|**********************************************
 49|********************************************
 53|************************************
 56|******************
 60|**********************************
 63|*********************************
 66|**********************************
 70|*********************************************
 73|****************************************************************
 77|**********************************************************************
 80|********************************************************************
 83|***********************************************************
 87|*********************************************************************
 90|*********************************************************
 94|*********************************************
 97|******************************************
100|*********************************************
```

Figure 4-3. *Sensitivity of long lookback*

```
Sensitivity curve for real parameter 2 (optimum=88.4591)

 0.010|*********************************************
 3.423|***************************
 6.837|*****************************
10.250|*******************************************
13.664|*****************************************************
17.077|**********************************
20.491|**************************
23.904|*****************************
27.318|*************************
30.731|*****************
34.144|***********
37.558|*************
40.971|***********************
44.385|************************
47.798|********************************
51.212|*****************************
54.625|****************************************
58.039|********************************************
61.452|*****************************
64.866|******************************************
68.279|*************************************************
71.692|**************************************************
75.106|***********************************************
78.519|*************************************************
81.933|****************************************************************
85.346|******************************************************************
88.760|*****************************************************************
92.173|**********************************************************
95.587|*****************************
99.000|**********************************************
```

Figure 4-4. *Sensitivity of short lookback pct*

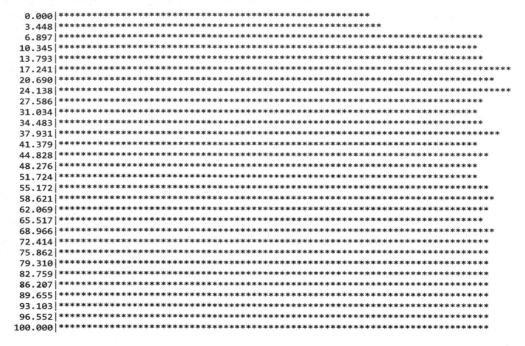

Figure 4-5. *Sensitivity of short threshold*

Figure 4-6. *Sensitivity of long threshold*

CHAPTER 5

Estimating Future Performance I: Unbiased Trade Simulation

The title of this chapter is optimistic, perhaps shamefully so. Financial markets are notoriously fickle. They are nonstationary (their statistical properties change over time), vulnerable to unforeseeable outside shocks, polluted by occasional wild swings for no apparent reason, and generally uncooperative. The idea that we can actually estimate the future performance of a trading system to any great degree is ludicrous. But what we often accomplish is to identify trading systems that have a painfully *small* expected future return, so we can be wary. Naturally, what we would really prefer is the ability to identify systems that have a high likelihood of *large* future return. And we may occasionally get lucky and enjoy this rare reward. It doesn't hurt to try. But the reader must understand that the real goal of this chapter is to use rigorous statistical methods to weed out those superficially promising systems that in reality should be discarded, or at least revised before being put to work with real money.

In-Sample and Out-of-Sample Performance

It is rare that a developer will dream up a trading system in *exactly* what will be its final form. The vast majority of time, the developer will hypothesize a *family* of trading systems. Any particular member of this family will be defined by the value(s) of one or more parameters. To take a rather mundane example, a developer may hypothesize that if a short-term moving average of recent market prices crosses above a long-term moving average, the tide has turned in this market and it is time to take a long position and to go short if the opposite happens. But what do *short-term* and *long-term* mean?

© Timothy Masters 2018
T. Masters, *Testing and Tuning Market Trading Systems*, https://doi.org/10.1007/978-1-4842-4173-8_5

The lookback period of each moving average must be specified before we have an actual trading system.

How do we choose effective lookback periods? The obvious method is to try as many values as computer time and other resources allow, and choose whichever pair of long-term and short-term lookbacks gives the best results. I'll parenthetically add that the criterion we use for defining "best results" can be important and will be discussed later. For now, just assume that we have a way of measuring trading system performance that allows us to choose the best parameters.

If we were working with perfect, noise-free data, the performance results we get from optimizing the short-term and long-term lookbacks for a dataset would usually be reflective of the results we would see in the future. Unfortunately, financial market data is about as noisy as its gets. In practice, market prices are dominated by noise, with just tiny bits of authentic patterns hidden deep under the noise.

The implication of this noisy situation is that our "optimal" parameters end up being chosen in such a way that our trading system fits patterns of noise in the training set as well as or even better than it fits the authentic market patterns. By definition, noise does not repeat. As a result, when we put our promising trading system to work, we may discover that it is nearly or completely worthless. This is a problem in any application, but it is particularly devastating in market trading because of the fact that financial markets are dominated by noise.

These two environments in which the trading system operates have standard names. The dataset that we use to optimize system parameters (such as short-term and long-term lookbacks in a moving-average-crossover system) is called the *in-sample* (*IS*) dataset. Any dataset that did not participate in the parameter optimization is called *out-of-sample* (*OOS*). The degree to which IS performance exceeds OOS performance is called *training bias*. This chapter is largely dedicated to quantifying and dealing with this effect.

It's worth mentioning that training bias can be caused by at least two entirely different effects. We have already discussed the most "famous" cause, learning unrepeatable noise patterns as if they were authentic market price patterns. This can be particularly severe when the model is excessively powerful, a situation called *overfitting*. A more subtle but equally problematic cause is under-representation of patterns in the training (in-sample) data. If the market history on which the trading system is trained does not contain sufficient representation of every possible price pattern that may be encountered in the future, then we cannot expect the system to correctly handle omitted patterns when they are eventually encountered. Thus, it is in our interest to develop our trading system using as much market history as possible.

The TrnBias Program to Demonstrate Training Bias

My web site contains source code for a small console application that demonstrates training bias for the primitive moving-average-crossover system just described. It can be easily modified by the reader to experiment with various optimization criteria. This complete source code is in TRNBIAS.CPP.

I will not explore this program in detail here because it is well commented and should be understandable to anyone who wants to modify it for their own purposes. However, I will briefly discuss its operation.

The program is invoked from the command line as follows:

TrnBias Which Ncases Trend Nreps

Which specifies the optimization criterion:

> 0 = mean daily return

> 1 = profit factor (sum of wins divided by sum of losses)

> 2 = raw Sharpe ratio (mean return divided by standard deviation of returns)

Ncases is the number of trading days.

Trend is the strength of the varying trend.

Nreps is the number of replications, typically at least several thousand.

The program generates a set of Ncases logarithmic daily prices. The prices consist of random noise plus an alternating trend that reverses direction every 50 days. The strength of this trend is specified as a small positive number, perhaps 0.01 (weak) to 0.2 (strong) or so. A Trend of 0.0 means that the price series is fully random. Then a complete set of trial moving-average lookbacks, ranging up to 200 days, is tested to find the combination of a short-term and a long-term lookback that gives the best in-sample performance. The user specifies the criterion by which this performance is judged. Finally, a new set of prices, using the same strength of trend, is generated. Its distribution is identical to the in-sample set, but its random components are different. The moving-average-crossover rule is applied to this OOS dataset, using the optimized short-term and long-term lookbacks, and its mean daily return is computed.

This process is repeated Nreps times, and the in-sample and out-of-sample average daily returns are averaged over the replications. The in-sample value minus the out-of-sample value is the training bias. These three quantities are reported to the user.

123

If you experiment with this program, you will discover several effects that are similar to what I have seen in actual trading system development.

- If you have a large number of cases, the choice of optimization criterion has relatively little effect. In fact, all three of these different methods have a tendency to provide the same optimal lookbacks for large datasets, regardless of the strength of the trend.

- If you have a small dataset, the optimization criterion has a huge effect on results.

- There is a slight though not universal tendency for the largest OOS mean daily return to be obtained by optimizing the profit factor. I have seen the same effect in my real-life development.

- In nearly every test that I ran, the training bias for the mean daily return was highest (worst) when optimizing mean daily return. This is almost certainly because mean daily return does not account for risk (losses) other than indirectly. Profit factor and Sharpe ratio both favor consistent, reliable returns, making them superior optimization criteria for a trading system. Also, profit-factor nearly always has the smallest training bias. It is my favorite optimization criterion.

Readers may want to modify the TrnBias program to incorporate the types of price patterns that they hypothesize, their trading system rules, and their preferred performance criteria to study the nature of training bias in their situation.

Selection Bias

Agnes heads up a company's division for trading system development. She has two people working for her, each of whom is charged with independently developing a profitable trading system based on historical data up to the current date. Soon, John presents her with outstanding backtest results, while Phil's results, while decent, are not nearly as impressive. Naturally, she chooses John's trading system and puts it to work with real money.

A few months later, their trading capital is largely gone. Wiped out. John's wonderful system tanked. Agnes thoroughly chews out John, but she's fired anyway, and they bring in Mary to replace her.

Mary examines John's system and sees the problem immediately: he has used an enormously powerful prediction model, one that did a great job of modeling the noise inherent in the market data. Moreover, because Agnes had given both of these guys complete market history up to the current date, they had used it all in developing their trading systems. Neither of them expended any effort at evaluating the out-of-sample performance of their system. Thus, neither of them had any idea how well their trading system had captured authentic market patterns, rather than just modeling noise.

After slapping both of their hands, she tells them a vitally important principle that Agnes ignored and in which they were complicit: *when selecting from among competing systems, **always base the selection criterion on out-of-sample results**, ignoring in-sample results.*

Why? The reason is that if the selection is based on IS results, the selection process favors overfit models. If model *A* primarily captures authentic market patterns, while model *B* not only captures these patterns but also does a great job of capturing patterns of noise, then model *B* will outperform model *A* on IS results and be selected, only to fail later when the noise does not repeat for real trading.

This principle is so important that Mary wisely chooses to hold back the most recent year of market history. She gives John and Phil market data that ends a year prior to the current date and tells them to try again.

Some time later, they both come to her with their systems, proudly showing off their spectacular results. (These guys just never learn!) So, she takes John's trading system and tests it on the year of data that she held back from them. It's fairly decent. This makes her happy, because the result she just observed is a truly fair, unbiased estimate of what John's system can do in the future. That test year played no role whatsoever in his system development, so it could not influence his choices or training procedures, and hence it has no optimistic bias. This is exactly the information she needs to make an intelligent decision about the true quality of his trading system.

Interlude: What Does *Unbiased* Really Mean?

Let's step aside for a moment and give a brief, intuitive clarification of the term *unbiased* that just appeared. We posit an imaginary universe of an infinite number of Johns, operating in an infinite number of different noisy market histories, with each John developing his own trading system based on his own universe's unique noisy market history. By *unbiased* in this example (and also generally), we mean that, *on average*, these different John-produced trading systems' OOS results would neither overestimate nor underestimate actual expected future performance. Because of random variation across universes, it is nearly certain that *the trading system produced by any single John will in truth over-estimate or under-estimate expected future performance in its OOS results*. Being "unbiased" does *not* mean that we can expect about the same performance in the future. That's much too much to hope for in a random universe. John's trading system's OOS performance will overestimate or underestimate the actual expected future performance of the system. But *unbiased* does mean that there will be no inherent bias one way or the other. The in-sample results have a strong optimistic bias because of the training bias already discussed. Out-of-sample results have no such bias. Roughly speaking, we could say that John's OOS results are just as likely to overestimate future performance as underestimate it. This is the best we can do.

Selection Bias, Continued

Okay, enough diversion; let's get back to the story in progress. We have John's OOS performance. Mary now goes on to test Phil's lovingly developed trading system on the recent year of data that she held out from both guys. It's OOS performance, which like John's is also unbiased and is slightly superior to John's. So, she wisely chooses Phil's system to trade.

We come now to the key point of this section: the OOS performance of Phil's system that the company is now trading is optimistically biased! Huh? How can this be? A moment ago, Phil's OOS performance was an unbiased measure of his system's expected future performance. But now that it has been chosen for trading and put to work, that same performance figure is suddenly biased? That makes no sense!

Actually, it does make sense. What we are experiencing is called *selection bias*. It came into play the moment Mary examined both OOS performances (John's and Phil's) and chose the better performer. The act of choosing one over the other introduces optimistic bias. The OOS performance of Phil's system that Mary just measured will now, on average, *overestimate* the expected future performance of his system.

How can such a bizarre transformation from unbiased to biased occur in the blink of an eye? It's because both of these competing systems (John's and Phil's) have their OOS performance influenced by two separate effects: true skill and dumb luck. These two systems will doubtless be based on slightly (or greatly!) different authentic patterns. Random noise in one system will be a little more like that system's authentic pattern compared to the other system. Thus, all other things being equal, the choice of the better system will tend to favor the *luckier* system. In the event that both systems have equal (though unmeasurable) true power, then the luckier system will have the superior OOS performance and hence be chosen by Mary. Only if their true powers are widely different, swamping out luck, will the truly better system be nearly guaranteed to be chosen.

By definition, noise does not repeat. Any good luck that favored one system over the other will vanish. As long as we were concerned with each system on an *individual* basis, the good luck and bad luck across those imaginary universes would average out, and OOS performance would be unbiased. But the moment we compare the unbiased performance of two or more competing systems and select the superior system, luck no longer averages out; good luck is favored, and we thereby introduce selection bias. And it can be enormous in real life. Be warned.

It should now be apparent that if Mary wants an unbiased estimate of the future performance of the trading system she picks, she has to go even further in holding out data. Instead of keeping back just one year (or whatever time slice she wants), she needs to hold out *two* years of data. She gives John and Phil market history that ends two years prior to the current date. When they present their systems to her, she tests their systems on the year of data that follows their training years and that ends a year prior to the current date. Based on the performance of the competing systems in this "first OOS" year, she chooses the best system. Then she tests this selection on the most recent year of data, what might be called the "second OOS" year. This provides an unbiased estimate of the performance of the selected system. This estimate is not only free from training bias, but it is also free from the selection bias that resulted from her choosing the best system from among the competitors.

The SelBias Program

Before you skip this section, please let me encourage everyone to study this material, even those who have no interest in using or modifying the SelBias program. The reason is that the description of how the selection-bias demonstration program works will serve to reinforce the somewhat counterintuitive ideas presented in the prior section. The concept of selection bias is so foreign to many developers, yet so important, that it is difficult to overly emphasize this topic. That said...

My web site contains source code for a small console application that demonstrates selection bias for the primitive moving-average-crossover system just described. It can be easily modified by the reader to experiment with various trading systems and optimization criteria. This complete source code is in SELBIAS.CPP.

The program is invoked from the command line as follows:

SelBias Which Ncases Trend Nreps

Which specifies the optimization criterion:

    0 = mean daily return

    1 = profit factor (sum of wins divided by sum of losses)

    2 = raw Sharpe ratio (mean return divided by standard deviation
       of returns)

Ncases is the number of trading days.

Trend is the strength of the varying trend.

Nreps is the number of replications, typically at least several thousand.

The program generates a set of Ncases logarithmic daily prices. The prices consist of random noise plus an alternating trend that reverses direction every 50 days. The strength of this trend is specified as a small positive number, perhaps 0.01 (weak) to 0.2 (strong) or so. A Trend of 0.0 means that the price series is fully random.

The previously discussed TrnBias program employs a two-sided (long and short positions) trading system. But the SelBias program of this section splits this into two separate, independent trading systems, one taking strictly long positions and the other taking strictly short positions.

For each of these two competing systems, a complete set of trial moving- average lookbacks, ranging up to 200 days, is tested to find the combination of a short-term and a long-term lookback that gives the best in-sample performance of each. These optimal lookbacks are found separately for each system (long-only and short-only). The user specifies the criterion by which this performance is judged.

A new set of prices, using the same strength of trend, is generated. Its distribution is identical to the in-sample set, but its random components are different. This set corresponds to the "first-OOS" dataset mentioned in the prior section. In the Mary-John-Phil example, this would be the year following the data given to John and Phil. The moving-average-crossover rule for each of the two competing systems is applied to this OOS dataset, using the optimized short-term and long-term lookbacks for each system. The mean daily return for each system is computed for this new dataset, giving us an unbiased estimate of future performance for each of the two systems.

Then we generate a third independent dataset, what has previously been referred to as the "second-OOS" dataset. Whichever of the two competing models performed best on the prior dataset is evaluated on this third dataset to provide an unbiased estimate of performance after selecting the superior model. The selection bias is the performance of the winning model on the second (first-OOS) dataset minus its performance on the third (second-OOS) dataset.

This process is repeated Nreps times, and the in-sample and out-of-sample average daily returns for the two competing systems, the grand OOS return, and the selection bias are averaged over the replications. The in-sample value minus the out-of-sample value for each competitor is the training bias. Each competitor has its own training bias, but there is only one selection bias. These averaged quantities are reported to the user, along with a t-score for the selection bias.

Walkforward Analysis

Most trading system developers are familiar with using walkforward analysis to estimate future performance. Despite this ubiquity, we will present the algorithm here, both to clarify any misconceptions and as a vehicle for pointing out several potential flaws in the most commonly employed version of the algorithm.

The idea behind walkforward analysis is that, given a historical dataset, we simulate how a trading system would have performed if it had been executed in real time (no knowledge of the future) during that market history. In other words, at any specified historical moment in time, we have at our disposal all available market history up to and including that specified time, and we pretend that we have no knowledge of market prices later than that time. We devise our trading system (usually by optimizing parameters) using the data up through the specified time and then test this trading system's performance over an immediate future time period (which is OOS) in the history. This simulates how our system would have performed in real life back at that historical time. We temporarily stash this future performance somewhere. We then move everything forward in time and repeat the process, exactly as a real trader would do when continually updating the trading system to keep up with evolving market conditions. When the end of the historical data is reached, we pool all of the individual OOS results and compute whatever performance measures we want. The most basic version of this algorithm can be stated as shown here. A more advanced version will appear later.

1) Set OOS_START to the bar of the user's desired starting date for testing.

2) Create the trading system based on market history over a desired lookback period that ends just *prior* to OOS_START.

3) Execute the trading system over a desired time period NTEST beginning at OOS_START. Save the system's performance. Note that NTEST need not be fixed. For example, we may want to do day trades over a calendar year, so NTEST will depend upon the number of trading days in the year being tested.

4) If more market data remains, advance OOS_START by NTEST and loop back to step 2.

When the previous algorithm is complete, we examine the performance results saved in step 3 for each pass through the loop. Most people call a single such pass a *fold*, and we will occasionally use this terminology.

Observe that because of the way this algorithm is constructed, the pooled OOS results are contiguous (no missing data), and they appear in the order in which they would have occurred if this process had been real life instead of a simulation. This means that even order-dependent performance statistics such as drawdown can be legitimately computed.

We may want to continue this walkforward testing even after the trading system is in use. This way, we can keep track of its ongoing performance to determine whether perhaps the system is deteriorating (a common occurrence!). In this case, we have one more consideration. Contiguity assumes that step 2, creation of the trading system, can occur fast enough for the next trade decision to be made. If we are doing end-of-day trading, we can likely retrain the system overnight. On the other hand, if we are doing intraday trading of price ticks as they occur in both day and night sessions, we must define the folds so that the system is re-created during times that the market is idle, such as on weekends. In practice this is rarely, if ever, an issue, because we can nearly always find blocks of idle time sufficiently long to retrain the system. But the key point is that *if we wish to pursue ongoing evaluation, we must perform development walkforward analyses using the same granularity that would be imposed on us during real-time use.*

Just to be clear, suppose our system is so slow to train relative to trade speed that updating the parameters must be done over weekends during actual use. In this situation, if we want to evaluate ongoing performance (always wise!), then during development we should do our walkforward analysis also using Monday to Friday blocks as folds. This way, real-time results are comparable to historical results.

Future Leak by Unobvious IS/OOS Overlap

A popular and powerful method for developing a trading system is to build a dataset of *predictors* and a *target* based on market history. The predictors are typically indicators such as RSI, trendline slopes, and so forth. The target is some measure of future market price change, such as the change from the current price to the price ten days out. Each case in the dataset contains the values of all predictors and the target for a single instance in the market, such as a day bar or an intraday bar. The developer then supplies this dataset to a modeling algorithm, which may be as simple as ordinary linear regression or as complex as a deep belief net. When the prediction model has been trained, the trading system is executed each day by computing the model's prediction for the current day's set of predictors. Based on the prediction made by the model, a position in the market may or may not be taken. This lets us harness the power of sophisticated modern machine learning techniques to drive our trading system.

A serious potential problem with this approach arises when the lookback period for indicators exceeds one bar, virtually always true, *and* the lookahead period for the target also exceeds one bar, which is often true. When indicators look back more than one bar, they have serial correlation because adjacent database cases share one or more market price observations. For example, suppose we have an indicator that measures the slope of a linear trend line across a 50-bar lookback period. When we advance to the next case, 49 bars are shared between the two adjacent cases. As a result, the trend indicator will change very little from one case to the next.

The same effect arises with the target. Suppose our target is the price change from now until ten days from now. When we advance from one case to the next, these two cases have nine bars of market change in common. The net market change for these two cases will be quite similar most of the time.

Now think about what happens at the boundary separating the end of the training set for a fold and the start of the test set for that fold. If we have serial correlation in *both* the indicators and the target, then late cases in the training set will be similar to early cases in the test set because neither the indicators nor the target will have changed much. The effect is that information about the test set has leaked into the training set, meaning that the supposedly fair OOS test is now optimistic since at training time we will have some information about the test set going into the optimization process.

The implication of this situation is that we must separate the training-set block from the test-set block by omitting some cases at the end of the training-set block, those which are contaminated by future leak. How many do we omit? We find the minimum of the indicator lookback and the target lookahead and subtract one. Of course, if the indicators have different lookbacks, we consider the indicator lookback to be the maximum across all indicators.

For example, suppose we have three indicators with lookbacks of 30, 40, and 50 bars, respectively. Our target has a lookahead of 80 bars. The maximum of (30, 40, 50) is 50. The minimum of 50 and 80 is 50. So, we must omit 49 bars from the end of each training-set block.

Where does this formula come from? Deriving it is a simple but educational exercise for the reader. Suppose we are about to test an OOS set beginning at Bar 100. Pick a small lookback and a small lookahead. Does the potential training case at Bar 99 have prices in common with the test case at Bar 100 for both the IS and the OOS blocks? How about Bar 98? How many of those ending cases have to be omitted before either the IS price set or the OOS price set no longer has prices in common with the first test case? Remember that we have a problem only if *both* an indicator and the target share price history between the IS and OOS sets, because this is how test-set information leaks into the training set. If one or the other (indicator set or target) is independent for two cases, then these cases share no prejudicing information between the IS and OOS sets.

Two things are worth noting here. First, in nearly all practical situations, the indicator lookback will exceed the target lookahead, usually by a lot. Thus, the lookahead is the limiting quantity. Second, if the target lookahead is just one bar, a common situation, we do not have to omit any training data. In the next section we will explore another advantage of looking ahead just one bar.

Error Variance Inflation with Multiple-Bar Lookaheads

In the prior section we saw that if the target lookahead is greater than one bar, we must remove from the training set those cases closest to the fold boundary in order to avoid disastrous optimistic bias in what are supposed to be unbiased results. In this section we explore a different problem with multiple-bar lookaheads, one with a very different solution.

Random variation in the noise that happens to contaminate our market data will result in our walkforward performance figures to also be contaminated with random variation; the performance figure we get after pooling all OOS fold data, though unbiased if we do it right, will almost certainly overestimate or underestimate the true value. We touched on this on page 125 when we discussed the meaning of the term *unbiased*. Naturally, we would like for this *error variance* to be as small as possible. Moreover, responsible developers will try to supplement the performance results with other useful information, such as the probability that results this good could have been obtained through random good luck if the system were truly worthless (a *p-value*). We might even attempt to compute confidence intervals or perform any of the sophisticated tests discussed starting on page 283.

The problem is that nearly all statistical tests of the sort that we would like to perform require that the observations on which the tests are based be independent. (There are some tests that do not require independence, but they are tricky to perform and often of questionable value.) Now think about what happens when we have a lookahead greater than one bar. The target values of adjacent bars will be strongly related because of the sharing of overlapping price history. Thus, the observations (trade returns) that we have available for computing performance statistics are not independent.

This is more serious than just vaguely "violating" assumptions of various statistical tests. It turns out that the violation is of the worst possible sort: tests become anti-conservative. This means that if we compute a p-value, the computed probability will be too small, leading us to conclude that our trading system is better than it really is. If we compute confidence intervals for the purpose of bounding wins and losses, the obtained intervals will be too narrow, with the true intervals potentially much wider than those computed.

Even if we do not perform any statistical tests (irresponsible!) and just contemplate the unbiased OOS performance, we still pay a price for using multiple-bar lookaheads without the remedy we'll describe soon. The issue that underlies all of our woes is the fact that the error variance, which is the degree to which our unbiased performance estimate randomly varies around its true value, is larger than it would be if the individual trade returns were independent.

When the returns are independent and pooled into a single performance statistic, random errors in the returns tend to cancel. Some errors are positive and some are negative, and they wash one another out. But when the returns have serial correlation, they have less opportunity to cancel. There are clumps of positive errors and clumps of negative errors, making smooth cancellation more difficult.

The result is that even though the OOS performance is unbiased, its troublesome error variance is inflated. Its over-estimation or under-estimation of the true performance is greater than it would otherwise be. With a large lookahead, this inflation can be severe. In severe cases, the error variance may be so large as to render the OOS performance estimate nearly worthless, despite being unbiased.

The usual method for solving this problem is to use test folds only one bar long and, instead of advancing the folds by one bar, advance them by the lookahead. This guarantees that OOS test cases will not share any market information. For example, suppose the lookahead is 5 and we are about to start an OOS fold at Bar 100. The training block would end with Bar 95, omitting the 4 most recent cases to prevent bias. After making our trade decision for Bar 100, we would move the OOS fold ahead to Bar 105.

A side benefit of this approach is that it mimics what most traders would do in real life. Most traders would not want to keep building up their position during the lookahead period, even if the model suggested doing so. The risk of catastrophic loss would be too great.

The General Walkforward Algorithm

We begin by defining some quantities that must be specified by the user.

> LOOKBACK is the number of bars of price history (including the current bar) used to compute the indicator.

> LOOKAHEAD is the number of future price bars, which does not include the current bar, used to compute the target.

> NTRAIN is the number of cases used in the training set (before omitting any recent cases) for the prediction model on which trade decisions are based. The total distance we look back from the current bar in the price history is LOOKBACK + NTRAIN - 2. The actual number of training cases will be NTRAIN - OMIT.

> NTEST is the number of test cases in each OOS test block.

> OMIT is the number of most recent training cases omitted from the training set to prevent optimistic bias when LOOKAHEAD is greater than one.

EXTRA is the number of cases, in addition to NTEST, advanced for the next fold. In other words, each fold will be advanced by NTEST + EXTRA cases in the dataset, with each case corresponding to a price bar.

As discussed in prior sections, if LOOKAHEAD is greater than one (something we should avoid if at all possible), there are several precautions we should take if we are to do the walkforward intelligently.

1) We must set OMIT = min (LOOKAHEAD, LOOKBACK) – 1 to avoid deadly optimistic bias. This is crucial.

2) We must set NTEST = 1 and EXTRA = LOOKAHEAD – 1 if we are to avoid dangerous serial correlation in trade results. Serial correlation alone does not introduce bias, but it increases the error variance that impacts our OOS performance figures, and it precludes most traditional statistical tests.

The general walkforward algorithm is as follows:

1) Set OOS_START to the bar of the user's desired starting date for testing. If the entire dataset is to be used, set OOS_START = NTRAIN.

2) Create the trading system based on market history over cases running from OOS_START – NTRAIN through OOS_START – OMIT – 1.

3) Execute the trading system over cases running from OOS_START through OOS_START + NTEST - 1. Save the system's performance. Note that NTEST need not be fixed. For example, we may want to do day trades over a calendar year, so NTEST will depend upon the number of trading days in the year being tested.

4) If more market data (cases in the dataset) remains, advance OOS_START by NTEST + EXTRA and loop back to step 2.

C++ Code for the Algorithm

The file OVERLAP.CPP, which we will explore soon, contains an example of the fully general version of the walkforward algorithm. Here is a code fragment that illustrates the algorithm. We will break it into sections, explaining each section separately.

The complete dataset is in data. This matrix contains ncols columns, with the last column being the target variable (typically a measure of near-term future market price change) and all prior columns being predictors. This matrix has ncases rows, each corresponding to a single bar or trading opportunity. We initialize the start of the current training set, trn_ptr, to be the start of the dataset. The OOS test set begins at index istart, just past the user-specified ntrain cases that make up the training set. We will count OOS cases in n_OOS.

```
trn_ptr = data ;      // Point to training set, which starts at the beginning of the data
istart = ntrain ;     // First OOS case is immediately past training set
n_OOS = 0 ;           // Counts OOS cases as they are processed
```

The main fold loop is shown next. Rather than having to compute in advance the number of folds, we will just leave it open-ended and stop the walkforward when we run out of historical data.

```
for (ifold=0 ;; ifold++) {
   test_ptr = trn_ptr + ncols * ntrain ;        // Test set starts right after training set
   if (test_ptr >= data + ncols * ncases )      // No test cases left?
      break ;                                    // Then we are finished
```

At the beginning of the loop just shown, we set the test-set pointer to be ntrain cases past the start of the current training set. We could just as well use istart to set this pointer, but I believe this formula is clearer. If the start of the test set is past the end of our historical data, we are finished.

The call to find_beta() is the training phase, to be discussed soon. We have ntrain–omit training cases, which begin at trn_ptr. The other two variables are the optimized parameters returned by the training algorithm. We then set nt to be the number of test cases in the OOS block. This will normally be the user-specified quantity, ntest. But the last OOS block may be shorter, so we trim it back as needed.

The test loop makes a prediction for each case. If the prediction is positive, we take a long position, recording the target. Otherwise, we take a short position (minus target). Finally, we advance the training and test blocks.

```
find_beta ( ntrain - omit , trn_ptr , &beta , &constant ) ;
nt = ntest ;
if (nt > ncases - istart)                // Last fold may be incomplete
   nt = ncases - istart ;
```

```
for (itest=0 ; itest<nt ; itest++) {        // For every case in the test set
   pred = beta * *test_ptr++ + constant ; // test_ptr points to target after this line
   if (pred > 0.0)
      oos[n_OOS++] = *test_ptr ;
   else
      oos[n_OOS++] = - *test_ptr ;
   ++test_ptr ;                             // Advance to indicator for next test case
   }
istart += nt + extra ;                      // First OOS case for next fold
trn_ptr += ncols * (nt + extra) ;           // Advance to next fold
} // Fold loop
```

Date-Dependent Walkforward

It is common to perform a walkforward analysis based on dates. For example, we may want to test one year at a time: we train through the end of a calendar year and test the following year. Then we advance the training and test windows one year and do the same. This has the advantage of minimizing the number of times the model must be trained, which can be good when the training time is problematic. It also makes for an intuitive presentation of results. The general walkforward algorithm just shown can be used, setting NTEST for each fold according to the number of bars in the test year. Moreover, it is easy to set OMIT so as to prevent optimistic bias. However, we must use a LOOKAHEAD of one if we are to avoid variance inflation that precludes most statistical tests.

If we must have LOOKAHEAD greater than one and we also must present annual or other date-dependent walkforward results, then we need to break up each test period into single-bar tests (NTEST=1), each separated by LOOKAHEAD, and pool results into each year. Best results will be obtained if the model is retrained for each subfold, but this is not required.

Exploring Walkforward Blunders

In this section we use a small console program to explore the impact of lookaheads greater than one bar when proper measures are not taken to eliminate harmful effects. This program is called OVERLAP.EXE, and its complete source code is in OVERLAP.CPP. We begin with the calling parameter list and then explain the program's operation in detail.

We will conclude with a series of experiments to demonstrate the various relevant issues. To begin, the program is invoked from the command line as follows:

OVERLAP nprices lookback lookahead ntrain ntest omit extra nreps

> nprices is the number of market prices (bars) in the market history. For the most accurate results, this should be large, at least 10,000.

> lookback is the number of bars of history used to compute the indicator.

> lookahead is the number of future bars used to compute the target.

> ntrain is the number of cases used in the training set (before omitting any) for the prediction model on which trade decisions are based. The actual number of training cases will be ntrain minus omit.

> ntest is the number of test cases in each OOS test block.

> omit is the number of most recent training cases omitted from the training set to prevent bias when lookahead is greater than one.

> extra is the number of cases, in addition to ntest, advanced for the next fold. If lookahead is greater than one, then ntest should be one, and extra should be lookahead minus one if we are to avoid dangerous serial correlation in trade results.

> nreps is the number of replications used to compute the median t-score and the tail fraction described later. It should be fairly large and odd, at least 1001, for accurate results.

First, the program computes a price history that is a random walk, completely unpredictable. The implication is that no trading system would, on average, provide an expected return other than zero. The degree to which the actual return exceeds zero indicates the degree to which optimistic bias has crept in.

After the price history has been generated, a database consisting of a single indicator and the target is created. This indicator is the linear slope of the price history across the lookback period. The target is the market price lookahead bars in the future, minus the current price. Each case in the database corresponds to a single bar in the price history.

The walkforward now begins, starting with the first case in the database. We use the first ntrain minus omit cases in the database as a training set to compute the linear regression equation (slope and intercept) for predicting the target from the single indicator. The test case(s) in the OOS block are then processed by applying this regression equation to predict the target. If the prediction is positive, we take a long position, and if the prediction is negative, we take a short position.

The philosophy behind this primitive model is that during at least some time periods the market will be in a trend-following mode, which will result in the regression equation picking up the relationship between the most recent price trend and continuation of the trend into the future. Of course, because the market prices in this simulation are a random walk, this situation will not happen except by random chance, and so the expected return of this trading system should be zero.

After all test cases in this OOS block are processed, the fold is advanced by moving the training and test windows forward by ntest plus extra cases, and the training/testing is repeated for this next fold. This continues until all prices are exhausted.

The entire process just described, beginning with market price history generation, is repeated nreps times. For each replication, a t-score is computed for the pooled OOS trade results, and the median t-score across all replications is printed. Because the market prices are a random walk, we would expect this median to be about zero, but we will see that incorrect structuring of the walkforward will result in optimistic bias. Also, for each replication, the right tail p-value (probability that results at least this good could have been obtained by pure luck) is computed. (Actually, for simplicity the normal CDF is used instead of the t CDF, but this is an excellent approximation when a large number of market prices are used.) A counter is incremented each time this p-value is less than or equal to 0.1. Because the market prices are a random walk, we would expect this event to happen in about 0.1 times nreps replications. The observed fraction of times is printed. We will see that this fairly significant p-value will occur more frequently than 0.1 if the walkforward is not structured correctly.

Here are a few experiments that demonstrate the consequences of improper walkforward when using the database/model approach. In all of these experiments, we use the following parameters:

nprices = 50,000   *Using a long price history provides accurate results.*
lookback = 100   *This has almost no impact on relative results.*
lookahead = 10   *Any value greater than 1 demonstrates the issues.*
ntrain = 50   *This is fairly unimportant.*
nreps = 10001   *A large value reduces the effect of random error on results.*

As a reminder, the program will print two results, the median (across replications) t-score for OOS returns and the fraction of these replications for which the p-value associated with the t-score is less than or equal to 0.1. Because the market is a true random walk (unpredictable), we expect the former to be near 0.0 and the latter to be near 0.1. Any increase beyond these expected values results from dangerous optimistic bias due to improper walkforward.

Experiment 1: Optimistic Bias from IS/OOS Overlap with Large Test Set

> *ntest* = 50
> *omit* = 0
> *extra* = 0

For this test we make the test set be the same size as the training set and take no action to counter the problems induced by the lookahead exceeding 1. A test set this large (the same size as the training set) would not usually be done in real life because late observations in the test set would be so far from the training set that any nonstationarity in the market could reduce predictability. But it may be necessary when the model requires massive training time and we simply do not have the computational resources to retrain more often.

We find that the median t-score is 5.35, severe bias, and the fraction of replications whose t-score is significant at the 0.1 level is 0.920, a ridiculous amount of bias.

Experiment 2: Optimistic Bias from IS/OOS Overlap with 1-Bar Test Set

> *ntest* = 1
> *omit* = 0
> *extra* = 0

This is the ideal test and real-time situation, retraining the model after every single use. This would often be practical when trading day bars; we retrain the model every night for making a prediction about the next day.

We find that the median t-score is 74.64 (!), extreme bias, and the fraction of replications whose t-score is significant at the 0.1 level is 1.0, perfect failure. Why is this bias so much more severe than in the prior experiment? The reason is that when we have a large test set in each fold, as cases get further into the future from the training set, the number of overlapping prices decreases, thus reducing the optimistic bias. But when we test only the single case immediately past the training set, we have the maximum possible number of overlapping prices.

Experiment 3: Optimistic Bias from IS/OOS Overlap, fully handled

> *ntest* = 1
> *omit* = 9
> *extra* = 0

In this experiment we explore the subject described starting on page 131, optimistic OOS performance when multiple-bar lookahead creates unobvious future leak. Recall that the target lookahead is 10 bars, so to fully eliminate future leak we must omit 10-1=9 of the most recent training cases. We do so in this test.

We find that the median t-score is -0.023, which is zero except for random variation in the test. So we have completely eliminated the bias in OOS results. However, the fraction of replications whose t-score is significant at the 0.1 level is 0.314. How can this happen when the OOS results are unbiased? This is because of variance inflation, discussed on page 133. We will explore this subject in Experiment 5.

Experiment 4: Optimistic Bias from IS/OOS Overlap, partly handled

> *ntest* = 1
> *omit* = 8
> *extra* = 0

This test is identical to the prior experiment, except that we almost, but not quite, omit enough training cases. We need to omit nine cases, but we omit only eight.

We find that the median t-score is 1.88, which is not huge but still a problem. Cheating by failing to omit the required number of cases, even if we come very close, still introduces dangerous optimistic bias. Moreover, the fraction of replications whose t-score is significant at the 0.1 level is 0.588, worse than in the prior experiment.

Experiment 5: Optimistic Bias and Variance Inflation, fully handled

> *ntest* = 1
> *omit* = 9
> *extra* = 9

In this experiment we handle both of the issues involved in multiple-bar target lookahead. Recall that the target lookahead is ten bars, so to fully eliminate future leak bias we must omit 10-1=9 of the most recent training cases. Also, we must jump an extra nine cases as we advance folds in order to avoid variance inflation from serial correlation in OOS trade results. We do both in this test.

We find that the median t-score is -0.012, which is zero except for random variation in the test. So we have completely eliminated the bias in OOS results. Moreover, the fraction of replications whose t-score is significant at the 0.1 level is 0.101, as perfect as we can expect in a random trial.

Testing Robustness Against Nonstationarity

The curse of trading system developers (well, one of the curses, anyway) is nonstationarity in financial markets. Patterns that allow great predictability for months may suddenly vanish. This may be because of changing economic environments, such as times of unusually high or low interest rates. It may also be because of the discovery of these predictable patterns by large institutions, resulting in predictability being arbitraged out of existence. Regardless of the cause, it is important that we test how well our trading system holds up against changing markets.

It should be noted that different trading systems really do have different degrees of robustness against common types of market changes. This is often by design. Some developers deliberately design trading systems that have a fast response to changing conditions but that also require frequent modification to keep up with evolving market patterns. Others design systems that capitalize on patterns that, while often less prominent, are present in markets for years or even decades. Regardless of our choice or even if we make no deliberate choice, we need to know how long a trained model will retain its predictive power as market patterns evolve.

One effective way to evaluate robustness against nonstationarity is to perform multiple walkforward analyses, each having a different testing period. For example, we might retrain a day-bar system every night, testing it for only the next day. Then we test the same system with an OOS period of two days, retraining it every other day. Continue this testing pattern, lengthening the test period until performance severely drops off.

When we plot OOS performance versus the test period, we will typically see peak performance at the shortest test period (most frequent retraining). Performance will drop off as we lengthen the test period. Often, the drop-off will be slow at first, and then plummet, giving the developer a rough idea of how frequently the system must be retrained.

An even more sensitive, though slightly more complex approach, is to base performance on only the *last* bar in each test fold. This eliminates the influence of earlier, superior results, though at the (minor) expense of more variation in the performance curve.

Cross-Validation Analysis

A major disadvantage of walkforward analysis is that it fails to efficiently use all of the available market history. For every walkforward fold, all information past the end of the OOS block is ignored. We can solve this problem by means of cross validation. The idea is that instead of using only training data *prior* to the OOS test block, we also include data *past* the OOS block in the training set. This is often extremely useful in applications that do not involve time-series data. However, when cross validation is applied to time-series data, such as market histories, several subtle issues can bite us. In this section we explore these issues.

Unobvious IS/OOS Overlap

If you've forgotten about how a lookahead greater than one bar can induce optimistic bias from future leak in walkforward analysis, please review the material starting on page 131. I'll leave it as an exercise for the reader to show that, just as we had to omit *min (lookback, lookahead) – 1* cases from the end of the training set in walkforward analysis, when we do cross validation, we also have to omit this many cases from the beginning of the part of the training set that is past the OOS test block. To show this, use the same technique you employed in showing it for walkforward analysis.

Figure 5-1 shows how this works for a fivefold cross validation. The full left-right extent of the rectangle represents the historical extent of the available data. The four hash marks above the long rectangle delineate the five folds. In the fold shown, we are testing the middle block.

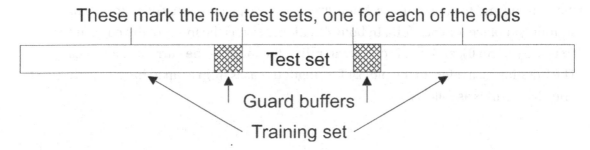

Figure 5-1. *Guard buffers in cross validation*

If our target variable had a lookahead of just one bar, we could use all of the data on both sides of the OOS test set as training data. But this figure illustrates the situation of having a longer lookahead. Thus, we need to omit training cases on both sides of the test set, acting as guard buffers to prevent inadvertent IS/OOS overlap that would cause dangerous optimistic bias.

The Fully General Cross-Validation Algorithm

In some cases, the programmer may find it easiest to avoid all the shuffling involved in the algorithm about to be shown. This can be done by incorporating the starting and stopping boundaries of the training set, test set, and guard buffers directly into the training and testing code. But this can be tricky itself. Moreover, it requires highly customized training and testing code; canned or general-purpose algorithms are out of the question. The algorithms shown in this and the next section are designed to consolidate all training data into a single array of contiguous cases, and the test data into another contiguous block. This greatly simplifies the separate training and testing code.

In this section we state the general cross-validation process in simple algorithmic form to provide an overview. In the next section we'll see C++ code that clarifies the details. The algorithm is simple if no guard buffer is needed (omit=0). But if we need a guard buffer, compressing the training data into a single contiguous block requires either complex shuffling in place or keeping a separate copy of the dataset, copying from a source array to a destination array as needed. We choose the latter approach, as it is not only simpler to program but also faster to execute.

Thus, if omit>0, we have two arrays. The one that we call SRC contains the entire historical dataset. The other is called DEST, and it is the array that will be passed to the training and testing routines. But if omit=0, we use just the array of historical data, shuffling in place for each fold. In both situations, istart is the index of the current first test case (origin 0), and istop is one greater than the index of the current last test case. The notation m::n refers to the block of contiguous cases from m up to but not including n. The algorithm is as follows:

istart = 0   *First OOS test block is at start of dataset.*

ncases_save = ncases ;   *We'll temporarily reduce this, so must restore.*

For each fold...

  Compute n_in_fold and istop   *Number of test cases; one past end of test set.*

  if omit   *We need guard buffers.*
    copy SRC[istart::istop] to end of DEST   *This is the OOS test block.*

    if first fold   *The training set is strictly after the test set.*
      copy SRC[istop+omit::ncases] to beginning of DEST *This is the training set.*
      ncases -= n_in_fold + omit   *This many cases in training set.*

    else if last fold   *The training set is strictly before the test set.*
      copy SRC[0::istart-omit] to beginning of DEST   *This is the training set.*
      ncases -= n_in_fold + omit   *This many cases in training set.*

    else   *This is an interior fold.*
      copy SRC[0::istart-omit] to beginning of DEST   *First part of training set.*
      copy SRC[istop+omit::ncases] to DEST[istart-omit] *Second part of training set.*
      ncases -= n_in_fold + 2 * omit   *This many cases in training set.*

  else   *omit=0 so we just swap in place.*
    if prior to last fold   *We place OOS block at end; already there if last fold.*
      swap istart::istop with end cases
    ncases -= n_in_fold   *This many cases in training set.*

  Train   *Training set is first ncases cases in new data matrix.*

  ncases = ncases_save   *Restore to full dataset (it was reduced for training).*

  Test   *Test set is last istop–istart cases in new dataset.*

  if (not omit AND not last fold) *If we shuffled in place, unshuffle.*
    swap istart::istop with end cases   *swap OOS back from end.*

  istart = istop   *Advance OOS test set for next fold.*

C++ Code for the General Algorithm

The previous algorithm is intended to give a rough overview of the relatively complex shuffling process used to consolidate training and test data for each fold, facilitating use of general-purpose training and testing algorithms. But that overview omitted many details that will now be presented using actual C++ code.

We begin with some initializations. Throughout the entire algorithm, istart is the index of the current first OOS test case, and istop is one greater than the index of the current last test case. The total number of OOS cases completed after each fold will be in n_done, and they will be counted up one at a time for indexing purposes in n_OOS_X. If we are using guard buffers (omit>0), then we need to save the total number of cases, because ncases will be reduced to the actual number of training cases employed for each fold.

```
istart = 0 ;            // OOS start = dataset start
n_done = 0 ;            // Number of cases treated as OOS so far
n_OOS_X = 0 ;           // Counts OOS cases one at a time, for indexing
ncases_save = ncases ;  // Save so we can restore after every fold is processed
```

This is the fold loop. The number of OOS test cases in this fold is the number of cases not yet done, divided by the number of folds remaining to be processed.

```
for (ifold=0 ; ifold<nfolds ; ifold++) {   // Processes user's specified number of folds

  n_in_fold = (ncases - n_done) / (nfolds - ifold) ;      // N of OOS cases in fold
  istop = istart + n_in_fold ;                            // One past OOS stop
```

The following if statement takes care of the situation of having to deal with guard blocks. First, we copy the current OOS test set to the end of the destination array, where it will be tested.

```
  if (omit) {
    memcpy ( data+(ncases-n_in_fold)*ncols , data_save+istart*ncols ,
             n_in_fold*ncols*sizeof(double) ) ;
```

If this is the first (leftmost) fold, the entire training set for this fold lies to the right of the OOS block. Copy it to the beginning of the destination array. The number of training cases is the total number of cases, minus those in the OOS set and the guard block cases.

```
if (ifold == 0) {   // First (leftmost) fold
  memcpy ( data , data_save+(istop+omit)*ncols ,
            (ncases-istop-omit)*ncols*sizeof(double) ) ;
  ncases -= n_in_fold + omit ;
  }
```

If this is the last (rightmost) fold, the entire training set is prior to the OOS block. Copy those cases.

```
else if (ifold == nfolds-1) { // Last (rightmost) fold
  memcpy ( data , data_save , (istart-omit)*ncols*sizeof(double) ) ;
  ncases -= n_in_fold + omit ;
  }
```

Otherwise, this is an interior fold. Here we deal with an issue not explicitly stated in the algorithm outline shown previously. It may be that the user specified so many folds that each fold has a tiny OOS test set, perhaps even just one case. It can then happen that on one side of the test set there are no cases after the guard block is excluded. We must handle that.

```
else {                // Interior fold
  ncases = 0 ;

  if (istart > omit) { // We have at least one training case prior to OOS block
    memcpy ( data , data_save , (istart-omit)*ncols*sizeof(double) ) ;
    ncases = istart - omit ;   // We have this many cases from the left side
    }

  if (ncases_save > istop+omit) { // We have at least one case after OOS block
    memcpy ( data+ncases*ncols , data_save+(istop+omit)*ncols ,
      (ncases_save-istop-omit)*ncols*sizeof(double) ) ;
    ncases += ncases_save - istop - omit ;   // Added on this many from right
    }
  } // Else this is an interior fold
} // If omit
```

The following else block handles the situation of omit=0: no guard blocks. This is much easier. We don't even have a separate source array. Everything is swapped in place. For each fold, we swap the OOS test set to the end of the array. After training and testing are complete for a fold, the data is swapped back the way it was. Note that for the last (rightmost) fold, the test set is already at the end, so we do not swap.

```
      else {
        // Swap this OOS set to end of dataset if it's not already there
        if (ifold < nfolds-1) {                // Not already at end?
          for (i=istart ; i<istop ; i++) {     // For entire OOS block
            dptr = data + i * ncols ;          // Swap from here
            optr = data + (ncases-n_in_fold+i-istart) * ncols ;  // To here
            for (j=0 ; j<ncols ; j++) {
              dtemp = dptr[j] ;
              dptr[j] = optr[j] ;
              optr[j] = dtemp ;
              }
            } // For all OOS cases, swapping
          } // If prior to last fold

        else
          assert ( ncases-n_in_fold-istart == 0 ) ;

        ncases -= n_in_fold ;
        } // Else not omit

/*
   Train and test this XVAL fold
   When we prepared to process this fold, we reduced ncases to remove
   the OOS set and any omitted buffer.   As soon as we finish training,
   we restore it back to its full value.
*/

      find_beta ( ncases , data , &beta , &constant ) ;  // Training phase
      ncases = ncases_save ; // Was reduced for training but now done training

      test_ptr = data+(ncases-n_in_fold)*ncols ;  // OOS test set starts after training set
      for (itest=0 ; itest<n_in_fold ; itest++) {  // For every case in the test set
        pred = beta * *test_ptr++ + constant ;     // test_ptr points to target after this
        if (pred > 0.0)                            // If predicts market going up
          OOS[n_OOS_X++] = *test_ptr ;             // Take a long position
```

```
    else
      OOS[n_OOS_X++] = - *test_ptr ;          // Take a short position
    ++test_ptr ;   // Advance to indicator for next test case
    }

/*
  Swap this OOS set back from end of dataset if it was swapped there
*/

    if (omit == 0  &&  ifold < nfolds-1) {  // No guard buffers and prior to last fold
      for (i=istart ; i<istop ; i++) {          // This is the same code that swapped before
        dptr = data + i * ncols ;
        optr = data + (ncases-n_in_fold+i-istart) * ncols ;
        for (j=0 ; j<ncols ; j++) {
          dtemp = dptr[j] ;
          dptr[j] = optr[j] ;
          optr[j] = dtemp ;
          }
        }
      }

    istart = istop ;              // Advance the OOS set to next fold
    n_done += n_in_fold ;         // Count the OOS cases we've done
    } // For ifold
```

In the previous code, note that we use the same "model" as was used in the
OVERLAP program discussed in detail on page 138. Subroutine find_beta() is the training
phase, using the first ncases cases in data to compute a linear function for predicting the
next data value (the price change for the next case). In the OOS testing phase of each
fold, we pass through the test set. For each case in the test set, we make a prediction of
the upcoming market move. If the prediction is positive, we take a long position, and if
it's negative, we take a short position. These facts are of little importance to the current
discussion, because the focus here is on the cross-validation swapping. Just be aware of
when training and testing happen amid all the swapping.

Cross Validation Can Have Pessimistic Bias

There is widespread belief that cross validation produces an unbiased estimate of population performance. At first glance, this makes sense: we are always testing a model that was trained on data that is separate from the test data (assuming that appropriate guard buffers were used if needed). But the subtle issue at play in cross validation is the size of each training set. The training set in each fold is smaller than the entire dataset, while we would typically train with the entire dataset when the model is put to use. When we have a smaller training set, the model parameter estimates are less accurate than they would be if we trained with the entire dataset. And of course, having less accurate model parameter estimates means that the model will have reduced accuracy, which translates to inferior OOS performance on average. Thus, all else being equal, we can expect cross validation to slightly underestimate the performance that will be obtained when we finally train using the entire dataset and then put the model to work.

Cross Validation Can Have Optimistic Bias

If the data is nonstationary, which is pretty much the rule in market trading applications, this nonstationarity can be a source of optimistic bias in cross validation. The idea is that by including future market data in the training set, even if individual cases are properly excluded, we provide the training algorithm with valuable information concerning the future distribution of the data, information that would not be available in real life.

As a simple example, suppose your historical data has steadily increased volatility from beginning to end. With walkforward analysis, as well as in real life, each test set (and real-life trading period) would have volatility exceeding that in the training set, which might be problematic. But the numerous interior test folds in cross validation would be tested on models trained with data from the future as well as the past, thus providing a variety of volatility examples that bracket the volatility in the test set. This is a subtle form of future leak, even though no actual cases are shared.

Cross Validation Does Not Reflect Real Life

As should be apparent from the previous two sections, cross validation is highly suspect compared to walkforward analysis when it comes to simulating real life. Granted, cross validation does allow the use of more training data than walkforward analysis, especially in early folds when walkforward analysis is forced to make due with meager historical data. In fact, for this reason, walkforward analysis can have even worse pessimistic bias than cross validation. On the other hand, most developers perform walkforward analysis using a training set size equal to that which will be used to train the final production model. This is because they are hesitant to span too wide of a historical period, which may encompass too many market regimes because of nonstationarity. In this common situation, the data advantage of cross validation is wiped out. And once that advantage is gone, there is no incentive to tolerate the sort of subtle future leak discussed in the prior section, in which hints of future nonstationarity issues are provided to the training algorithm. Thus, I cannot recommend cross validation analysis in trading system development, except in the most unusual special situations.

Special Precautions for Algorithmic Trading

First, let's be clear on the meaning of *algorithmic trading*. Much of the recent discussion has been focused on the increasingly popular and powerful *model-based trading*. In model-based trading, we build a dataset of predictors and targets and then train a powerful model to predict the target, given the predictors as of a trading opportunity. This is in sharp contrast to the older, more traditional algorithmic trading, in which a rigorously defined algorithm makes trading decisions on the fly. One venerable chestnut of algorithmic trading is a moving-average crossover system: we take a long position when a short-term moving average is above a long-term moving average, and we take a short position when the reverse is true. To train such a system, we find short-term and long-term lookbacks that optimize some measure of performance. We now investigate the potentially deadly issue of unobvious future leak in algorithmic trading systems.

Recall from the discussion that began on page 131 that for both walkforward analysis and cross validation, we may need a guard buffer removed from the training set where it touches the test set. The number of cases removed is one less than the minimum of the lookback and the lookforward distance used in computing the model-training database.

With model-based trading, it is nearly always the case that the lookback exceeds the lookforward distance, usually to a considerable degree. We may look backward in history for hundreds of bars to compute measures of trend, volatility, and more sophisticated indicators. But when we take a position in the market, we typically hold it for at most a few bars so that the model may quickly respond to changing market conditions.

But with algorithmic systems, the reverse is often true, sometimes to the degree that the lookforward distance must be assumed to be infinite! For example, suppose our trading system operates with the following rule: if a short-term moving average just now (on this current bar) crosses a threshold 2 percent above a long-term moving average, we open a long position. We hold that position until the short-term moving average crosses below the long-term moving average. The key point to note in this example system is that *we don't know how long the position will be open.*

Let's examine walkforward testing of this system. Suppose we arbitrarily impose an upper limit of 150 bars for the long-term moving average lookback. After training, we may well find that the actual lookback is less than this, but it can perhaps be this extensive, so we must be prepared.

What about the lookahead? Unfortunately, the rule for closing the position may fire just a few bars after entry, or we may still be in our position 1,000 bars later. We just don't know in advance.

The implication is that unlike with model-based trading, in which the lookahead almost always determines the size of the guard buffer, for open-ended algorithmic trading it will often be the lookback that determines the guard buffer size, and this will usually be depressingly large.

Pursuing this example will clarify the situation. Suppose we are at the last bar of the training block in this fold, say Bar 1000. To find optimal short-term and long-term lookbacks, we try a large number of candidate pairs, perhaps even every possible pair of short-term and long-term lookbacks. For each candidate pair we start at the earliest possible bar in the training block for which we could compute the long-term moving average. We evaluate the entry rule, take a position if it passes, and hold the position until the exit rule fires. We move along through the training block, trading as decreed by the rules. When the trade-opening process reaches Bar 1000, we stop and compute a performance figure for this short-term/long-term lookback pair. Then we repeat the process for a different pair of lookbacks. Eventually, we have in hand the lookback pair that gives the best trading performance in the training block.

Then we go to Bar 1001, the first bar in the OOS test set for this fold. We evaluate the entry rule using the previously determined optimal lookbacks and act accordingly. If the test set size is more than one bar, we repeat for the next bar, cumulating net performance across the test set.

Astute readers have noticed that we glossed over a crucial aspect of this algorithm: during training, what do we do with the position when we hit the end of the training block for the fold? There are at least five ways we could handle issues near the training/ testing boundary, four of which are good and one of which is disastrous.

1) ***If a position is open at the end of the training block, we leave it open and keep advancing, closing it only when the closing rule fires.*** This provides an honest outcome, the profit that would have been obtained in real life. But suppose a position opens on Bar 1000, the last bar in the training block, and it is an extremely profitable trade. The training algorithm will favor lookbacks that capture that great trade. Now consider what happens at Bar 1001, the first bar in the OOS test set. This trial will share a lot of past price history with the prior bar, one bar less than the optimal long-term lookback. Thus, it will almost certainly open a trade there. Moreover, this trade will share the same future bars that produced a huge profit in the training phase, and hence it will be very profitable. This past-and-future price sharing between the training and test periods is serious future leak, and it will produce significant optimistic bias. Don't do it.

2) ***Force the training algorithm to close and mark-to-market the position when the end of the training block is reached.*** This eliminates future leak and makes the trading system consistent with what could be achieved in real life, because no future information ever takes part in training. But it does distort trades near the end of the training period by closing them in a different manner from how they are closed earlier in the training period, when positions are unlikely to be prematurely closed. This may or may not adversely impact computation of optimal lookback pairs. It certainly deserves contemplation.

3) ***Modify the closing rule to close the position if it has been open a specified number of bars, and use a guard buffer that size.*** In the example under discussion, we might make the closing rule be "We hold the position until the short-term moving average crosses below the long-term moving average, or the position has been open for 20 bars." Then we cease opening new positions (have a guard buffer) when we pass this many bars prior to the end of the training period. This, too, prevents future leak and is consistent with what could be achieved in real life. It has the advantage over method 2 in that all trades are consistent with the same rule,

which avoids distortion in the optimization process. But unless the bar limit is very large, this may be an unwelcome infringement on the developer's trading hypothesis.

4) *Act as in method 1, freely advancing open trades past the end of the training period. However, stop opening positions (guard buffer) when we reach the end of the training period minus one less than the maximum lookback.* In our current example, the last bar at which we might open a position is 1000–(150–1)=851. This is safe because when we begin the test set at Bar 1001, we will be examining Bars 852 through 1001. Thus, the prices on which entry decisions during training were done, and those on which testing entry decisions are made, are completely disjoint. Despite avoiding future leak and hence providing unbiased results, this method has the philosophical annoyance that it does not imitate real life; we access prices beyond the end of the training period during the training process. However, this is more of a philosophical problem than an actual problem.

5) *Use the "single-bar-lookahead" method of the next section.*

Which method is best? It depends (of course!). I tend to favor method 3 for several reasons. All trades follow the same rules, regardless of whether they are early or late in the training period. (Method 2 violates this nice property.) It does not peer into the future like method 4, even though method 4's future-gazing does not introduce harmful future leak. But perhaps most of all, in my own work over the years I have found that automated trading systems lose accuracy fast as they march away from their opening bar. If a trade is not at or at least near its goal soon after opening the position, it rapidly devolves into a crap shot, maybe winning, maybe not. So by introducing a time limit on how long a position can be open, we reduce the impact of randomness.

There is one situation in which method 4 is likely superior to method 3. Both methods require that we cease opening trades some time before the end of the training period. In method 3 we lose the trade time limit, while in method 4 we lose the lookback. It may be that our trading plan requires a long time for the trade to be open. In my experience, this is not a good thing, but other developers may differ. If the required time period is longer than the lookback, method 4 will lose fewer trading opportunities than method 3. Despite being vaguely uncomfortable with method 4 looking into the future during training, we might consider method 4 to be the superior choice in such situations.

Converting Unknown-Lookahead Systems to Single-Bar

We just explored four different methods for handling boundary regions near the training/test border, three of which are practical and effective. We now introduce a fifth method, which can sometimes be more complicated but which avoids the use of any guard buffer at all and hence increases the effective size of each training fold. It does distort end-of-training-set trades like method 2, but in a frequently more innocuous way. Moreover, it generates a long, continuous series of single-bar returns rather than fewer multiple-bar returns. This is necessary to perform the CSCV superiority test and several other procedures described later.

To implement this conversion, we modify the trading rule to be a series of single-bar trades, with the first trade opening in response to the opening rule and subsequent trades being just a continuation of the prior bar's position. In other words, suppose our desired trading rule is to open a position when no position is currently open (to prevent simultaneous open trades) and the OpenPosition condition becomes true, and then close the position when the ClosePosition condition becomes true. The modified rule requires that we perform the following at the close of each bar:

> *If no position is open*
>> *If OpenPosition is true, open a position to extend through the next bar*
> *Else*
>> *Close the position and record this bar's return on the trade*
>> *If ClosePosition is false, re-open the same position that was just closed*

This complexity is needed only if you are using commercial software that requires explicit opening and closing of positions in order to record trades. Of course, if you are writing your own software, it is much simpler: just record an open trade's marked-to-market return on each bar!

This is often the best method because it provides the finest granularity in returns. This is important to stable profit factor calculations, it enables more accurate drawdown calculations (it's essentially marking-to-market every bar), and it is mandatory for some of the most powerful statistical tests (CSCV) described elsewhere in this text. Please consider it seriously. A practical example of this, with C++ code, will appear on page 198.

Unbounded Lookback Can Subtly Happen

We saw in method 4 earlier that the number of trading opportunities is reduced according to the lookback for trading decisions. We would be inclined to use this method when we have an open-ended trading system and we do not want to impose a time limit on how long trades may remain open. But in this case, we must be careful that we do not have a lookback that is, at least in theory, unbounded. If we cannot establish a firm bound on the lookback, a bound that is not impractically large, then we cannot use method 4.

How can our lookback ever be unbounded? One obvious way is if some component of our decision computation has unbounded lookback. For example, we've been talking about moving-average crossover systems in which the lookbacks of the moving averages are bounded. That's good. But what if we used exponential smoothing, or a recursive filter, for our long-term and short-term smoothing? The value of such filters is computed based on data all the way back to the first price in the market history. Granted, the contributions of really early prices may be very small. But remember that when it comes to market trading, seemingly innocuous sources of bias can have shockingly serious impact.

A much more subtle source of unbounded lookback is when trading decisions are based on prior trading decisions. For example, our system may include a safety valve that shuts down all trading for a month if four losing trades in a row occur. Now, the lookback for the current bar goes back to the prior trade, and the one before that, and so on.

Or consider these entry and exit rules: we open a position if some rigorously defined condition that cycles on and off frequently is true *and* we do not currently have a trade open. We close the trade when some other rigorously defined condition is true. In this situation, our current trade decision depends on whether we opened a trade at the prior opportunity, which in turn depends on the opportunity prior to that, ad infinitum. The lookback is unbounded.

Sceptics may scoff at this concept. I do not, as I was badly burned by this very issue early in my career, and I no longer underestimate its impact.

Comparing Cross Validation with Walkforward: XVW

On page 138 we presented the OVERLAP program to explore the bias introduced by unobvious IS/OOS overlap. Here we expand this program in the XvW program, which operates similarly but whose primary purpose is to demonstrate the great disparity possible between walkforward and cross-validation analysis of exactly the same trading system. Please feel free to use this program (the complete source code is in XvW.CPP) as a template to explore this phenomenon with your own trading system ideas.

Here is the calling parameter list. Much of the program's operation is described in detail in the section that begins on page 138, so we will omit redundant details here. The program is invoked from the command line as follows:

XvW nprices trend lookback lookahead ntrain ntest nfolds omit nreps seed

> nprices is the number of market prices (bars) in the market history. For the most accurate results, this should be large, at least 10,000.

> Trend is the strength of a trend that reverses every 50 bars. A trend of 0.0 means that the market price series is a random walk.

> lookback is the number of bars of history used to compute the indicator.

> lookahead is the number of future bars used to compute the target.

> ntrain is the number of cases used in the training set (before omitting any) for the prediction model on which trade decisions are based. The actual number of training cases will be ntrain minus omit.

> ntest is the number of test cases in each OOS test block.

> nfolds is the number of cross-validation folds.

> omit is the number of most recent training cases omitted from the training set to prevent bias when lookahead is greater than one. Ideally it should be one less than the lookahead.

> nreps is the number of replications used to compute the several t-scores and the tail fraction described later. It should be fairly large, at least 1000, for accurate results.

> seed is the random seed and may be any positive integer. This facilitates repeating the test with different seeds to confirm results.

As was described starting on page 137, the program repeatedly generates market histories. One difference between this XvW program and the OVERLAP program is that OVERLAP always generates random walks, while XvW can optionally generate price histories having a user-specified degree of trend that reverses every 50 bars.

This introduces a degree of predictability in market prices, producing positive average returns. A dataset consisting of a predictor and target for each bar is created. A simple linear regression model is tested with both walkforward and cross-validation testing. When complete, a line similar to the following will be printed:

Grand XVAL = 0.02249 (t=253.371) WALK = 0.00558 (t=81.355) StdDev = 0.00011 t = 150.768 rtail = 0.00000

This information is:

- Mean OOS return and associated t-score for cross validation

- Mean OOS return and associated t-score for walkforward

- Standard deviation of the difference between the two methods, the t-score for this difference, and its right-tail p-value

If you specify a trend of 0.0, producing a pure random walk, all t-scores will be insignificant except for natural random variation. When you increase the trend, t-scores will rapidly become significant. The t-score for the difference between walkforward and cross validation is highly dependent on the lookback, on the lookahead, and to some degree on the number of folds. The main takeaway from this demonstration is that in nearly all practical situations, walkforward and cross validation analysis produce significantly different results, often wildly different.

Computationally Symmetric Cross Validation

I've already pointed out (with multiple justifications) that I do not favor cross validation for performance analysis of market trading systems. However, there is one interesting application of a special form of cross validation that I have found to be frequently useful. This application is inspired by a fascinating 2015 paper, "The Probability of Backtest Overfitting" by David H. Bailey et al. It is widely available for free downloading on the Internet.

Computationally symmetric cross validation (CSCV) largely or completely eliminates one aspect of ordinary k-fold cross validation that can be problematic in some situations: unequal training-set and test-set sizes. Unless we use just two folds (generally unrecommended due to instability), for each fold the test set will be much smaller than the training set. In the extreme, when we use hold-one-out cross validation, each test set consists of a single case. Usually we pool all OOS returns into a single testing pool the same size as the original dataset, so there is no problem. But occasionally we may want to compute a separate performance criterion of each fold's OOS data, perhaps to get an idea of the fold-to-fold variation. Some criteria, especially those involving ratios, are compromised by small sets. For example, the Sharpe ratio requires that we divide by the standard deviation of returns within the sample. If the sample is small, this denominator may be tiny, or even zero. If the sample consists of a single case, we cannot do it at all. The profit factor (wins divided by losses) also requires large datasets, as do measures involving drawdown.

CSCV works by partitioning the collection of individual trade returns (nearly always one-bar-ahead returns) into an even number of subsets that are equal or nearly equal in size. Then, these subsets are combined in every possible way, making half of them be a training set and the other half a test set. For example, suppose we partition the returns into four subsets. We combine subsets 1 and 2 into a training set, and we combine 3 and 4 into the corresponding test set. Then we combine 1 and 3 into a training set, and we combine 2 and 4 into the corresponding test set. We repeat this recombination until every possible arrangement has been used.

It should be clear that unless the number of partitions is small and the number of returns far from an integer multiple of the number of partitions, all training sets and test sets will be nearly equal in size, each about half of the total number of returns.

We digress briefly to emphasize that this partitioning is done on the individual bar returns, not on the price data. For example, consider our good old moving-average crossover system, and suppose we have specified short-term and long-term lookbacks for computing the moving averages. We do not partition the price histories because the recombination would produce deadly discontinuities that would wreak havoc on moving average computation. Rather, we process the entire market history, beginning to end, and keep track of the return captured from each bar. This set of individual bar returns is partitioned.

So, how is model optimization for each training set accomplished? Unfortunately, CSCV does not allow us to use any "intelligent" training algorithm, one that uses performance criteria from prior trial parameter sets to guide the selection of future trial parameter sets. So, for example, we cannot use genetic optimization or hill climbing. Each trial parameter set or other model variation must be independent of results obtained from prior trials. Thus, either we will almost always use a large number of randomly generated model parameters, or we will do an exhaustive grid search across the valid parameter space. After evaluating some measure of performance for each trial parameter set, we choose the parameter set that has optimal performance in the training set.

The CSCV Algorithm: Intuition and General Statement

Let's recap what we have so far. We have created a (usually large) number of candidate sets of model parameter sets. For example, if we have a moving-average crossover system, a trial parameter set would consist of a long-term lookback and a short-term lookback. These numerous parameter sets may have been generated randomly or in a grid search.

For each trial parameter set, we evaluate the trading system across the entire available market price history. We must specify a fixed granularity for evaluating returns. This granularity is typically every bar: for each bar, we compute the contribution to the equity of the position (long/short/neutral) provided by that bar. But it need not be every bar; it could just as well be hourly for intraday trading, weekly for day bars, or whatever. However, finer granularity is better. The important thing is that the granularity be defined in such a way that we have a profit figure available at the same time for every competing system. This is almost never a problem; we just evaluate the profit changes at the same points in time (such as every bar or for the week on every Friday) for every competing system.

To keep things simple, from here on I will assume that we are evaluating returns on every bar, understanding that coarser granularities are legal though less desirable. When we have evaluated every trading system (every parameter set) at every bar, we can represent these returns as a matrix. Each row of the matrix will correspond to a single trading system (parameter set), with its bar-by-bar returns spanning the row. Our matrix will have one row for each parameter set and as many columns as we have bars where the trading systems are active. (This is the transpose of the matrix in the [Bailey et al.] article, but it is more computationally efficient to do it this way.)

Note that we will virtually always have fewer bars of returns than we have bars of price history, due to lookback for making trading decisions, and lookahead for evaluating the one-bar return due to the trade decision. For example, suppose we need the most recent 10 bars of price history to make a trade decision. We will lose 10 bars of price history.

If we now want to find the optimal parameter set for the entire available history (as opposed to implementing the CSCV algorithm), we compute our optimization criterion separately for each row of this return matrix and see which row (parameter set) produces the best criterion. For example, if our performance criterion is total return from the trading system, we just find the sum across each row and choose the system whose row sum is greatest. If our criterion is the Sharpe ratio, we compute this quantity for the returns of each row and find the row that has the greatest value, and so on. That tells us the optimal parameter set.

To implement the CSCV algorithm, we partition the columns of this return matrix into an even number of subsets, as described earlier. These subsets will be recombined, half of them defining a training set and the remaining half being the OOS test set. Every possible combination will be processed. For the moment, consider a single such combination.

We now compute two criteria for each row, the performance criterion for the pooled training set and that for the pooled test set. For example, suppose our criterion is the mean return per bar. For each row (trading system) we sum the columns of that row that make up the training set and divide by the number of such columns, giving us the IS mean return per bar for that trading system. We similarly sum the columns that make up the test set and divide by the number of such columns, giving us the OOS mean return per bar. When we have done this for each row, we have two vectors, one for the training set and one for the test set, with each vector having as many elements as we have competing trading systems (parameter sets).

To find the best IS trading system for a single training/testing partitioning, we simply locate the element in its performance vector that has the best performance. Then we examine the corresponding element in the OOS vector. This is the OOS performance attained by the IS-optimal trading system in this particular partitioning.

Now here is the key part of the CSCV algorithm: we consider the OOS performance of *all* trading systems. If our model and parameter-selection procedure are truly effective, we would expect that the IS-optimal model would also have superior OOS performance relative to the OOS performance of the IS-suboptimal systems. After all, if this model is superior to its competitors in-sample *and* it truly is capturing authentic predictable market patterns, then it should usually do a good job of capitalizing on those market patterns out-of-sample. We set a fairly low but reasonable bar for defining what we mean by performing relatively well out-of-sample: the OOS performance of the IS-best system should exceed the median OOS performance of the other systems.

Consider for a moment what we would expect if the model were worthless; it fails to capture any authentic market patterns: there would be no reason to expect that the best IS performer would also be superior OOS. The relative OOS performance of the best IS performer would be random, sometimes outperforming the other systems and sometimes underperforming. We would expect about a 50-50 probability that this "best" system would lie above the median OOS performance. But if the model were wonderful, doing a great job of predicting market movement, we would expect its OOS performance to be great as well, at least most of the time.

How can we estimate the probability that the OOS performance of the best IS performer will be above the median OOS performance? Combinatorially symmetric cross validation, of course! Recall from early in this discussion that we will form every possible combination of the subsets, placing half of them in the training set and the other half in the test set. For each such combination, we perform the operation just described: find the best IS system and compare its OOS performance to that of the other systems. Count how many times the OOS performance of the IS-best exceeds the median of the others. These operations are not independent, but each of them is unbiased. Thus, if we divide the count of superior OOS performances and divide by the total number of combinations tested, we have a reasonably unbiased estimate of the probability that the OOS performance of a trained system will outperform the median of its competitors in the simulation.

I say *reasonably* unbiased because there are two source of bias, discussed earlier, to consider. First, each training set in CSCV is half the size of the complete dataset, which causes a pessimistic bias compared to training with the entire dataset. See Page 150. Also, if the market prices (and hence returns) are nonstationary, cross validation of any sort can have slight optimistic bias compared to the performance that could be attained in real life. Also see Page 150.

Finally, it should be noted that to avoid inadvertent IS/OOS overlap (page 131), we would almost always employ a lookahead of one bar, which is what I present in this book. The recombination algorithm can be modified to shrink training segments, but the modification would be cumbersome and generally not worthwhile in this situation anyway.

We are now ready for a brief statement of the algorithm just described intuitively.

Given:
  n_cases: Number of cases (columns in returns matrix), ideally a multiple of n_blocks
  n_systems: Number of competing systems (rows in returns matrix)
  n_blocks: Number of blocks into which the n_cases cases will be partitioned (even!)
  returns: n_systems by n_cases matrix of returns.
    Returns [i,j] is the return from a decision made on trading opportunity j for system i.

Algorithm:

```
nless = 0
for all 'n_combinations' training/testing combinations of subsets
  Find the row which has maximum criterion in the training set
  Compute the rank (1 through number of test cases) of the test-set criterion in this
    row (system) relative to the test criteria for all 'n_systems' rows
  Compute fractile = rank / (n_systems + 1)
  If fractile <= 0.5
    nless = nless + 1
Return nless / n_combinations
```

Note that we can precompute the number of combinations using the standard formula for the number of combinations of n_blocks things taken n_blocks/2 at a time (Equation 5-1).

$$Ncombinations = \frac{Nblocks!}{(Nblocks/2)!(Nblocks/2)!} \tag{5-1}$$

In the intuitive description of the algorithm, we compared the OOS performance of the best IS performer to the median of the other OOS performances. In the previous algorithm, we compute the relative rank and the corresponding fractile, counting failure if the fractile is less than or equal to 0.5. The two operations are equivalent, but the approach shown in the previous algorithm is faster than computing the median.

It should be apparent that what we hope for is a small value of the ratio nless / n_combinations because this is the approximate probability that our best IS performer will *underperform* its competitors out-of-sample. Expressing it this way makes it vaguely similar to an ordinary p-value.

What Does This Test Actually Measure?

The intuition behind the test just described makes sense, but the vital subtleties may not be obvious. We now explore this in more depth.

The key point to understanding the nature of this test is to realize that its results are *entirely relative to the set of competitors* being evaluated. In the most common (though not mandatory) situation, these competitors are all the same model but with different values of one or more parameters. The domain over which we select trial parameters is of paramount importance if the test is to be truly useful. If the domain is overly broad, including numerous unrealistic parameter values, or if is overly restrictive, failing to cover the complete range of possible parameter values, the test loses a good deal of its applicability.

When we say that the test's results are relative to the set of competitors, what we mean is that this test can be thought of as measuring a sort of dominance. It answers the following question: how much does the IS-optimal model dominate its competitors in terms of real-world performance, when the real-world performance is measured by OOS performance in the test? The key word here is *competitors*.

Suppose we dilute the field of competitors by including a large number of systems that any reasonable developer would know in advance to be worthless. In terms of parameterization, this would equate to testing many parameter sets that are wildly beyond reasonable norms. These systems will perform poorly, both in and out of sample. Thus, even a slightly decent system's OOS performance will be above the median performance of all systems, resulting in a great score on this test, possibly undeserved.

Conversely, suppose we limit our field of competition to only systems known in advance to likely be good, with little variety. No one system, not even the IS-best, will dominate the others OOS, leading to a poor score.

The bottom line is that we must understand that the score on this test tells us how well the best-IS model outperforms the competing poorer-IS models OOS. Thus, we should strive to ensure that the competitors thoroughly but not unrealistically represent the parameter domain.

C++ Code for the CSCV Superiority Test

In this section we present C++ code (CSCV_CORE.CPP) to implement the test just described. This code will be broken into sections, each having its own explanation. We begin with the function and local variable declarations. This subroutine assumes that the returns from the competing trading systems have already been computed and stored in a matrix as described earlier.

```
double cscvcore (
    int ncases ,          // Number of columns in returns matrix (change fastest)
    int n_systems ,       // Number of rows (competitors)
    int n_blocks ,        // Number of blocks (even!) into which cases will be partitioned
    double *returns ,     // N_systems by ncases matrix of returns, case changing fastest
    int *indices ,        // Work vector n_blocks long
```

```
   int *lengths ,         // Work vector n_blocks long
   int *flags ,           // Work vector n_blocks long
   double *work ,         // Work vector ncases long
   double *is_crits ,     // Work vector n_systems long
   double *oos_crits      // Work vector n_systems long
   )
{
   int i, ic, isys, ibest, n, ncombo, iradix, istart, nless ;
   double best, rel_rank ;
```

The first step is to partition the ncases columns of returns in n_blocks subsets of equal or approximately equal size. In the [Bailey et al.] paper, the assumption was that ncases is an integer multiple of n_blocks so that all subsets are the same size. However, I believe that this is not strictly necessary, and it is certainly restrictive. Therefore, I use the array indices to point to the starting case of each subset and use lengths to be the number of cases in each subset. The number of cases in each subset is the number of cases remaining divided by the number of subsets remaining.

```
   n_blocks = n_blocks / 2 * 2 ;    // Make sure it's even
   istart = 0 ;
   for (i=0 ; i<n_blocks ; i++) {    // For all blocks (subsets of returns)
      indices[i] = istart ;           // Block starts here
      lengths[i] = (ncases - istart) / (n_blocks-i) ; // It contains this many cases
      istart += lengths[i] ;          // Next block
      }
```

We initialize to zero the counter of the number of times the OOS performance of the IS-best system underperforms the OOS performance of the others. We also initialize a flag array that identifies which subsets are currently in the training set and which in the test set.

```
   nless = 0 ;   // Will count the number of times OOS of best <= median OOS

   for (i=0 ; i<n_blocks / 2 ; i++)   // Identify the training set blocks
      flags[i] = 1 ;

   for ( ; i<n_blocks ; i++)        // And the test set blocks
      flags[i] = 0 ;
```

The main outmost loop passes through all possible combinations of blocks (subsets of returns) into a pooled training set and a pooled test set. The first act in this loop is to compute the in-sample performance of each system. To do this, gather all n returns of the system being evaluated into a single work array, and then call an external subroutine criter() to compute the performance criterion.

```
for (ncombo=0; ; ncombo++) {   // For all possible combinations

/*
   Compute training-set (IS) criterion for each candidate system
*/

   for (isys=0 ; isys<n_systems ; isys++) {   // Each row of returns matrix is a system
      n = 0 ;                                 // Counts cases in training set
      for (ic=0 ; ic<n_blocks ; ic++) {       // For all blocks (subsets)
         if (flags[ic]) {                     // If this block is in the training set
            for (i=indices[ic] ; i<indices[ic]+lengths[ic] ; i++) // For every case in this block
               work[n++] = returns[isys*ncases+i] ;
            }
         }

      is_crits[isys] = criter ( n , work ) ;  // IS performance for this system
      }
```

Then we do the same thing for the test set. The code is nearly identical to that shown earlier, but we'll show it anyway.

```
   for (isys=0 ; isys<n_systems ; isys++) {   // Each row of returns matrix is a system
      n = 0 ;                                 // Counts cases in OOS set
      for (ic=0 ; ic<n_blocks ; ic++) {       // For all blocks (subsets)
         if (! flags[ic]) {                   // If this block is in the OOS set
            for (i=indices[ic] ; i<indices[ic]+lengths[ic] ; i++) // For every case in this block
               work[n++] = returns[isys*ncases+i] ;
            }
         }

      oos_crits[isys] = criter ( n , work ) ;  // OOS performance of this system
      }
```

Search through all systems and find the one that has the maximum in- sample performance.

```
for (isys=0 ; isys<n_systems ; isys++) { // Find the best system IS
  if (isys == 0 || is_crits[isys] > best) {
    best = is_crits[isys] ;
    ibest = isys ;
    }
  }
```

Compute the rank of the OOS performance of the best system within the population of OOS performance of all systems. Mathematically, best >= oos_crits[ibest] is true, but to guard against floating-point ambiguities we pre-test for this. Then we compute the fractile (rel_rank) and increment our failure counter if this performance does not exceed the median.

```
best = oos_crits[ibest] ;        // This is the OOS value for the best system in-sample
n = 0 ;                          // Counts to compute rank
for (isys=0 ; isys<n_systems ; isys++) {   // Universe in which rank is computed
  if (isys == ibest || best >= oos_crits[isys]) // Insurance against fpt error
    ++n ;
  }

rel_rank = (double) n / (n_systems + 1) ;
if (rel_rank <= 0.5)   // Is the IS best at or below the OOS median?
  ++nless ;
```

We come now to the only truly complex part of this algorithm: advancing to the next combination of blocks that define the training and test sets. Many readers will want to take its operation on faith. I'll provide a brief explanation after the code. Readers who want to plug through its operation would be advised to get out pencil and paper and work out the succession of combinations. After all combinations have been tested, we divide the failure count by the total combination count to get the approximate probability of underperformance. Here is the code:

```
n = 0 ;
for (iradix=0 ; iradix<n_blocks-1 ; iradix++) {
  if (flags[iradix] == 1) {
    ++n ;                // This many flags up to and including this one at iradix
```

```
        if (flags[iradix+1] == 0) {
          flags[iradix] = 0 ;
          flags[iradix+1] = 1 ;
          for (i=0 ; i<iradix ; i++) {  // Must reset everything below this change point
            if (--n > 0)
              flags[i] = 1 ;
            else
              flags[i] = 0 ;
            } // Filling in below
          break ;
          } // If next flag is 0
        } // If this flag is 1
      } // For iradix

    if (iradix == n_blocks-1) {
      ++ncombo ;   // Must count this last one
      break ;
      }
    } // Main loop processes all combinations

  return (double) nless / ncombo ;
}
```

This code passes through the blocks, looking for the first occurrence of a $(1,0)$ pair and counting 1s as it goes. The first time it finds a $(1,0)$ pair, it propagates the 1 to the right, replacing this $(1,0)$ pair with a $(0,1)$ pair. Then, just as when the algorithm began, it moves the requisite number of 1s to the beginning of the array prior to this pair and fills in the rest of this prior section with 0s. So, these operations do not change the count of 1s and 0s. This swapping sets us up for an entirely new, unique family of combinations, because it is impossible for the new $(0,1)$ pair to ever change back to $(1,0)$ and then to $(0,1)$ without at least one flag beyond it changing. The algorithm is inherently recursive, with the rightmost 1 slowly advancing and all flags below it changing in the same way recursively.

If you are the sort who prefers heuristic validation, know that you can explicitly compute the number of combinations from the number of blocks by means of Equation 5-1. Program the advancing algorithm and test it for a variety of number of blocks, confirming that you get the correct number of combinations. You know that there could be no duplicates because if any combination reappeared, the algorithm would go into an endless loop. Thus, if you get the correct number of combinations, you know that they are unique and hence cover every possible combination.

An Example with SPX

We now look at a moving-average crossover example with SPX, the S&P 500 index. I chose this "market" because it has a long history and it is exceptionally broad, thus avoiding any individual equity issues. As a point of interest, I reran this test on a variety of individual equities and indices and found two general effects. First, moving-average crossover systems tend to work very well until the last few decades, when their performance drops off precipitously (at least in the tests I ran; I am not claiming that this is universal). Second, individual equities have tremendous variation, with some issues responding beautifully to this system, and others not so much. So, my goal in this example is to demonstrate the CSCV dominance algorithm, not to promote or discourage use of any particular trading system.

We begin with a subroutine (in CSCV_MKT.CPP) that shows how we can compute the returns matrix needed by CSCV_CORE.CPP. This routine is called with the array of price histories and the maximum lookback desired by the user. It computes the returns matrix. Note that we need to supply it with the log of the actual prices so that moves when a market is at 1000 are commensurate with moves when the market is at 10. We will index the items in returns with iret, which advances across rows (bars) fastest.

```
void get_returns (
   int nprices ,          // Number of log prices in 'prices'
   double *prices ,       // Log prices
   int max_lookback ,     // Maximum lookback to use
   double *returns        // Computed matrix of returns
   )
{
   int i, j, ishort, ilong, iret ;
   double ret, long_mean, long_sum, short_mean, short_sum ;

   iret = 0 ;  // Will index computed returns
```

We have three nested loops. The outermost loop varies the long-term lookback from a minimum of two bars to the user-specified maximum. The next loop varies the short-term lookback from a minimum of one to one less than the long-term lookback, ensuring that the short-term lookback is always less than the long-term lookback. The innermost loop marches across the price history, making trade decisions and computing the return attributable to each. We must not begin this price march at ilong-1, even though valid return data begins there. This is because the returns matrix must be a true matrix, with each row having the same number of properly aligned columns. Thus, we need to start at the same bar for every system.

```
for (ilong=2 ; ilong<=max_lookback ; ilong++) {  // Long-term lookback
   for (ishort=1 ; ishort<ilong ; ishort++) {          // Short-term lookback
      for (i=max_lookback-1 ; i<nprices-1 ; i++) {  // Compute returns across history
```

We could explicitly compute the moving averages at each bar, but this would be excruciatingly slow. A much faster method, though trivially less accurate because of floating-point error buildup, is to compute the two moving sums once, on the first bar, and update them from then on. For each bar, divide the moving sums to get the moving averages.

```
if (i == max_lookback-1) {     // Find the moving averages for the first valid case.
   short_sum = 0.0 ;              // Cumulates short-term lookback sum
   for (j=i ; j>i-ishort ; j--)
      short_sum += prices[j] ;
   long_sum = short_sum ;   // Cumulates long-term lookback sum
   while (j>i-ilong)
      long_sum += prices[j--] ;
   }

else {                                    // Update the moving averages
   short_sum += prices[i] - prices[i-ishort] ;
   long_sum += prices[i] - prices[i-ilong] ;
   }

short_mean = short_sum / ishort ;  // Convert sums to averages
long_mean = long_sum / ilong ;
```

The trading rule is that we take a long position if the short-term moving average is above the long-term moving average, and conversely. If the two moving averages are equal, we remain neutral. I left in my assert() to clarify to the reader exactly how many items are now in the returns matrix.

```
      // We now have the short-term and long-term moving averages ending at bar i

      if (short_mean > long_mean)        // Long position
        ret = prices[i+1] - prices[i] ;
      else if (short_mean < long_mean)   // Short position
        ret = prices[i] - prices[i+1] ;
      else                               // Be neutral
        ret = 0.0 ;

      returns[iret++] = ret ;            // Save this return
      } // For i (decision bar)

    } // For ishort, all short-term lookbacks
  } // For ilong, all long-term lookbacks

  assert ( iret == (max_lookback * (max_lookback-1) / 2 * (nprices - max_lookback)) ) ;
}
```

When I ran this program on SPX, I tried several different numbers of blocks and maximum lookbacks. The following results were obtained, providing significant evidence that a moving-average crossover system provides useful predictive information in this market.

Blocks	Max lookback	Probability
10	50	0.008
10	100	0.016
10	150	0.036
12	50	0.004
12	100	0.009
12	150	0.027

This tells us nothing about the risk/reward ratio, so the system may not be worth trading. But it does show that an optimally trained model greatly outperforms its suboptimal competitors out-of-sample. This is valuable information, as it tells us that the model has real potential; if the model were flawed, training would add little or no value (OOS performance), and the probabilities would be closer to 0.5.

Nested Walkforward Analysis

Sometimes our development procedure requires us to nest one layer of walkforward analysis inside another such layer. The classic example of this situation is portfolio construction. We have a collection of candidates for inclusion in a portfolio, each of which requires some degree of performance optimization (maybe separately, maybe as a group with common parameters). We also have some criterion for portfolio performance that we use to select a subset of these candidates for inclusion in a trading portfolio. Whatever the case, two stages of optimization are occurring (portfolio components and the portfolio as a whole), so to estimate real-world performance of the portfolio, we must perform a nested walkforward analysis. Here are a few examples (far from complete!) where this would be necessary:

- We have a variety of trading systems whose performance is dependent on slowly varying market regimes. For example, we may have a trend-following system, a mean-reversion system, and a channel-breakout system. We keep track of which of these three systems has been performing best in recent times, and when we make our trade decisions, we use the currently superior system.

- We have a trading system that is applicable to nearly any equity, but we know from experience that different families of equities (transportation, financial, consumer staples, and so on) have superior performance with this system at different times. We keep track of which equities have been responding best to our trading system recently, and these are the equities that we trade.

- One of your colleagues insists that mean return is the best measure of how well a market or trading system is performing. Another argues for Sharpe ratio, while another likes profit factor. You, in your wisdom, suspect that the ideal measure may change over time. So, rather than running three separate tests and comparing start-to-end performance, you keep track of which performance measure is currently most accurate and use this measure to select the system or market for your current trading.

Why do we need to use nested walkforward in such situations? Why can't we just optimize the entire process, pooling parameterization of individual components and group performance into one big pot of optimizable parameters? The answer is that the second stage of these operations, whether it be selection of individual systems or portfolio components or a second round of pooled optimization, *must be based on OOS results from the first stage.*

Let's consider a simple example in which we avoid the complexity of evolving market conditions. This topic of selection bias was introduced on page 124, and now might be a good time to review that section. The members of your department have given you, the department head, a variety of models that they developed and propose the company trade. You must select the best of these models. Would you examine the in-sample performance of the competitors and choose whichever is best? Certainly not, and with good reason: if this system is overly powerful (typically because it has too many optimizable parameters), it would overfit the market history, modeling noise in addition to any authentic patterns. When this system is put to work in real-world trading, the noise patterns will vanish (that's the definition of noise), and you will be left with rubbish. The intelligent approach is to compare the OOS performance of the competing systems and base your choice on this quantity.

The situation does not change when you are dealing with a constantly evolving situation. You still need to base your regular, repeated decisions of what to trade or what markets to include in your portfolio on the OOS performance of the competitors. This is because *in-sample performance tells us little about how a trading system will perform in the real world.*

This, then, is the reason we need nested walkforward. We need an inner level (I like to call this *Level-1*) of walkforward to provide the OOS results on which the *Level-2* optimization will be based. And of course, the Level-2 trade decisions will themselves need to be OOS validated with walkforward analysis. Thus, we nest two levels of walkforward analysis.

To prepare for and clarify the algorithms that will soon appear, we present a small example of how this procedure works. We will assume for this example that the lookback for the Level-1 training (typically optimizing individual trading systems) is 10 bars, and the lookback for the Level-2 optimization (typically selection from competing trading systems) is 3 bars. Then we proceed as follows:

Use Price Bars 1-10 to train the individual competitors.
Test each competitor with Bar 11, giving our first Level-1 OOS case
Use Price Bars 2-11 to train the individual competitors.
Test each competitor with Bar 12, giving our second Level-1 OOS case

Use Price Bars 3-12 to train the individual competitors.

Test each competitor with Bar 13, giving our third Level-1 OOS case

We now have enough Level-1 OOS cases to commence Level-2 testing

Use Level-1 OOS Bars 11-13 to train the Level-2 procedure

Test the Level-2 procedure on Bar 14, giving our first totally OOS case

Use Price Bars 4-13 to train the individual competitors.

Test each competitor with Bar 14, giving a new Level-1 OOS case

Use Level-1 OOS Bars 12-14 to train the Level-2 procedure

Test the Level-2 procedure on Bar 15, giving our second totally OOS case

Repeat the prior four steps, advancing the price and Level-1 OOS windows, until the historical data is exhausted

The Nested Walkforward Algorithm

Experienced programmers should be able to program nested walkforward given only the prior explanation and example. But for the sake of clarity, I'll state the algorithm in a fairly general way. This is in the framework of the most common use of nested walkforward: you have two or more trading systems that, on each bar, look at recent market history and make a decision on the position to take (long/short/neutral) on the next bar. You also have a scoring system that examines the recent OOS performance of each of these systems and chooses an apparently superior subset of these trading systems (perhaps just one) to use for the next trade. Your goal is to collect OOS trades from this best subset. This lets you evaluate the performance of your entire trading system, both the foundation systems and the method for scoring and selecting the best. The following variables are especially important:

n_cases: Number of market price history bars in the prices array.

prices: Market history (log of prices). We call the units here *bars*, but this information could also include other measures such as volume and open interest.

n_competitors: Number of competing trading systems.

IS_n: User-specified lookback of trading systems; number of recent market history bars used to make trade decisions.

OOS1_n: User-specified lookback of system selector; number of recent OOS returns produced by the multiple trading systems and used by the system selector to choose the best system(s).

OOS1: OOS returns of the trading systems, an n_competitors by n_cases matrix. Note that the first IS_n columns in this matrix are not used because they are undefined. Column j of this matrix contains the returns produced by Bar j as a result of a decision made on Bar j–1.

OOS2: OOS returns of the selected best system(s); our ultimate goal.

IS_start: Starting bar of the training set. It advances with the window.

OOS1_start: Index in OOS1 of the starting bar of the current system OOS set used by the system selector. It advances with the window as soon as the system selector has OOS1_n cases to look back at.

OOS1_end: One past last bar of current system OOS set used by the system selector. It advances with the window. This also serves as the current OOS1 case index. When the algorithm starts, this equals OOS1_start, and it increments each time the window advances.

OOS2_start: Starting index of complete OOS set 2; it remains fixed at IS_n + OOS1_n.

OOS2_end: One past its last case in OOS2. This also serves as the current OOS2 case index.

The algorithm shown next in sections is heavily edited to be widely applicable. In the next section, we will present a complete C++ program that uses nested walkforward in a slightly different but comparable application. Here, we begin by initializing the starting index in the systems' price history to be the first case in the history. The system OOS returns begin immediately after the systems' lookback period. The selector's OOS returns, our ultimate goal, begin immediately after the system OOS period. Then we begin the main loop that moves a window across the price history series.

```
IS_start = 0 ;                              // Start training with first case
OOS1_start = OOS1_end = IS_n ; // First OOS1 case is right after first price set
OOS2_start = OOS2_end = IS_n + OOS1_n ;// First OOS2 case is after OOS1 complete

for (;;) {   // Main outermost loop advances windows
```

The first step for each window position is to evaluate all competitors (trading systems) at this bar and store the results in OOS1, which is a two-dimensional array having the system down the rows and the bar across the columns, with that index changing fastest. The routine criterion_1() handles all systems, so we must tell it which system we want to evaluate. To evaluate a system, it looks at IS_n bars beginning with Bar IS_start and ending with Bar IS_start+IS_n-1. Note that it does not look at Bar OOS1_end, which will always be the next bar after this in-sample period.

In the vast majority of applications, criterion_1() will use those IS_n bars of market history to find model parameters that maximize the performance of the trading system within those IS_n bars. It will then make a decision as to the position to take for the next bar, which is at Bar OOS1_end=IS_start+IS_n. As its last step in the majority of applications, criterion_1() will return the profit/loss generated by that trade on this Bar OOS1_end. If the optimized model said to take a long position, this return would be prices[OOS1_end] – prices[OOS1_end–1]. (Recall that prices would almost always be the log of actual prices.) If the model said to take a short position, criterion_1() would return the negative of that difference, and of course if the position is to be neutral, the return would be zero. Rather than including this typical behavior explicitly in the algorithm shown here, I left it general to allow for more complex trading systems that might double up on some trades, and so on.

```
for (icompetitor=0 ; icompetitor<n_competitors ; icompetitor++)
   OOS1[icompetitor*n_cases+OOS1_end] =
                              c riterion_1 ( icompetitor , IS_n , IS_start , prices ) ;
```

We have finished traversing the price history with the moving window when in the prior step we computed the OOS1 value at the last history bar. At that point there is nothing more to do because there is not another bar to use for computing OOS2, the performance of the selected best system.

```
if (OOS1_end >= n_cases-1)  // Have we hit the end of the data?
   break ;                             // Stop due to lack of another for OOS2
```

We now take care of part of the task of advancing the moving window. There is a warm-up period at the beginning of the algorithm while we build up enough OOS1 cases to allow the selector function to make a decision. Regardless of whether we have enough OOS1 cases, we increment the starting price index for training the component trading systems, and we also increment the OOS1 index where the next OOS return will be placed. But if the number of OOS1 bars computed so far, OOS1_end – OOS1_start, has not yet reached the required number for the selector, OOS1_n, we have nothing more to do yet, and we just keep advancing the window.

```
++IS_start ;      // Advance training window start
++OOS1_end ; // Advance current OOS1 case

if (OOS1_end - OOS1_start < OOS1_n)  // Are we still filling OOS1?
   continue ;  // Can't proceed until we have enough cases to compute an OOS2 return
```

When we get here, we have enough cases in OOS1 to invoke the system selector and compute an OOS2 case. First we find the best trading system, using the most recent OOS1_n values in OOS1 for each system. Remember that OOS1_end now points one past what we have in OOS1 (we incremented it a couple lines ago). Thus, the price at Bar OOS1_end is out-of-sample.

The selector function here is criterion_2(). Its first parameter is the number of OOS1 values to examine, and its second parameter is the starting address of that vector of values. If necessary, look back to see how these values are arranged as a matrix in OOS1.

In this algorithm, we find the single best trading system and evaluate its return. Readers who want to find a portfolio of systems instead should have little trouble modifying this presentation. Just call criterion_2() for each system, save the values in an array, and sort the array. Keep however many of the best you want.

```
best_crit = -1.e60 ;
for (icompetitor=0 ; icompetitor<n_competitors ; icompetitor++) {  // Find the best
   crit= criterion_2(OOS1_end-OOS1_start, OOS1+icompetitor*n_cases+OOS1_start);
   if (crit > best_crit) {
      best_crit = crit ;
      ibest = icompetitor ;
      }
   }
```

We now know the best competitor, so find its OOS return. The function trade_decision() here uses the optimized trading system ibest to decide on a position to take. Back when I discussed criterion_1(), I pointed out that I made it general to allow different sized positions. I did not make this version general simply because I want to be perfectly clear on how returns are computed for a trade decision. If your system possibly opens multiple positions in response to differing confidences, you will have to modify this code appropriately. This routine examines the most recent IS_n prices prior to Bar OOS2_end to make its decision. Note that Bar OOS2_end is not included in the decision process, so it is out-of-sample.

```
position = trade_decision ( ibest , IS_n , OOS2_end - IS_n , prices ) ;
if (position > 0)        // Long
  OOS2[OOS2_end] = prices[OOS2_end] - prices[OOS2_end-1] ;
else if (position < 0)   // Short
  OOS2[OOS2_end] = prices[OOS2_end-1] - prices[OOS2_end] ;
else                     // Neutral
  OOS2[OOS2_end] = 0.0 ;
```

We can complete the process of advancing the moving window. Before OOS1 contained enough values (OOS1_n are needed for the selector criterion_2()) we did not advance OOS1_start. But we advance it now that the OOS1 window is full. And of course we advance OOS2_end.

```
++OOS1_start ;   // Finish advancing the windows
++OOS2_end ;
} // Main loop
```

We have traversed the entire market history. At this time, OOS1_end and OOS2_end both equal n_cases because they always point one past the last entry, and we processed every possible bar.

Now that the entire market history is processed, we can compute some things that likely would be of interest. First, we compute and save the mean OOS performance of each system. The information for each bar is in OOS1. We could include every entry in OOS1, and some developers might be interested in this figure. However, for our purposes here, we want to have a level playing field, so we include only those bars that are also available in OOS2, which starts later than OOS1. In this demonstration, our computed performance measure is just the mean return per bar, but we could just as well compute profit factor, Sharpe ratio, or anything else. After all, the cumulative sum of each row of OOS1 is just a bar-to-bar equity curve that we can evaluate any way we want.

```
for (i=0 ; i<n_competitors ; i++) {
  sum = 0.0 ;
  for (j=OOS2_start ; j<OOS2_end ; j++)
    sum += OOS1[i*n_cases+j] ;
  crit_perf[i] = sum / (OOS2_end - OOS2_start) ;
  }
```

The last step is to compute our ultimate goal, the OOS performance of the selected best system. Those returns are in OOS2. As with OOS1, we compute mean return here, but feel free to compute other measures.

```
sum = 0.0 ;
for (i=OOS2_start ; i<OOS2_end ; i++)
  sum += OOS2[i] ;
final_perf = sum / (OOS2_end - OOS2_start) ;
```

A Practical Application of Nested Walkforward

In the prior section we saw an outline of the most common use of nested walkforward, presented as a series of C++ code fragments. Now we present a somewhat different use for this technique, this time in the form of a complete program that the user can modify if desired, compile, and use in practical applications. This program can be downloaded as CHOOSER.CPP and is complete, ready to compile and run.

The motivation behind this application is that the markets in a universe of equities take turns being the best performers. During some time periods, banks may be stellar performers, while at other times technology may reign supreme. The general idea is that every day (or other time period if we want) we examine every equity in a universe and select the one that has the best recent performance. We buy and hold this one currently superior equity during the next day and then re-evaluate the situation.

This nested walkforward demonstration moves a lookback window bar-to-bar. Scaling of printed results assumes that these are day bars, but of course they could be minute-bars in a higher-speed situation, weekly bars in a more relaxed environment, or whatever the developer wants.

At each bar it examines recent long performance for multiple markets. It collects the performance of each individual market that would have been obtained by simply buying and holding that market during the historical window period. It then purchases and holds for the next bar whichever market had the best recent performance. But how do we measure the performance of each competing market to choose the best market? Do we use mean return per bar? Sharpe ratio? Profit factor? That's the selection aspect of this application. At each bar we try several different performance measures and see which measure provides the best OOS return over a separate historical window. When we buy the best market for the next bar, we base that decision on whichever performance measure has the best recent OOS track record. Thus, we need an OOS performance figure for this second-level choice, in which we use a "best measure" to choose a "best market." Nested walkforward is required.

To use the command-line CHOOSER program, the user provides a list of market history files, each of whose filename specifies the name of the market. For example, IBM. TXT contains the market history prices for IBM. Each line of a market history file has the date (YYYYMMDD), open, high, low, and close. Any additional numbers on the line (such as volume) are ignored. For example, a line in a market history file might look like this:

```
20170622 1075.48 1077.02 1073.44 1073.88
```

In addition to providing the name of the text file that lists the market files, the user also specifies IS_n, the lookback in market price history for finding the currently best performing market; OOS1_n, the lookback in market-level OOS results for selecting the currently best performing criterion; and the number of Monte Carlo replications (discussed later). For example, the user might invoke the CHOOSER program from the command line as follows:

```
CHOOSER Markets.txt 1000 100 100
```

The Markets.txt file might look like this:

```
\Markets\IBM.TXT
\Markets\OEX.TXT
\Markets\T.TXT
etc.
```

The previous command line also says that 1,000 bars of recent market history will be examined to find the best market, and 100 bars of the OOS performance of that market selection process will be used to select the best performance criterion. It also says that

100 Monte Carlo replications will be performed to test the statistical significance of results. This subject will be introduced on page 283.

Here we will present the nested walkforward part of the CHOOSER.CPP code in more detail than we used in the prior general algorithm. But note that the complete program includes a Monte Carlo permutation test that we will not discuss until page 316, so those parts of the code will be omitted for now to avoid confusion.

Just to be clear, here are the three different performance criteria that will be used to decide which of the many markets is currently the most promising. They take two parameters: the number of (log) prices to examine and a pointer to the array of prices. The price array must actually be the log of the real prices to make them scale independent as well as enjoy other properties discussed in the Introduction.

The total return of a market segment is just its last price minus its first. To compute the raw (unnormalized) Sharpe ratio, we first compute the mean return per bar and then the variance of the bar-to-bar changes. The raw Sharpe ratio is the mean divided by the standard deviation. The profit factor is the sum of all up moves divided by the sum of all down moves. Finally, criterion() calls whichever of these routines is specified.

```
double total_return ( int n , double *pric es )
{
  return prices[n-1] - prices[0] ;
}

double sharpe_ratio ( int n , double *prices )
{
  int i ;
  double diff, mean, var ;

  mean = (prices[n-1] - prices[0]) / (n - 1.0) ;

  var = 1.e-60 ;  // Ensure no division by 0 later
  for (i=1 ; i<n ; i++) {
    diff = (prices[i] - prices[i-1]) - mean ;
    var += diff * diff ;
    }

  return mean / sqrt ( var / (n-1) ) ;
}
```

```
double profit_factor ( int n , double *prices )
{
   int i ;
   double ret, win_sum, lose_sum ;

   win_sum = lose_sum = 1.e-60 ;

   for (i=1 ; i<n ; i++) {
     ret = prices[i] - prices[i-1] ;
     if (ret > 0.0)
       win_sum += ret ;
     else
       lose_sum -= ret ;
     }

   return win_sum / lose_sum ;
}

double criterion ( int which , int n , double *prices )
{
   if (which == 0)
     return total_return ( n , prices ) ;

   if (which == 1)
     return sharpe_ratio ( n , prices ) ;

   if (which == 2)
     return profit_factor ( n , prices ) ;

   return -1.e60 ;   // Never get here if called correctly
}
```

The code for reading the market histories is straightforward but tedious, so it is omitted from this discussion. Also, bars for all markets must be aligned in time, so if any market is missing data for a bar, that bar must be removed from all other markets to preserve time alignment. This would be a rare event among major markets. This code, too, is tedious and hence omitted from this discussion; see CHOOSER.CPP for this code, highly commented. Here we focus on the nested walkforward code, which uses the following variables:

n_cases: Number of market price history bars.

market_close[][]: Market history (log of prices). The first index is the market, and the second is the bar.

n_markets: Number of markets (rows in market_close).

IS_n: User-specified number of recent market history bars for each selection criterion to examine.

OOS1_n: User-specified lookback of market selector; number of recent OOS returns from markets and used to choose the best market-selection method.

n_criteria: Number of competing market selection criteria.

OOS1: OOS returns of the "best" markets as determined by each competing criterion, an n_criteria by n_cases matrix. Column j of this matrix contains the returns produced by Bar j as a result of a "best market" decision made on Bar j–1.

OOS2: OOS returns of the markets selected with the best criterion.

IS_start: Starting bar of the current market performance window.

OOS1_start: Index in OOS1 of the starting bar of the current window. It advances with the window as soon as the system selector has OOS1_n cases to look back at.

OOS1_end: One past last bar of current OOS1 window. It advances with the window. This also serves as the current OOS1 case index.

OOS2_start: Starting index of complete OOS set 2; it remains fixed at IS_n + OOS1_n.

OOS2_end: One past the last case in OOS2. This also serves as the current OOS2 case index.

Users will find it interesting to compare performance obtained by the market selection procedure of this section to performance obtained by buying and holding individual markets or a basket of all competing markets. So, we print this information.

To facilitate a fair comparison, we should consider exactly the same bars that will take part in OOS2 calculations. The first bar in OOS2 will be at IS_n + OOS1_n, and its return is relative to the price at the prior bar. The last bar in OOS2 will be at n_cases–1 because bar indices are zero origin. We multiply the mean-per-bar return by 25200. This is reasonable when the prices are day bars, as there are typically about 252 trading days in a year. The prices are actually log prices, which are close to fractional returns relative to the prior price. Thus, the printed values are close to annualized percent returns. Here is this code:

```
fprintf ( fpReport, "\n\n25200 * mean return of each market in OOS2 period..." ) ;
sum = 0.0 ;
for (i=0 ; i<n_markets ; i++) {
  ret = 25200 * (market_close[i][n_cases-1] - market_close[i][IS_n+OOS1_n-1]) /
                (n_cases - IS_n - OOS1_n) ;
  sum += ret ;
  fprintf ( fpReport, "\n%15s %9.4lf", &market_names[i*MAX_NAME_LENGTH], ret ) ;
  }
fprintf ( fpReport, "\nMean = %9.4lf", sum / n_markets ) ;
```

Do some initializations. Users may be interested in knowing how many times each market selection criterion was selected as the best based on its OOS performance, so we zero an array of counters. We also initialize the various indices that let us traverse the market history.

```
for (i=0 ; i<n_criteria ; i++)
  crit_count[i] = 0 ;    // Counts how many times each criterion is chosen

IS_start = 0 ;              // Start market window with first case
OOS1_start = OOS1_end = IS_n ; // First OOS1 case is right after first price set
OOS2_start = OOS2_end = IS_n + OOS1_n ; // First OOS2 case after complete OOS1
```

The main loop that marches across the market history is next. The first step for each pass through the loop (window placement) is to evaluate the recent historical performance of each market, as measured by each competing criterion. For each criterion, find the market that had the best recent performance, motivated by the hope that the outstanding performance of this market will continue, at least until the next bar. We measure this next-bar performance as the change from the current bar to the next bar, which is Bar OOS1_end. We save this OOS performance in OOS1.

```
for (;;) {          // Main loop marches across market history

  for (icrit=0 ; icrit<n_criteria ; icrit++) {   // For each competing performance criterion
    best_crit = -1.e60 ;
    for (imarket=0 ; imarket<n_markets ; imarket++) {
      crit = criterion ( icrit , IS_n , market_close[imarket]+IS_start ) ;
      if (crit > best_crit) {
        best_crit = crit ;
        ibest = imarket ;   // Keep track of which market is best according to this criterion
        }
      }
    OOS1[icrit*n_cases+OOS1_end] =
                market_close[ibest][OOS1_end] - market_close[ibest][OOS1_end-1] ;
    }
```

At the end of the icrit loop shown previously, we have in OOS1 the next-bar (OOS) performance of whichever market each criterion found to be most promising. We now break out of the history-traversing loop if we have reached the end of the market data. Otherwise, advance those window pointers that always advance. Then check to see whether we have enough bars (OOS1_n) in OOS1 to be able to select the best criterion.

```
if (OOS1_end >= n_cases-1) // Have we hit the end of the data?
  break ;          // Stop due to lack of another for OOS2

++IS_start ;     // Advance training window
++OOS1_end ;  // Advance current OOS1 case

if (OOS1_end - OOS1_start < OOS1_n) // Are we still filling OOS1?
  continue ;      // Cannot proceed until enough cases to compute an OOS2 return
```

When we reach this point, we have enough bars in OOS1 to compare the competing criteria to see which one did the best job of selecting a market whose outstanding performance would continue on into the next bar. Our measure of criterion competence here is just the total OOS return of each competing criterion over the lookback window. Purely for the user's edification, count how many times each criterion is selected as the most reliable.

```
for (icrit=0 ; icrit<n_criteria ; icrit++) {        // Find the best criterion using OOS1
  crit = 0.0 ;                                       // Measures competence of icrit
  for (i=OOS1_start ; i<OOS1_end ; i++)              // Lookback window for competence
    crit += OOS1[icrit*n_cases+i] ;                  // Total return is a decent measure
  if (crit > best_crit) {
    best_crit = crit ;
    ibestcrit = icrit ;                              // Keep track of most reliable criterion
    }
  }

++crit_count[ibestcrit] ;   // This is purely for user's edification
```

At the end of the loop just shown, we know that ibestcrit is the criterion that, at least recently, proved to be the most reliable way of selecting the best market to buy. So we use this criterion to evaluate the recent performance of every market and select the best market to buy. We examine the IS_n prices prior to Bar OOS2_end, which will be this second-level OOS bar.

```
best_crit = -1.e60 ;

for (imarket=0 ; imarket<n_markets ; imarket++) { // Use best crit to select market
  crit = criterion ( ibestcrit , IS_n , market_close[imarket]+OOS2_end-IS_n ) ;
  if (crit > best_crit) {
    best_crit = crit ;
    ibest = imarket ;  // Keep track of best market as selected by best criterion
    }
  }
```

We now know which market has been selected as the best recent performer, and we have made this selection based on the criterion that has recently performed most reliably. So hopefully, this was a great choice; it's the best market, chosen by the most reliable criterion. We test this by computing the price change moving from the last bar in OOS1 that was checked to the next bar, OOS2_end. Save this return in OOS2. Finally, advance the window indices that we did not advance earlier.

186

```
OOS2[OOS2_end] =
                market_close[ibest][OOS2_end] - market_close[ibest][OOS2_end-1] ;

++OOS1_start ;   // Finish advancing window across market history
++OOS2_end ;

} // Main loop that traverses market history
```

The hard work is done. We have in OOS2 the bar-ahead OOS returns from our double-selection process, using the currently best criterion to choose the currently most promising market. Now it's time to compute and print summary results. You can refer to CHOOSER.CPP to see how I print these results if you want; their computation is shown here. Recall that just as we did for the raw markets at the beginning of this presentation, performances take into account only those bars that are available for OOS2. This makes all performance figures comparable. Also, as we did for raw market returns, we multiply by 25,200 to make these figures approximately annualized percent returns for day bars.

```
for (i=0 ; i<n_criteria ; i++) {      // Provide separate results for each criterion
  sum = 0.0 ;
  for (j=OOS2_start ; j<OOS2_end ; j++)
    sum += OOS1[i*n_cases+j] ;
  crit_perf[i] = 25200 * sum / (OOS2_end - OOS2_start) ;
  }

sum = 0.0 ;
for (i=OOS2_start ; i<OOS2_end ; i++)
  sum += OOS2[i] ;
final_perf = 25200 * sum / (OOS2_end - OOS2_start) ;
```

An Example Using S&P 100 Components

I ran the CHOOSER program just described on a large subset of the S&P 100 components, those whose history extends back to at least late 1986. This provides somewhat over 20 years (7725 days) of data in 65 markets. The market lookback (the number of prices examined by each performance criterion) was 1000 bars (days), and the OOS1 lookback (the number of best-market OOS bars used to compare performance criteria) was 100. A Monte Carlo permutation test with 1000 replications was performed. See page 316 for a discussion of these p-values. The results obtained were as follows:

```
Mean =    8.7473
```

```
25200 * mean return of each criterion, p-value, and percent of times
chosen...
```

```
 Total return    17.8898    p=0.076    Chosen 67.8 pct
 Sharpe ratio    12.9834    p=0.138    Chosen 21.1 pct
Profit factor    12.2799    p=0.180    Chosen 11.1 pct
```

```
25200 * mean return of final system = 19.1151 p=0.027
```

This tells us the following things in regard to this test:

- If we had simply purchased and held an equal basket of all these equities over the OOS2 period, we would have obtained an approximate annual return of 8.7473 percent.

- If we had used only total return to select the currently best performing market, we would have obtained an approximate annual return of 17.8898.

- Using only Sharpe ratio or only profit factor would have provided somewhat lower returns of 12.9834 and 12.2799 percent, respectively.

- When we put all three criteria into competition, they are chosen as most reliable 67.8, 21.1, and 11.1 percent of the time, respectively.

- If we also keep track of which criterion is currently most reliable, our approximate OOS annual return increases to 19.1151 percent.

Cross Validation Nested Inside Walkforward

It is often the case that we want to nest cross validation inside a walkforward analysis. To understand when this would be appropriate, recall the fundamental trade-off between cross validation and walkforward analysis in testing automated trading systems: cross validation makes far more efficient use of available data than walkforward testing, but it does not reflect real life. It can suffer from pessimistic or optimistic bias, and its results are often quite different from results obtained from the generally more "legitimate" walkforward analysis.

This trade-off inclines us toward cross validation instead of walkforward testing when its weaknesses are not critically important issues. In the example of nested walkforward presented in the prior two sections, bias and "real-life applicability" were vital considerations not only in the final result but also in the OOS1 inner result because that inner result is what enables us to choose from among competing performance evaluation functions. But there are situations in which lack of real-life conformity, including small bias issues, are less serious.

The two classic such situations are optimization of model complexity and selection of predictor variables. Obviously, both of these apply to model-driven trading systems, rather than rule-based algorithmic systems. However, there are some (rare) situations in which it may be useful to embed cross validation inside walkforward testing of algorithmic systems.

Admittedly, the decision to embed cross validation versus walkforward inside an outer walkforward analysis is often unclear and arguable. Still, as an example, consider optimizing the number of hidden neurons in a multiple-layer feedforward network that predicts market movement. If we have too few neurons, the model will be too weak to find predictive patterns. If we have too many, the model will overfit the data, learning random noise in addition to authentic patterns. We need the sweet spot.

This sweet spot is fundamentally dependent on the nature and degree of the noise in the data, so we want to employ as much data as possible in making this complexity decision, thus favoring cross validation. Moreover, we don't much care if the optimization process does not reflect real-life progress across time; we're just finding the ideal structure of the model as determined by the nature of the data. Also, it's not unreasonable to expect that any pessimistic bias due to using less than the full dataset (page 150) will be reflected roughly equally in all complexity trials, and any optimistic bias due to nonstationarity leakage (page 150) will also be fairly balanced. Our only goal in this test is to assess optimistic bias due to overfitting, which will be prominent when comparing models of varying complexity. So in this situation we would be inclined to favor cross validation.

To be clear on the process of embedding cross validation inside walkforward analysis, consider the following tiny example. We want to decide whether we should use three or five hidden neurons in our neural network. We divide the historical dataset into ten sections (1–10) and choose to use threefold cross validation. So, we do the following:

1) Configure the model to have three hidden neurons.

2) Train the model with sections 2 and 3, and predict the cases in section 1.

3) Train the model with sections 1 and 3, and predict the cases in section 2.

4) Train the model with sections 1 and 2, and predict the cases in section 3.

5) Pool the predictions for sections 1–3, and compute the OOS performance for this three-neuron model.

6) Configure the model to have five hidden neurons.

7) Repeat steps 2–5 to get the five-neuron performance.

8) Choose whichever model (three or five hidden neurons) had the better OOS performance. Train that model with sections 1–3.

9) Use this model to predict section 4, our first ultimate OOS set.

10) If we have not yet reached section 10 (the last section), repeat steps 1–9, except that every section number is incremented to the next, moving the entire window of operations one section forward in time.

11) When we reach the end, we have walkforward OOS data for sections 4–10. Pool it to get a grand performance figure. If it is not satisfactory, go back to the drawing board.

12) If we are satisfied with the grand performance, use cross validation on the entire dataset (any reasonable number of folds) twice, computing OOS performance of the three- and five-neuron models.

13) Choose whichever model was the better performer and train it with the most recent three sections (for consistency with how we tested) or the entire dataset (for maximum data usage) for use in trading.

That last step deserves a bit of discussion. How much of the data should we use when training the final model for production use? During walkforward testing in this example we trained each model with three blocks of data for OOS testing. To be consistent, our production model should also be trained with the most recent three blocks. This is good if we fear significant nonstationarity in the market. But by using all available data, we create a more stable model. Either choice is defensible.

In earlier sections we presented a general algorithm and a specific example of how to nest walkforward inside walkforward. That process involved some fairly complex manipulation of starting and stopping indices of lowest-level market data, mid-level OOS results, and outer-level OOS results. In most applications, this is the easiest and clearest way to approach the problem, despite the moderate complexity.

But when embedding cross validation, things become more complex. For this reason, as well as because in most applications the cross validation is part of the model-training process, we nearly always take a different and much simpler approach. Steps 1–8 of the example shown on the prior page are typically performed in a single subroutine call rather than being mixed up in the entire process as was done for embedded walkforward.

In other words, we have a single subroutine (likely calling other routines) that handles the training of individual folds, supervises the cross-validation competition between model architectures, and trains the final model. This single subroutine is then called in a simple walkforward implementation; it is called with a chunk of the earliest market history, and then the trained model is used to make trades for one or more bars of market data, that test set being however long the user wants the testing window to be. Those OOS results are preserved, and the entire training/testing window is moved forward so that the first bar in the next test window immediately follows the last bar in the current test window. This window is shifted forward until the end of the data is reached. The upshot is that as far as the walkforward analysis goes, it's just primitive single-layer walkforward of a predictive model, with the walkforward algorithm being blissfully unaware that there is cross validation going on inside the training routine.

CHAPTER 6

Estimating Future Performance II: Trade Analysis

Handling Dynamic Trading Systems

In the prior chapter, we focused mainly on how to collect unbiased, true-to-life trades from systems that made a position decision on each bar and produced a measurable return on each bar. Many trading systems, especially those that are algorithmic rather than model-based, make a decision to open a position and hold this position until a closing rule fires at some indeterminate future time. During that holding period, adjustments to the system may even be made, such as moving a trailing stop. This complicates things.

The focus of the current chapter is how to analyze the unbiased trades that we collected using the techniques of the prior chapter and use this analysis to estimate various aspects of future performance of our trading system. But before delving into this topic, we need to learn how to deal with trades produced by dynamic trading systems and explore several very different ways of analyzing these trades. For this reason, our first example will show an effective way to do this, and we will compare different ways to score trades.

© Timothy Masters 2018

T. Masters, *Testing and Tuning Market Trading Systems*, https://doi.org/10.1007/978-1-4842-4173-8_6

Unknown Lookahead to Single Bars, Revisited

On page 155 we saw an excellent technique for converting algorithmic trading systems having indeterminate lookahead into systems that look ahead one bar; please review that section now. This is wonderful, because when we do walkforward analysis of such systems, we do not need to deal with data-wasting guard buffers, regardless of how long the lookback is. Also, this technique provides the finest possible granularity, enabling the use of some of our most powerful statistical analysis algorithms.

There is yet another huge attraction to this technique, not mentioned in that section because I wanted to wait until I could present a detailed example. Now is the time. Of course, if our trading system is intrinsically a one-bar-ahead system, such as those that make a bar-by-bar decision about the position to take as we complete the next bar, we already have what we need, so we don't need to worry about conversion. But if we are in the common situation of having a rule that opens a position, another rule that closes a position an undefined time later, and perhaps even rules that change the exit rule as the trade progresses, we should be strongly inclined to use the conversion algorithm given on page 155.

The attraction of this algorithm that we mention now is that the transition from the training period to the testing period is simple, despite the complexity of the dynamic trading system. Moreover, if the training process is fast enough to be performed between bars (such as overnight in day-trading systems), we can seamlessly blend from the last fold of walkforward into final training and immediate use of the trading system.

As a small example to demonstrate how this works, consider the last fold of a walkforward test. Suppose we have 120 bars of data numbered 1 through 120 and we want to use the first 100 bars as a training period, the remaining 20 bars as a test period, retrain immediately upon completion of the test, and have an order ready to be placed to have a position open through the next bar, 121.

In this example, our last trade decision during training would be made on Bar 99, because we will need the price on Bar 100 to compute the final bar's contribution to our performance measure in the training period, the measure that is being optimized by parameter adjustment. When the optimal parameters are found and we prepare to advance to the test period, we also need to know the last position in the training period, that which was in effect for the move from Bar 99 to Bar 100 in the optimal model. The easiest approach is just to save it along with the optimal parameter updates during training. Then, when we advance to Bar 101 for the beginning of the test period, we use the optimized model to make a trade decision on Bar 100 and use the price on Bar 101 to compute the first return in the test period. If the reason for preserving the last position in the training period is not clear, refer to the algorithm on page 155 to see why we need the prior position. We need this for the Bar 100 decision.

It gets even better. Suppose we have data through Bar 120 and have finished the walkforward with good results. We retrain the system, making decisions through Bar 119, preserve the last position, and use the optimized model to make a decision on this Bar 120. This is the first position we take in real-life trading, ready for Bar 121 tomorrow. Smooth!

Profit per Bar? Per Trade? Per Time?

When we complete a walkforward test and have in hand a pooled collection of bar-by-bar OOS returns, we have several choices of what we can do to this data in preparation for statistical analysis.

- Remove all bars on which a position was not open. Their returns are zero anyway, so they dilute the dataset. Keep only the individual bar returns for all bars on which a position was open. This is probably the most common approach, as it provides data in fine granularity, but only data from times we were actually in the market. Most of the techniques in this book will use this approach.

- Keep all bars, even those that have a return of zero because no position was open. This provides the maximum possible detail, because it includes the data in the prior technique, along with information about how often we were in the market. Some analyses that we will see later care about differentiating between systems that are almost always in the market versus those that trade infrequently. We should consider the common trade-off between systems that trade rarely but have a high success rate versus those that trade often, have a lower success rate, but make up for that by sheer mass of trades.

- Pool small sets of contiguous bars into numerous "summary" returns. For example, we might sum the returns of the first ten bars (including those with no position open) into a single return, the next ten bars into a second return, and so forth, across the entire dataset.

Or the pooling might be date-based, perhaps summing into weekly or monthly returns. This has the disadvantage of discarding much potentially useful information, the details of what's happening inside those packets. It also reduces the quantity of data available for analysis, always a negative. But it has several big advantages. Wild bars (those with an abnormally large price movement) have their effects diluted, always a good thing in statistical analysis. Also, randomness is reduced. We can't tell much about the performance of a system by examining a half-dozen individual bar returns. But if we have a half-dozen returns, each of which is the sum of ten bar returns, we can tell a bit more. We will see this approach used later when we examine ways to see whether a trading system is still performing as expected or whether its performance is significantly deteriorating.

- Treat each completed trade (often called a *round turn*) as a single return. We note the price when the trade opens and the price when the trade closes. The return is the closing price minus the opening price.

This last approach is by far the most common in the industry because it is intuitive. And it doesn't hurt that this approach tends to exaggerate returns, both wins and losses; if a developer has a winning system, exaggeration is welcome, while if the developer has a losing system (with exaggerated losses), we'll never see it. But this completed-trade approach is terrible for statistical analysis, both because of the exaggeration and because of the loss of information. We'll explore these issues now.

Analyzing Completed Trade Returns Is Problematic

When we pool all individual bar returns into a single quantity spanning the complete trade, the reduction in quantity of data points can be huge. If the average trade lasts for 50 bars, our number of data points for analysis is reduced by a factor of 50. For statistical analysis, the difference between having 10 data points and 500 data points is enormous.

Equally serious is the loss of information about what happens in the market as the trade progresses. Perhaps we take a long position and the market slowly and steadily rises in a direct march to a profitable exit. Or maybe after our long entry the market gyrates wildly, shooting up, then plunging far below our entry, and then recovering at the close of the trade to show a profit. These two scenarios have extremely different implications in terms of trade analysis, but when we pool the bar returns into a single net figure, we lose this information, so we don't know which scenario took place.

The loss of fine-granularity information is especially problematic when computing the profit factor, one of my favorite performance measures. Recall that the profit factor is defined as the sum of wins divided by the sum of losses. Consider some numbers fabricated to demonstrate the problem. Suppose our system has two trades, each spanning multiple bars. The two trades are identical in that their total bar wins are 101 points and their total bar losses are 100 points. Thus, each trade has a net win of 1 point. There are no losing trades, so the profit factor based on trades is (1+1)/0; it is infinite. But if we compute the profit factor from individual bars, the profit factor is (101+101) / (100+100) = 1.01, essentially worthless.

This problem is equally severe with the Sharpe ratio, because the essence of the problem is loss of information about internal volatility. We can have two competing systems that have identical Sharpe ratios based on completed trade returns, but if one has high internal volatility and the other's is low, their bar-based Sharpe ratios will be very different (and more accurate!).

What we usually see (and the earlier profit-factor demonstration was a perfect example) is that for any trading system, computing performance measures based on completed trade returns will provide values that are more extreme than we would obtain if the measures were based on individual bar returns within the trade. This is partly because the number of returns going into the computation is smaller with trade returns, leading to greater instability, and partly because natural market variation within a trade is washed out. This can and will lead to erroneous conclusions.

In summary, I cannot emphasize strongly enough that you should pay minimal attention to performance metrics that are based on the net returns of trades. Whenever possible, you should break trades into as fine a granularity as reasonably possible and compute your metric based on these quantities. Of course, if you are making a proud presentation, you will probably want to put your trade-based results in big bold print on the handouts; everybody does, so you need to be on equal footing. But for your own internal research, ignore those numbers. Look at the fine-granularity returns that make up the complete trades. That's what counts.

The PER_WHAT Program

At the beginning of this section (page 195) we explored several methods for presenting returns (typically OOS returns) for statistical analysis. We also emphasized the importance of procuring bar-by-bar returns within an extended trade, using the algorithm shown on page 155 if necessary. This section presents a demonstration program that puts it all together: use the page 155 algorithm to convert an indeterminate-lookahead system to a one-bar-ahead system, and then restructure the bar returns according to the options laid out on page 195. The file PER_WHAT.CPP contains complete, ready-to-compile source code for this program.

The trading system in this example is a simple long-only moving-average breakout system. When the market price crosses above a threshold that is an optimizable distance above a moving average with optimizable lookback, a long position is opened. This position is kept open until the market price crosses below the moving average, even if the price is below the entry threshold. This indeterminate-lookahead system is walked forward, and the OOS results are cumulated using any of the methods shown on page 195. Finally, one of several user-specified performance criteria is computed. Readers should be able to modify the training, testing, and walkforward routines to suit their own needs or use segments of this program as templates for their own code.

We now work through the most important segments of the source code, beginning with the invocation parameters specified by the user.

PER_WHAT which_crit all_bars ret_type max_lookback n_train n_test filename

Let's break this command down:

- which_crit: Specifies which criterion will be used for computing optimal parameters and then evaluating OOS performance. 0=mean return; 1=profit factor; 2=Sharpe ratio.

- all_bars: Applies to training only, and for only the mean return and Sharpe ratio criteria. If nonzero, all bars, even those with no position open, go into computing the optimization criterion.

- ret_type: Applies to testing only. This selects which method we use for translating bar returns to analyzable returns, as described on page 195. 0=all bars; 1=bars with position open; 2=completed trades. If we want to use the third method shown on page 195, pooling returns into fixed blocks, we would use option 0 here and pool manually. Note that completed trades are never used during training, as this is a terrible approach because of massive information loss.

- max_lookback: Maximum moving-average lookback tried during training (parameter optimization).

- n_train: Number of bars in the training set for each walkforward fold. It should be much greater than max_lookback to get good parameter estimates.

- n_test: Number of bars in the test set for each walkforward fold. Smaller values (even just 1) make the test more robust against nonstationarity in the market, but take much longer to execute.

- filename: Name of the market file to read. It has no header. Each line in the file is for a single bar, and it has the date as YYYYMMDD and at least one price. Any numbers after the first number following the date are ignored. For example, a line in a market history file might look like the following, and only the first price (1075.48) would be read. Readers who would prefer to use the close for open/high/low/close files can easily modify this code.

```
20170622 1075.48 1077.02 1073.44 1073.88
```

We will not bother explaining the code that reads the market information and allocates memory; comments in the code make that self-explanatory. The only thing to note is the constant MKTBUF defined at the beginning of the source file. We don't know in advance how many records will be in the market history file, so prices are reallocated in chunks of this size. Its value is not critical.

We'll jump directly to the walkforward code. We have read and stored nprices market history prices and converted them all to logs. We initialize the index of the first price in the first training set to be the beginning of the array of prices. We also initialize to zero the count of the number of OOS returns cumulated during the walkforward.

```
train_start = 0 ; // Starting index of training set
nret = 0 ;        // Number of computed returns
```

Here is the walkforward loop. An explanation follows.

```
for (;;) {

  crit = opt_params ( which_crit , all_bars , n_train , prices + train_start ,
                      max_lookback , &lookback , &thresh , &last_pos ) ;

  n = n_test ;    // Test this many cases
  if (n > nprices - train_start - n_train) // Don't go past the end of history
    n = nprices - train_start - n_train ;

  comp_return ( ret_type , nprices , prices , train_start + n_train , n , lookback ,
                thresh , last_pos , &n_returns , returns + nret ) ;
  nret += n_returns ;

  train_start += n ;
  if (train_start + n_train >= nprices)
    break ;
  }
```

We'll look at the opt_params() parameter optimization code soon. Many of the key parameters in this call were defined at the beginning of this section. Note that we pass it prices+train_start as a pointer to the beginning of the training set for the current fold. It returns the optimal MA lookback and the optimal entry threshold. It also returns the position (long versus neutral) as of the end of the training set, because we'll want this to start the OOS test. Of course, we could alternatively always start the test fold with this position being zero, forcing the OOS test to always start from scratch. But in real life we would virtually always know this position or be able to quickly compute it, so it is more realistic to begin the test period with this useful past information in hand.

We let n be the number of OOS test cases for this fold. Normally it will be the user-specified value, n_test. But if we are doing the last fold, there may be fewer prices left in the market history, so we must limit the number of test cases accordingly.

The index in the history array of the first test case is train_start+n_train, the first price after the current training period. We pass this test routine the previously computed optimal lookback and threshold, as well as the market position as of the end of the training period. We also give it the next available slot in the OOS return array, returns+nret. It returns to us the number of OOS returns just computed for this fold.

The number of returns so far, nret, is updated per this fold. We also advance the index of the start of the training set so that the first bar in the next test fold will be immediately after the last bar in the current test fold. If we have reached the point that there will be no test cases in a subsequent fold, we are done. When the loop exits, we have nret contiguous OOS returns in returns.

The calling parameter list for the training (optimization) routine is as shown here. All of these parameters have been discussed already, some in the list at the beginning of this section and some in conjunction with the walkforward code just shown.

```
double opt_params (
    int which_crit ,        // 0=mean return per bar; 1=profit factor; 2=Sharpe ratio
    int all_bars ,          // Include return of all bars, even those with no position
    int nprices ,           // Number of log prices in 'prices'
    double *prices ,        // Log prices
    int max_lookback ,      // Maximum lookback to use
    int *lookback ,         // Returns optimal MA lookback
    double *thresh ,        // Returns optimal breakout threshold factor
    int *last_pos           // Returns position at end of training set
    )
```

The outermost loops in this routine try every combination of lookback and entry threshold, testing the performance of each. The user specifies which performance criterion will be optimized. To keep things simple, and with negligible loss of speed, we will continually update some things used by all three criteria even if they will not be used. Initialize these quantities. We also assume that no position is open as of when we begin the training period, certainly a reasonable assumption.

```
best_perf = -1.e60 ;                          // Best performance across all trials
for (ilook=2 ; ilook<=max_lookback ; ilook++) {    // Trial MA lookback
    for (ithresh=1 ; ithresh<=10 ; ithresh++) {    // Trial threshold is 0.01 * ithresh

        total_return = 0.0 ;                  // Cumulate total return for this trial
        win_sum = lose_sum = 1.e-60 ;         // Cumulates for profit factor
        sum_squares = 1.e-60 ;                // Cumulates for Sharpe ratio
        n_trades = 0 ;                        // Will count trades
        position = 0 ;                        // Current position
```

We have a pair of parameters (MA lookback and entry threshold) to try by cumulating performance for all valid cases. The index of the first legal bar in prices is max_lookback–1, because we need max_lookback cases (including the decision bar) in the moving average. Start at the same bar for all lookbacks to make them comparable. We must stop one bar before the end of the price array because we need the next price to compute the return from the decision. In the following loop, the decision is made at Bar i, and the return from this decision is the price change from Bar i to Bar i+1.

```
for (i=max_lookback-1 ; i<nprices-1 ; i++) { // Compute performance across history
```

Rather than taking the very slow approach of recomputing the moving average at each bar, we compute it once on the first bar and then update it for subsequent bars.

```
if (i == max_lookback-1) {    // Find the moving average for the first valid case.
  MA_sum = 0.0 ;              // Cumulates MA sum
  for (j=i ; j>i-ilook ; j--)
    MA_sum += prices[j] ;
  }
else                          // Update the moving average
  MA_sum += prices[i] - prices[i-ilook] ;
```

The moving average is the sum that we continually update divided by the lookback. We also compute the trial entry threshold from ithresh.

```
MA_mean = MA_sum / ilook ;        // Divide price sum by lookback to get MA
trial_thresh = 1.0 + 0.01 * ithresh ;
```

Now that we have the moving average and the trial threshold, we make a trade decision. The algorithm as implemented here looks slightly different from its presentation on page 155, but it really is exactly the same algorithm. The difference is that the version shown on page 155 is most general, applicable if we are restricted to a commercial platform in which we must explicitly open and close trades. But if we are writing our own code, we can simplify it. If the entry rule fires, flag that we have a position open. If the exit rule fires, flag that we are out of the market. If neither rule fires, just maintain the current position. Then compute the return to the next bar, according to the current position. Since the example system shown here is long only, it's just the positive difference. If the reader implements a short or dual system, modify this code accordingly.

```
if (prices[i] > trial_thresh * MA_mean)       // Do we satisfy the entry test?
   position = 1 ;
else if (prices[i] < MA_mean)                 // Do we satisfy the exit test?
   position = 0 ;

if (position)
   ret = prices[i+1] - prices[i] ;            // Return to next bar after decision
else
   ret = 0.0 ;
```

For simplicity, we compute all three criteria, even though we use only one of them. Change this if you want, but the time savings is marginal.

```
if (all_bars  ||  position) {
   ++n_trades ;
   total_return += ret ;
   sum_squares += ret * ret ;
   if (ret > 0.0)
      win_sum += ret ;
   else
      lose_sum -= ret ;
   }
```

Notice in the previous if() block that if the user specified all_bars=0, a bar's return will enter into the performance calculation only if a position was open on that bar. But if the user specified all_bars nonzero, then bars with no open position, and hence a zero return, will also take part. This has no impact on profit factor, but it does affect the other two criteria by making them sensitive to how often the trading system is in the market.

Now we keep track of the best performing parameter set. We update the best performance so far, as well as the MA lookback and entry threshold that gave this best performance. We also save the position of the trial system as of the last decision bar, because we will want this when we start the OOS test for the fold.

```
if (which_crit == 0) {                      // Mean return criterion
   total_return /= n_trades + 1.e-30 ;      // Don't divide by zero
   if (total_return > best_perf) {
      best_perf = total_return ;
      ibestlook = ilook ;
```

```
        ibestthresh = ithresh ;
        last_position_of_best = position ;
        }
      }

    else if (which_crit == 1  &&  win_sum / lose_sum > best_perf) { // Profit factor crit
      best_perf = win_sum / lose_sum ;
      ibestlook = ilook ;
      ibestthresh = ithresh ;
      last_position_of_best = position ;
      }
```

The following Sharpe ratio criterion needs a special mention. We compute the variance of the returns by subtracting from the mean-square the square of the mean return. This method is generally discouraged because subtraction of two similarly sized numbers can lead to floating-point inaccuracies. However, in this application the mean square will nearly always be much larger than the squared mean, so this issue will not be a problem in practice, and it is fast to compute and easy to understand.

```
    else if (which_crit == 2) {                     // Sharpe ratio criterion
      total_return /= n_trades + 1.e-30 ;           // Now mean return
      sum_squares /= n_trades + 1.e-30 ;
      sum_squares -= total_return * total_return ;   // Variance (may be zero!)
      if (sum_squares < 1.e-20)  // Must not divide by zero or take sqrt of negative
        sum_squares = 1.e-20 ;
      sr = total_return / sqrt ( sum_squares ) ;
      if (sr > best_perf) {                          // Sharpe ratio
        best_perf = sr ;
        ibestlook = ilook ;
        ibestthresh = ithresh ;
        last_position_of_best = position ;
        }
      }

    } // For ithresh, all short-term lookbacks
  } // For ilook, all long-term lookbacks
```

After all lookbacks and entry thresholds have been tried, we are done. Return the optimal parameters and market position of the best system as of the last decision bar (the second-last training-set bar).

```
*lookback = ibestlook ;
*thresh = 0.01 * ibestthresh ;
*last_pos = last_position_of_best ;

return best_perf ;
}
```

The routine that takes these optimal parameters and applies them to the test fold is similar to what we just saw, but we'll examine it anyway to focus on the important differences.

Before studying the code, we must understand the algorithm for trading in the test period. The first OOS trade decision is made on the last bar of the training set. (Recall that when we trained using the code just shown, we did not make a trade decision on that last bar, because we did not have the next bar available to compute a return. That next bar is in the test set!) The return for this first OOS trade is the price change from the last bar of the training set to the first bar in the test set.

Also recall that the trade decision made on the last bar can depend on the market position as of the prior bar. This happens when neither the entry rule nor the exit rule fires, so we just continue the position. This dependency is why, in the training algorithm, we returned last_pos as the market position as of the last bar. We'll want to pass this to the OOS test routine to be available for that first trade.

With this understood, here is the calling convention for the test routine. All of these items have already been discussed in conjunction with the training routine, except ret_type, which was discussed on page 198. To review, ret_type selects which method we use for translating bar returns to analyzable returns, as described on page 195. The caller specifies 0, 1, or 2: 0=all bars; 1=bars with position open; 2=completed trades. If we want to use the third method shown on page 195, pooling returns into fixed blocks, we would use Option 0 here and pool manually.

The second parameter in this call list, nprices, is not used by the algorithm and can be removed by the reader if desired. However, an assert() statement appears at one place in the code where it looks ahead to compute a return, and this safety check makes sure that we are not looking past the end of the market price array. Readers who modify this code for their own trading system may want to leave it in place as cheap insurance against a careless mistake.

```
void comp_return (
    int ret_type ,          // Return type: 0, 1, or 2
    int nprices ,           // N of log prices in 'prices' used only for safety, not algorithm
    double *prices ,        // Log prices
    int istart ,            // Starting index in OOS test set
    int ntest ,             // Number of OOS test cases
    int lookback ,          // Optimal MA lookback
    double thresh ,         // Optimal breakout threshold factor
    int last_pos ,          // Position in bar prior to test set (last training set position)
    int *n_returns ,        // Number of returns in 'returns' array
    double *returns         // Bar returns returned here
    )
```

We begin by initializing some key variables. The counter nret is the number of returns that are computed for the caller. If the return type specifies that we keep all bars (ret_type=0), this will equal ntest. Otherwise, it can be less, often much less. The optimization routine gave us the optimal system's market position at the last bar, which we get as last_pos. We need prior_position only for the completed trades option (ret_type=2). When the position goes from zero to nonzero, we just opened a new position, and when it goes from nonzero to zero, we closed the position. If your trading system has undefined lookahead and can go directly from long to short or short to long, you will need to slightly modify this code according to how you want to record completed trades. Typically this closes the old trade and opens a new trade on the same bar. But other accounting practices are possible, including situations in which additional trades open or a set of open trades partially closes. Note that for the "completed trades" option we must keep the opening price in the test block to avoid future leak, so prior_position=0.

```
nret = 0 ;                      // Counts returns that we output
position = last_pos ;           // Current position
prior_position = 0 ;            // For completed trades, always start out of market
trial_thresh = 1.0 + thresh ;   // Make it multiplicative for simplicity
```

In the main loop we make our trade decision on bar i. The first decision is made on the last bar of the training set (istart–1), and we make ntest decisions. As was the case in the training routine, instead of recomputing the moving average from scratch at each bar, we compute it once on the first bar of the test and update it thereafter.

```
for (i=istart-1 ; i<istart-1+ntest ; i++) { // Compute returns across test set

   if (i == istart-1) {          // Find the moving average for the first valid case.
      MA_sum = 0.0 ;             // Cumulates MA sum
      for (j=i ; j>i-lookback ; j--)
         MA_sum += prices[j] ;
      }

   else                         // Update the moving average
      MA_sum += prices[i] - prices[i-lookback] ;

   MA_mean = MA_sum / lookback ;      // Divide price sum by lookback to get MA
```

As we did in the optimization algorithm, we execute the algorithm of page 155 slightly differently than shown there, though with identical results. If the open rule fires, we make sure a position is open (it may already be open). If the exit rule fires, we close the position. If neither rule fires, we maintain the prior position. The assert() here is cheap insurance against algorithm or caller errors, and of course it may be omitted (and the nprices parameter removed) if the programmer is confident in correctness. We then compute the return for this bar according to the position.

```
   assert ( i+1 < nprices ) ;              // Optional cheap insurance

   if (prices[i] > trial_thresh * MA_mean)    // Do we satisfy the entry test?
      position = 1 ;

   else if (prices[i] < MA_mean)            // Do we satisfy the exit test?
      position = 0 ;

   if (position)
      ret = prices[i+1] - prices[i] ;
   else
      ret = 0.0 ;
```

At this time we know our position and return for this bar. Save (or not) the appropriate outputted return.

```
if (ret_type == 0)              // All bars, even those with no position
   returns[nret++] = ret ;

else if (ret_type == 1) {       // Only bars with a position
   if (position)
     returns[nret++] = ret ;
   }

else if (ret_type == 2) {                       // Completed trades
   if (position  &&  ! prior_position)          // We just opened a trade
     open_price = prices[i] ;
   else if (prior_position  &&  ! position)     // We just closed a trade
     returns[nret++] = prices[i] - open_price ;
   else if (position  &&  i==istart-2+ntest)    // Force close at end of data
     returns[nret++] = prices[i+1] - open_price ;
   }
```

The "completed trades" code deserves additional attention. If our position has changed from zero to nonzero, we just opened a trade, so we record the opening price, which is the decision bar. If our position changed from nonzero to zero, we just closed a trade, so we record its profit. This demonstration system is long only, with just one position open at any time, so this trade's return is the price on which the decision to close is made, minus the price at which the trade opened. If your system can also be short, you'll need to add an extra check and flip the sign of the return for short positions. If your system can go directly from long to short or short to long or have multiple positions open, more extensive modifications to this short block of code are needed.

The last else if() code handles the situation of having a position still open when the end of the OOS test block is reached. (In the main program we made sure ntest would not overrun the full price history array, so we need not check that now.)

We are now essentially done. Set prior_position to the current position and continue the loop. When the loop exits, after having processed all ntest bars in the OOS test set, we pass back the count of returns.

```
    prior_position = position ;
    } // For i, computing returns across test set

  *n_returns = nret ;
}
```

Although this PER_WHAT program facilitates some interesting experimentation, many readers will want to hold off on building and using this program, instead focusing on the BOUND_MEAN program that will appear on page 232. That program implements the same trading system as the PER_WHAT program, and it takes things further by using several methods to compute probable lower bounds for this trading system in any market supplied by the user.

A Lower Bound for Mean Future Returns

In prior sections we have explored trading systems that make bar-by-bar decisions and hence provide bar-by-bar returns. We also presented an example of how to take a trading system that uses entry and exit rules, and hence may have unknown lookahead, and compute its returns on a bar-by-bar or complete-trade basis. One performance measure that we would find useful is a lower bound for the long-term mean of these returns in the future. (We may rarely be interested in an upper bound as well.) If we achieve great walkforward test results, but then we find that a reasonable lower bound on the true mean value of the returns that we can expect in the future is small, we would do well to go back to the drawing board. In short, excellent backtest performance is wonderful but not enough. We want high confidence that this outstanding performance will continue. This is the topic of this section.

First, at the risk of being overly pedantic, I'll briefly review the more important types of returns we may be dealing with, and I'll throw in some commentary.

- Everybody would like to have bounds for the returns of completed trades. Unfortunately, in most practical situations, this is the most difficult figure to obtain with great reliability. The primary reason for this difficulty is the paucity of data. In statistical analysis, quantity equals reliability. We have only as many data points as we have trades, and unless the system trades frequently, we will often have too few returns to compute a useful bound. Still, this is such a useful and meaningful figure that we must not write it off.

- My favorite return to bound is the mean return per bar for bars on which a position is open. This will provide many more data points than returns of completed trades. It is also a sensible performance metric, as it tells us our expected return in exchange for taking the risk (and possible margin expense) of having a position open.

- Another frequently useful mean return to bound is the return for subsets (such as weekly sums) of all bars. This is important if we are monitoring ongoing performance to detect deterioration.

Brief Digression: Hypothesis Tests

Having a lower bound on the mean return we can expect in the future is our ultimate goal, and we'll get to that soon. But there is a useful alternative that can also serve as a stepping-stone to confidence bounds, so we begin with the subject of *hypothesis tests*. By the way, for simplicity here we will focus on *one-sided* tests, those concerned with hopefully asserting that our achieved mean return is far enough above zero to provide confidence that we have a useful trading system. Later, we will generalize this to one-sided tests for "negative" measures such as drawdown and eventually look at bounding parameters in an interval, a task not often done in financial analysis but still useful in some situations.

A classical hypothesis test uses indirect reasoning to make a statement about the quality of our trading system as implied by the observed mean return. We need to define two hypotheses.

- The *null hypothesis* is usually the boring "default" assumption, the situation that we hope is not in effect. When evaluating the observed OOS return of a trading system, our null hypothesis is typically that the system is worthless: its true expected return is zero or less.

- The *alternative hypothesis* is usually the situation that we hope is in effect. In the current context, the alternative hypothesis is typically that our trading system is good, as evidenced by a significantly large positive observed sample mean return.

The indirect reasoning works like this:

1) Assume that the null hypothesis is true and compute the theoretical distribution of the mean return (or whatever our test statistic is) under this hypothesis. This is the hard part.

2) Using this distribution, compute the probability that we could
    have randomly observed a sample mean as large as (or larger
    than) that which we did obtain.

3) If this probability is tiny, conclude that the null hypothesis is false.

This works because we must always define the null and alternative hypotheses to be *mutually exclusive* and *exhaustive*. This means that it is impossible for both hypotheses to be true and that these two hypotheses cover all possibilities. The true situation is always either one or the other, never both and never neither.

The fundamental logic is this: suppose we see that if the null hypothesis were true, our observed return is highly unlikely to be this good. In this case, we conclude that the alternative hypothesis is probably true.

It is vital to understand that getting a result well in line with the null hypothesis does not let us assert that the null hypothesis is true, or even probably true. No matter what outcome we observe, *we can never assert that the null hypothesis is true*. We can only assert that the null hypothesis is probably false and thereby assert that the alternative is probably true.

Here are two examples that may illustrate the situation. Suppose someone fills two identical large jars with jelly beans, both to the same height. You look at them closely and try to make a statement. Can you say that they contain the same number of jelly beans? They certainly look very, very close. But it could easily be that one contains 1,000 and the other 1,001. You would never see the difference. You can't even say that they are *probably* the same, because you don't know if the filler had an agenda to fool people. On the other hand, suppose one jar is clearly filled much higher than the other. Then you can confidently say that they contain unequal numbers of jelly beans.

This second example is somewhat closer to the task at hand. Suppose we are testing the quality of our trading system. It has two trades, one a gain of 10 percent and one a loss of 8 percent. If the system were truly worthless, the probability of such an outcome (or better) from just two trades would be very high, and therefore we cannot use our indirect logic to reject the null hypothesis and thereby assert the alternative. So, does this mean that we can confidently assert that the null hypothesis is true, and the system is worthless? Or even probably worthless? Certainly not, because two trades are far too few trades on which to make such a decision. It may well be that if we had used a much longer market history, we would have obtained 100 returns of 10 percent and 100 losses of 8 percent. Under this circumstance, we would likely find that there is a very low probability that a truly worthless system would perform this well. We could thereby reject the null hypothesis that the system is worthless and decide that it probably has merit. Of course, we may still decide that it does not make enough money to justify the risk, but that's another issue.

The bottom line is that failure to reject the null hypothesis may have come simply because we did not do enough testing rather than because the null hypothesis is true. If we had extended our test period we might have concluded that the null hypothesis is false. Or perhaps we have selected an inappropriate testing procedure that failed to reject the null hypothesis. Thus, we must *never* assert the truth of the null hypothesis.

So, How Do We Use This Probability?

Let's briefly review the hypothesis test steps presented at the beginning of the prior section. First, we assume the null hypothesis (the boring situation) is true and compute the statistical distribution of our test statistic (the mean return in the current context). Second, we consider the observed value of our test statistic in the context of this null hypothesis distribution. Third, if our observed value (or better) would be highly unlikely under this assumption, we conclude that the alternative hypothesis (the interesting situation) is probably true. There are three specific things we can do to execute this process, one of which is fully legitimate, one of which is basically legitimate but in a gray area, and one of which is horribly wrong.

- The officially correct way to perform this test is to decide *in advance* what probability of incorrectly rejecting the null hypothesis we are willing to live with. Recall that the assumption is that the null hypothesis is true and we are computing the probability that our observed value (or better) could have been observed under this assumption. So if this observed probability is small and we thereby reject a true null hypothesis, we are mistaken in doing so. It is common to set a probability threshold of 0.05 in advance, deciding that if the probability of our observed value is 0.05 or less, we will reject the null hypothesis. The implication is that when we perform the test and the null hypothesis is true, we will have a 5 percent chance of incorrectly rejecting this hypothesis. In the current context, this means that if our trading system is truly worthless, we will have a 5 percent chance of incorrectly concluding that it legitimately makes money. We may be more conservative and demand only a 1 percent chance of falsely rejecting the null hypothesis when it is true, and this will give us a more stringent test, a test that is more difficult to pass. Or we may loosen our requirement, being willing to live with a 10 percent chance of falsely concluding that a truly worthless system makes money. In this case we would set our probability threshold at 0.1, concluding legitimacy if the probability of our observed mean return is 0.1 or less.

Equivalently, we could compute in advance the value under the null hypothesis distribution that corresponds to a probability of 0.1. Then we conclude legitimacy if our observed mean equals or exceeds this threshold. Please ponder this equivalency if you don't see it immediately. (Remember that larger observed means would have smaller probabilities.) It makes no difference which way you do the test; they are identical.

- Another approach to hypothesis testing is used by many people, including myself, because it provides a bit more information at the expense of opening the door to some abuse if one is not careful in how results are interpreted. In this approach, one does not specify an error probability threshold, like 0.05 or whatever, in advance. Instead, one just goes ahead and computes the probability under the null hypothesis of achieving a result as good as or better than what we obtained. In this context, this probability is called a *p-value*. This gives us not just the *reject/do-not-reject* decision that the first approach gave us. It gives us a quantitative figure. If we get a p-value of 0.049, we conclude that this test would have rejected the null hypothesis at the 0.05 error level, but just barely, and so we would rightly be cautious. On the other hand, if we get a p-value of 0.001, we rightly conclude that *if the null hypothesis were true*, it would be extremely unlikely for our trading system to do as well as it did. This is still not enough to trade the system; it may be that its risk/reward ratio is poor. But all other things being equal, we may legitimately conclude that a p-value of 0.001 is more encouraging than .049.

I mentioned that there are risks of using this approach. Here is a big and common one, and it's subtle. We may *not* use p-values as reliable measures of the relative values of systems. If we get a p-value of 0.001, we may legitimately get a warm, fuzzy feeling and have somewhat more confidence in our system than we would have with a p-value of 0.049. But that's it. Warm and fuzzy; nothing more. We may *not* conclude that we have a slam dunk decision on which is better. It may be that if we took the 0.049 system and tested it on a longer stretch of historical data, we would get a p-value of 0.001 as well. That's a big weakness of hypothesis tests: they are dependent on how much data is tested. So, be careful about interpreting p-values in a numerical sense. You can (and should) do it, but only with a very large grain of salt.

- The third occasionally used approach to hypothesis testing is *incorrect*! We will discuss it here, constantly reminding the reader that every bit of the "logic" presented in this bullet point is wrong. Let's say you obtain a p-value of 0.01, a very encouraging result (a legitimate conclusion). The *totally incorrect* logic used by many is that since a worthless system would have only a 1 percent chance of getting results this good by luck (true), if we conclude that the system is skilled, we have only a 1 percent chance of being wrong (false!). Some adventuresome developers may word the conclusion more aggressively: because there is only a 1 percent chance that we would be wrong in concluding that the system is skilled (false!), there is a 99 percent chance that the system is skilled (no way!).

This last point is hard for many people to swallow, so we'll expound on it. The key is that a p-value from a hypothesis test is *conditional*. It says that *if* the null hypothesis is true, the p-value is the probability of getting a result at least as good as that observed. There's nothing in that statement about whether the null hypothesis is true.

Here is a crude example. We have been told that after years of research, we know that 99 percent of all dogs have four legs. Because of unfortunate accidents, 1 percent of dogs have fewer than four legs. Every now and then, someone calls you and says that they have an animal with a certain number of legs, and they ask your opinion about whether it's a dog. Today they call and say that their animal has two legs. You know that dogs have fewer than four legs only 1 percent of the time. With this in mind, you legitimately conclude that it probably is not a dog, and you are comfortable with this conclusion because of the scarcity of two-legged dogs. Among all the times the animal truly is a dog, you will be fooled into calling it a non-dog only 1 percent of the time.

But you can say *nothing* about the probability that this animal is or is not a dog. What if unknown to you, the person who periodically calls you is from a dog shelter, and he's just messing with you. Every animal he calls you about, regardless of how many legs it has, is a dog. Then, every time he tells you the animal has less than four legs, and you therefore conclude that it is not a dog, you will be wrong. Always. The false logic of the third bullet point on the prior page says that you have a 99 percent chance of being right, while in fact you have a 0 percent chance of being right! That's pretty bad. On the other hand, if the calls come from a strictly cat shelter, every time you reject the null hypothesis you will be correct. Always. So, depending on where the calls are coming from, you are correct either never or always.

In summary, in the context of using a hypothesis test for the quality of our trading system based on mean return (or some other quantity discussed later), these points must be kept in mind:

- If our performance is so good that a worthless system would have scored at least this well with only small probability (p-value), we may have confidence that our trading system has true skill, not just good luck. If we set a p-value threshold in advance (the first bullet point in this section) and decide that the system is skilled if and only if our achieved p-value is this small or smaller, then among the universe of worthless systems on which our p-value is based, we will be fooled into falsely claiming skill with the prespecified p-value probability. This, of course, inspires us to set a low p-value threshold. We want a low probability of being fooled into declaring a worthless system to be skilled.

- If we do not obtain a small p-value, we may *not* conclude that the system is worthless. Perhaps we just didn't test correctly or test enough market history.

- Regardless of the size of our p-value, whether it is delightfully tiny or annoyingly large, we can say *nothing* about the probability that our system is worthless or skilled. Nothing.

Parametric P-Values

In the prior section, we wantonly threw around uses for a p-value, the probability that we would have gotten performance at least as good as we obtained if the null hypothesis were true. In the current context, this is the probability that our OOS mean return could have been at least as large as we obtained, merely as a result of a truly worthless trading system being lucky. But how do we compute this p-value? There are several common approaches, and this section discusses the easiest.

Arguably the most important distribution in all of statistics is the *normal distribution*. It achieves this lofty position because (very roughly stated) when you add together independent, identically distributed random variables, their sum (and mean) tends toward having a normal distribution. Even if the variables are not exactly independent or identically distributed, the distribution of their sum (and mean) has a strong tendency to approach the familiar bell curve shape of the normal distribution. With some caution, we may often assume that our trading system's returns follow a distribution that is close enough to normality that we can perform statistical tests based on this assumption. In particular, we will use the Student's t-test, a standard test that assumes normality of its data but that is fairly robust against moderate non-normality.

Before proceeding, we must be clear about the most significant issues involved in using the normality-based t-test on trading system returns. This test is surprisingly robust against *moderate* levels of common forms of non-normality, such as skewness (lack of symmetry in the shape of the distribution) and heavy tails (extreme values that are *not severely* extreme). It is very robust against unusually light tails (few or no extreme values). But the big killer for the t-test is truly wild extremes, or even a single wild extreme. If the vast majority of our wins and losses cluster in the range of, say, –5 to 5, and we have one return of 50, the t-test will be worthless. Thus, before using a t-test to compute a p-value for returns, one *must* plot a histogram of the returns to be tested. Extremes that fall within reasonable limits of a bell curve are fine (no need to be picky), but if one or more returns are crazy far from the bulk of returns, use one of the tests described later.

This is not the venue for digging into details of the t-test; references are widely available, and some readers may want to dig a bit deeper than the superficial treatment here. Now, we deal just with the mathematical formulas and a code snippet demonstrating how to compute a p-value for a collection of returns, in the context of deciding whether the returns are good enough to justify declaring that the trading system has skill rather than just luck. Most often, these returns would be the individual bar returns for those bars on which a position is open, although any of the other types of returns discussed in the prior chapter could be tested.

Let x_1, x_2, ...x_n be the returns whose p-value we are computing. Their mean is trivially given by Equation 6-1. We estimate the population standard deviation as the square root of the unbiased variance estimator, as given by Equation 6-2. The t-score for this set of returns is given by Equation 6-3. If we designate the cumulative distribution function of the t statistic having df degrees of freedom (typically n–1) as CDF(df,t), then Equation 6-4 is the associated p-value. This is the probability that a t-score will equal or exceed the specified value, which in our context is the probability that the mean return of a worthless trading system could equal or exceed our obtained mean return by luck alone.

$$Mean = \frac{1}{n}\sum_{i=0}^{n} x_i \tag{6-1}$$

$$StdDev = \sqrt{\frac{1}{n-1}\sum_{i=0}^{n}(x_i - Mean)^2} \tag{6-2}$$

$$t = \frac{\sqrt{n}\,Mean}{StdDev} \tag{6-3}$$

$$p - value = 1 - CDF(n-1, t) \tag{6-4}$$

Astute readers who are familiar with t-scores will have noticed that Equation 6-3 is the t-score under the null hypothesis that the true mean is zero. But on page 211 it was pointed out that the null and alternative hypotheses must be mutually exclusive and exhaustive. To satisfy the exhaustive part, the null hypothesis of worthlessness must be that the trading system has a true mean that is zero *or negative*. So, why can we get away with assuming the true mean is zero and ignoring the possibility of a negative true mean? The answer will become more clear when we present Equation 6-5, but for now understand that if the true mean were negative, the actual t-score would be even larger than that given by Equation 6-3, and the p-value would be even smaller. Thus, a true mean of zero is the most conservative case; if we reject under that null hypothesis, we would reject even more strongly under a negative-mean null hypothesis. So, it is legitimate to let the null hypothesis be that the true mean is zero. We can ignore the possibility of a negative true mean.

Here is a code snippet demonstrating these computations. This code is extracted from the program BOUND_MEAN.CPP, with some small modifications for clarity. The source code for the t_CDF() function can be found in the file STATS.CPP. The complete program, along with an example of its application, will be presented on page 233.

```
mean = 0.0 ;                      // Equation 6-1
for (i=0 ; i<n ; i++)
   mean += returns[i] ;
mean /= n ;

stddev = 0.0 ;                    // Equation 6-2
for (i=0 ; i<n ; i++) {
   diff = returns[i] - mean ;
   stddev += diff * diff ;
   }
stddev = sqrt ( stddev / (n - 1) ) ;

t = sqrt((double) n) * mean / stddev ;    // Equation 6-3

pval = 1.0 - t_CDF ( n-1 , t ) ;          // Equation 6-4
```

Parametric Confidence Intervals

Having a p-value by which we can test the null hypothesis that our trading system is worthless is nice, but even nicer would be having the range in which the true mean is likely to lie. In any hypothesis test in any field of endeavor, if we test enough cases, we will pick up even the faintest legitimate effect. This is particularly problematic in the analysis of automated trading systems, in which we may backtest over decades. It will often be the case that we have a trading system that does have a small amount of skill, and if we perform a hypothesis test using thousands of bars of trade returns, we will likely get a small p-value and hence correctly conclude that our system probably has legitimate skill. But what if the actual skill possessed by our system provides an expected annualized return of one-half of 1 percent? It's honest-to-goodness skill, and given a large enough sample set, a hypothesis test will detect it. But nobody would want to trade that system, skill or not. Its return, though real, is too small to be profitable. The subject of this section is a simple method for the computation of upper (rarely needed) and lower bounds for the true mean return of our system. On page 222 we will present a very different method for performing this computation, the bootstrap.

Look back for a moment at Equation 6-3. That showed how to compute a t-score from an observed mean return, under the null hypothesis that the true mean return of the system was zero. We now need the more general form of this equation, which does not assume that the true mean is zero. This is shown in Equation 6-5. In this equation, *ObsMean* is the observed mean, and it corresponds to *Mean* in Equation 6-3, the mean return from your OOS testing. *TrueMean* is the unknown true mean. Note that when it is zero, Equation 6-5 is identical to Equation 6-3.

$$t = \frac{\sqrt{n}\left(ObsMean - TrueMean\right)}{StdDev} \tag{6-5}$$

By definition, the cumulative distribution function CDF(df,t) appearing in Equation 6-4 is the probability that a randomly drawn t-score will be less than or equal to the specified t. Define the inverse of this function as InvCDF(df,p). This function, by definition, gives us the t-score threshold that has the property that a randomly drawn t-score will be less than or equal to this threshold with the specified probability p. For notational convenience, we designate InvCDF(df,p) as t_p where, as usual, $df=n-1$. This definition is stated in Equation 6-6, in which t is a randomly observed t-score.

$$P\left\{t \leq t_p\right\} = p \tag{6-6}$$

We collect our OOS returns and compute their mean *ObsMean*. We do not know the true mean of the population of future returns, but we would like to make a probability statement about it. To do so, take the t-score defined by Equation 6-5 and substitute it for t in Equation 6-6. This gives us Equation 6-7, and some simple algebraic rearrangement converts that to Equation 6-8.

$$P\left\{\frac{\sqrt{n}\left(ObsMean - TrueMean\right)}{StdDev} \leq t_p\right\} = p \tag{6-7}$$

$$P\left\{ObsMean - \frac{StdDev \cdot t_p}{\sqrt{n}} \leq TrueMean\right\} = p \tag{6-8}$$

We define in Equation 6-9 a figure called *LowerBound*. It is the quantity on the left side of the previous inequality. Note that it is easily computed; all we need is the mean of our OOS returns, their standard deviation as defined by Equation 6-2, the number n of returns, and the t-score threshold for our desired probability, as defined by Equation 6-6. We now discuss why we call this *LowerBound* and what it means.

$$LowerBound = ObsMean - \frac{StdDev \cdot t_p}{\sqrt{n}} \tag{6-9}$$

We don't know the true mean of the population from which future returns will be drawn. We do have the mean of the returns in our OOS test set, and it's reasonable to assume that the true population mean will be somewhere in this vicinity. But our OOS test data was just a random sample from the population. It may have been unlucky and thereby underestimate the true mean. Or it may have been lucky and given an optimistic view of the future. We would like to quantify this variability.

Suppose that the true mean, which we do not and cannot know, happens to be equal to the *LowerBound* defined in Equation 6-9 and which we just computed from our sample. Keep in mind that this true mean is an actual, fixed number, such as 5.21766 or whatever. We don't know what it is, but that doesn't make it any less real. Now look back at Equation 6-8. The number on the right side of the inequality is an unknown but fixed (assuming stationarity!) value. The quantity on the left side of the inequality is a random variable, subject to sampling error from our choice of OOS test period. The act of choosing our OOS test period for the experiment just run is a random sample, so Equation 6-8 applies: there is probability p that the computable quantity on the left side of the inequality is less than or equal to the true mean, which we are momentarily assuming is the value in Equation 6-9. We have likely set p to be large, say 0.95 for this example, so this inequality is likely to be true. In other words, if the true mean, *which we do not know*, happens to be equal to the value given by Equation 6-9, which we call *LowerBound*, there is probability 0.95 that the inequality in Equation 6-8 is satisfied. In fact, since *LowerBound* is the quantity on the left side of the inequality, we have perfect equality; the condition is satisfied but just barely.

Now consider the possibility that the true mean is actually larger than *LowerBound*. Clearly, the inequality in Equation 6-8 is easily satisfied, with true inequality. But what if the true mean as de is less than *LowerBound*? Now the inequality fails, which has small probability (1−0.95=0.05 in this example). In other words, **LowerBound is the threshold for the true mean satisfying the inequality in Equation 6-8, a situation which has high probability if we set p high.**

Some hard numbers may make this clearer. Suppose we sample 100 returns. We observe a mean return of 8, and the returns have a standard deviation of 5. We set $p=0.95$ so that we can be 95 percent sure of our lower bound for the true mean of returns. The associated t-score is approximately 1.66. Plugging these numbers into Equation 6-9 gives a *LowerBound* of 8 – 5 * 1.66 / sqrt(100) = 7.17.

This result can be interpreted in two ways. The common interpretation, which is reasonable though not strictly correct, is to say that there is a 95 percent chance that the true mean of returns, the value around which future returns will be centered, is at least 7.17. The problem with this interpretation is that it makes it sound as if the true mean is a random variable, and based on our OOS results, we have just computed a probability that the true mean has at least some minimum value. In fact, the true mean is a fixed number, not random. The OOS sample that we collected is the random quantity. Thus, the strictly correct interpretation is to say that 7.17 is the minimum value that the true mean could have for there to be at least a 95 percent probability of having observed an OOS sample of our obtained quality or better. Please don't stress over this concept too much. You are not committing a grave sin by using the first and most common interpretation.

Here is a code snippet demonstrating these computations, extracted from BOUND_ MEAN.CPP, with small modifications for clarity. Source code for inverse_t_CDF() is in STATS.CPP. The complete program, along with an example of its application, will be presented on page 233.

```
mean = 0.0 ;                          // Equation 6-1
for (i=0 ; i<n ; i++)
  mean += returns[i] ;
mean /= n ;

stddev = 0.0 ;                        // Equation 6-2
for (i=0 ; i<n ; i++) {
  diff = returns[i] - mean ;
  stddev += diff * diff ;
  }
stddev = sqrt ( stddev / (n - 1) ) ;

lower_bound = mean - stddev / sqrt((double) n) * inverse_t_CDF ( n-1 , 0.95 ) ;
```

One would almost never be interested in an upper bound for the true mean. However, for the sake of completeness, we note that the upper bound is given by Equation 6-9 except that the minus sign is changed to a plus sign. Interested readers will find it informative and possibly entertaining to derive this fact. The reasoning is essentially identical to that for the lower bound but with the direction of the inequality reversed.

Note that if you want an interior confidence interval as de, a pair of bounds such that you can say with specified probability that the true mean lies inside this interval, you must split the "failure" probabilities. For example, suppose you want a 90 percent probability that the true mean lies between lower and upper bounds. You must split that 10 percent failure into 5 percent failure on each side, using $p=0.95$ for both the lower and upper bounds. This gives a 5 percent chance that the true mean lies below the lower bound, and 5 percent that it is above the upper bound, leaving a 90 percent chance that it lies between them.

Lower Confidence Bounds and Hypothesis Tests

We conclude this discussion with a useful observation that is easily provable in the Student's-t scenario just discussed and that in fact is true more generally as well. Take a look back at Equation 6-3 on page 217. In that section we computed the t-score for testing the null hypothesis that the true mean was zero versus the alternative that the true mean is greater than zero. Now look at Equation 6-9 for computing the lower bound for the true mean. Easy algebraic manipulation of these two equations reveals the interesting (and perhaps not very surprising) fact that ***the null hypothesis would be rejected if and only if LowerBound is positive.*** So we don't actually need to do separate tests. All we have to do is use Equation 6-9 to compute the lower bound corresponding to some p, such as the 0.95 assurance that we used in the example. We can reject the null hypothesis of zero mean at the $1-p$ level (1-0.95=0.05) if and only if Equation 6-9 gives us a positive number. (Note that since we usually have a continuous distribution, the probability of the lower bound being exactly zero is zero, but to be conservative, we typically demand that it be positive in order to reject the null hypothesis.)

Bootstrap Confidence Intervals

The prior section's method for bounding the true mean of returns is easy to understand and program, fast to compute, and generally quite robust against any problems except the presence of one or more extreme outliers. But sometimes we do have some questionable outliers, or maybe we want to be extra cautious. In this case, at least for mean returns we have a considerably more complex but usually safer approach called the *bootstrap*.

There are primarily three different bootstrap methods for finding lower (and also upper, if we want) bounds for the true mean. For a fairly rigorous and quite accessible discussion of all three methods, please see my book *Assessing and Improving Prediction and Classification*. For an extremely rigorous presentation, see the excellent book *An Introduction to the Bootstrap* by Efron and Tibshirani. Here, we will briefly mention two of these methods but present in detail only the method that is almost always the best of the three in this application. Also, because the theoretical background for this best algorithm is brutal, readers who want to pursue the theory are referred to the Efron and Tibshirani source. Here we focus on the relevant equations and source code only.

The Pivot and Percentile Methods

The most easily understood idea behind bootstrapping is often called the *pivot* method. Consider first the situation we are in. Our trading system feeds us (and will continue to feed us, as long as the market characteristics remain stationary) a series of returns. When we use the Student's-t method of the prior section, we assume that the distribution of these routines is not terribly non-normal. In the more general case, we know nothing whatsoever about this distribution. We would like to have a good guess as to its true mean, and we would also like an estimate of the sample-to-sample variation of the mean return in OOS samples. If we know the size and nature of this variation, we can establish probabilistic bounds on the likely true mean.

Unfortunately, we have only one sample from the population of returns, namely, that obtained from the OOS test set. That's not much to work with for estimating the sample-to-sample variation or any possible over- or underestimation of the true mean by the sample mean. But there is something very clever that we can do (thank you, Bradley Efron). We can *pretend* that our *sample* of returns is actually an entire *population* of returns and that this pretend-population is at least somewhat similar to the parent population in some important ways. Of course, we cannot assume perfect similarity. The returns in our sample may on average be larger or smaller than those in the parent population. They may have larger or smaller variation. So, the bootstrap is far from perfect because of this unavoidable random variation. But we can usually gather some useful information by pretending that our sample is a representative parent population and then sampling from it.

The fundamental idea behind the pivot method of bootstrapping is that whatever effects we see in the samples from our OOS sample pretending to be a population would have been reflected in our original sample from the true population. For example, suppose we collect a sample of OOS returns and compute some test statistic from this sample. Currently our test statistic is the mean, but later we will explore other performance measures, so we use the general term *test statistic* instead of being specific. Now we draw a random sample of the same size, with replacement, from our OOS sample. Some returns in our original sample will not appear in this bootstrap sample, while others will appear multiple times. It's a random draw. We compute the test statistic for this bootstrap sample. Then we do it again, and again, hundreds or thousands of times. We thus have hundreds or thousands of values of the test statistic, each computed from a bootstrap sample.

We know the value of the test statistic in our original sample, which is now playing the role of a population. Suppose we find that, on average, the test statistic in our bootstrap samples underestimates the value of the test statistic in the original sample by a few percent. The bootstrap assumption is that the test statistic in our original sample will similarly underestimate the unknown true value in the population. Thus, to better estimate the true population value of the test statistic, we increase the computed value of the test statistic by a few percent, whatever amount would have been needed to increase the average in the bootstrap samples to bring that average up to the value for the original sample.

We do a similar thing in regard to variation. We assume that whatever variation we see in the test statistic among the numerous bootstrap samples, we have been subject to that same degree of variation when we collected our OOS test returns. This gives us a good idea of how far our sample's mean return may be from the true population mean return, and we can thereby compute probabilistic lower and upper bounds on the true mean.

The second major method for computing bootstrap confidence intervals is called the *percentile* method. The concept is easier to understand on a superficial level, but it's much more complex once one digs below the surface (which we shall not do here). The algorithm is simple: collect numerous bootstrap samples (ideally thousands) and compute the parameter of interest, which would be the mean in our context. Then the distribution of those computed values under bootstrap sampling from the original sample is assumed to be the distribution of the original sample's value under the unknown parent distribution. So, for example, the 5th percentile of this distribution becomes the 95 percent confident lower bound for the true mean, and the

95th percentile of this distribution becomes the 95 percent confident upper bound for the true mean. It's ridiculously easy, and amazingly enough, it works in a great many situations.

Ambitious readers with some modest degree of mathematical ability might want to work out the result that the confidence intervals produced by the pivot and the percentile methods are the reverse of each other: if one method produces a lower bound that is much further from the computed sample test statistic than is the upper bound, then the other method will produce bounds such that the upper bound is much further from the sample test statistic than is the lower bound. Given such a bizarre situation, it is a miracle that these two methods work at all, but they usually do quite well. On the other hand, the third method, described in the next section and used in this text, tends to be the most reliable of all.

The BC$_a$ Bootstrap Algorithm

The algorithm presented in this section is much more broadly applicable than the pivot and percentile methods of the prior section. The exact mathematical conditions under which it is valid are broad, though not universal. My book *Assessing and Improving Prediction and Classification* does quite a good job (if I do say so myself!) of laying out the exact conditions under which it is valid and does so in a manner that should be accessible to those with a moderate degree of mathematical training. However, that discussion is beyond the scope of this text, which is geared more toward practicalities and a target audience with limited mathematical background. Please see my *Assessing and Improving Prediction and Classification* book if you are interested, or see the Efron and Tibshirani book *An Introduction to the Bootstrap* if you want a fierce and thorough discussion. For now, note that the BC$_a$ bootstrap (short for "bias corrected and accelerated") easily handles the mean return as well as most other performance measures other than ratio measures, as will be discussed on page 238.

To compute confidence bounds using the BC$_a$ bootstrap, we need to perform four steps.

1) Compute the bias correction, which compensates for the degree to which the necessary implicit transformation is biased.

2) Compute the acceleration, which compensates for the degree to which the variance of the implicitly transformed parameter depends on its value.

3) Compute lower and upper bounds using the previously described percentile method and then modify the fractile points according to these corrections.

4) Get the fractiles from the sorted bootstrap parameter estimates.

We now describe these steps, one at a time. Throughout this discussion, $\Phi(z)$ represents the normal cumulative distribution function (CDF), and $\Phi^{-1}(p)$ is its inverse.

Step 1: The bias correction just involves simple counting. We see how many of the bootstrapped parameter estimates are less than the estimate for the original sample. The bias correction is the inverse normal CDF of the fraction of the replications less than the grand value. This is expressed in Equation 6-10. In this equation, $\hat{\theta}^{*b}$ is the parameter estimate (mean return or whatever other performance measure we are investigating) for the bth bootstrap sample, there being a total of B bootstrap samples taken. The parameter estimate for the original sample is $\hat{\theta}$, and the #[] operation just means to count how many times the inequality holds among the B bootstraps.

$$\hat{z}_0 = \Phi^{-1}\left(\frac{\#\left[\hat{\theta}^{*b} < \hat{\theta}\right]}{B}\right)$$

(6-10)

Step 2: To compute the acceleration, we need to perform a jackknife on the parameter estimator. Our set of OOS returns consists of n cases. We temporarily remove case i from the collection and compute the parameter using the remaining $n-1$ cases. Let $\hat{\theta}_{(i)}$ designate this parameter value. Let $\hat{\theta}_{(\cdot)}$ be the mean of these n jackknifed values, as shown in Equation 6-11. Then the acceleration is given by Equation 6-12.

$$\hat{\theta}_{(\cdot)} = \frac{1}{n}\sum_{i=1}^{n}\hat{\theta}_{(i)}$$

(6-11)

$$\hat{a} = \frac{\sum_{i=1}^{n}\left(\hat{\theta}_{(\cdot)} - \hat{\theta}_{(i)}\right)^3}{6\left[\sum_{i=1}^{n}\left(\hat{\theta}_{(\cdot)} - \hat{\theta}_{(i)}\right)^2\right]^{3/2}}$$

(6-12)

Step 3: We modify the percentile method's fractile points according to the bias and acceleration. For example, suppose we want a 90 percent confidence interval. The fractile points would be $\alpha=0.05$ and $\alpha=0.95$, assuming that we want to split the probability of failure equally above and below. (This splitting was discussed on page 222.) A modified fractile point, α', is computed from an original α by means of Equation 6-13. This equation is applied to the upper and lower endpoints separately. Note that if the bias correction and acceleration are both zero, $\alpha'=\alpha$.

$$\alpha' = \Phi\left(\hat{z}_0 + \frac{\hat{z}_0 + \Phi^{-1}(\alpha)}{1 - \hat{a}\left(\hat{z}_0 + \Phi^{-1}(\alpha)\right)}\right)$$ (6-13)

Step 4: The final step is just the ordinary percentile bootstrap algorithm, but using the modified fractile points provided by Equation 6-13 instead of the user's specified points. Sort the B values of $\hat{\theta}^{*b}$ into ascending order and select the lower and upper bounds from this array. The unbiased choice for the lower bound, in which $\alpha'<0.5$, is to select element k (indexed 1 through B), where $k = \alpha'(B+1)$, truncated down to an integer if there is a fractional remainder. For the upper bound, $\alpha'>0.5$, let $k = (1-\alpha')(B+1)$, truncated down to an integer if there is a fractional remainder. Element $B+1-k$ is the upper confidence bound.

As was noted in the section on confidence based on Student's-t, when a bootstrap algorithm is used to compute confidence intervals for the mean return, we only rarely would be interested in an upper bound. Our greatest interest is in how small the true mean return might be. Of course, if we also learned that the true return might be quite large, we would probably be happy. And as should be obvious, we've already done 99.9 percent of the work in computing the lower bound; also finding the upper bound is an insignificant amount of extra work. Thus, all routines presented compute both bounds. Use them as you want.

The BOOT_CONF.CPP Subroutines

The file BOOT_CONF.CPP on my web site contains subroutines for computing a small assortment of confidence intervals using the percentile and BC_a methods. In this section we work through this code.

To lay a foundation, we present the simple yet surprisingly effective percentile algorithm that lies at the core of the superior BC_a algorithm. Recall from the earlier short discussion that this algorithm just evaluates the parameter (such as mean return) being studied using a large number of bootstrap samples, and it assumes that the resulting distribution of parameter estimates directly provides confidence intervals for the true value of the parameter in the population. This algorithm is invoked with the following calling convention (and variable declarations):

```
void boot_conf_pctile ( // Percentile bootstrap algorithm
   int n ,                    // Number of cases in sample
   double *x ,                // Variable in sample
   double (*user_t) (int , double *) , // Compute parameter
   int nboot ,                // Number of bootstrap replications
   double *low2p5 ,           // Output of lower 2.5% bound
   double *high2p5 ,          // Output of upper 2.5% bound
   double *low5 ,             // Output of lower 5% bound
   double *high5 ,            // Output of upper 5% bound
   double *low10 ,            // Output of lower 10% bound
   double *high10 ,           // Output of upper 10% bound
   double *xwork ,            // Work area n long
   double *work2              // Work area nboot long
   )
{
   int i, rep, k ;
```

We would most likely call this routine with the n returns from our OOS test in x. The user_t() function would compute the mean of the vector given to it, assuming that our performance measure of interest is the mean return. We should set nboot to be very large; 10,000 is not unreasonable.

The first step is to draw a large number of bootstrap samples and compute the parameter of interest for each sample. We save them for sorting later. The outer loop in the following code draws each of the nboot (*B* in the preceding discussion) samples. For each replication, we draw n randomly selected cases from the original sample. It's important that each bootstrap sample contain the same number of cases as the original sample, because many parameters are sensitive to the number of cases in the sample.

```
for (rep=0 ; rep<nboot ; rep++) {    // Do all bootstrap reps (b from 1 to B)

   for (i=0 ; i<n ; i++) {           // Generate the bootstrap sample
      k = (int) (unifrand() * n) ;   // Randomly select a case from the sample
```

```
  if (k >= n)                            // Should never happen, but be prepared
    k = n - 1 ;
  xwork[i] = x[k] ;                      // Put bootstrap sample in xwork
  }

 work2[rep] = user_t ( n , xwork ) ;  // Save parameter from this bootstrap sample
 }
```

The parameter estimates are sorted. The qsortd() routine takes as its parameters the indexes of the first and last cases in the array to be sorted. The lower and upper bounds are pulled from this sorted array using the unbiased fractile estimators, as described in step 4 on page 227. Only one pair of bounds is shown here, because the others are identical except for the multiplier. Feel free to set whatever fractile multiplier you want, or make it a calling parameter.

```
 qsortd ( 0 , nboot-1 , work2 ) ;     // Sort ascending

 k = (int) (0.025 * (nboot + 1)) - 1 ; // Unbiased quantile estimator
 if (k < 0)
   k = 0 ;
 *low2p5 = work2[k] ;
 *high2p5 = work2[nboot-1-k] ;
```

By the way, if you want to use the generally inferior pivot method, those bounds are easily obtained from the percentile bounds. Let *Param* be the parameter value for the original sample. Then *PivotLower* = 2 * *Param* – *PctileUpper* and *PivotUpper* = 2 * *Param* – *PctileLower*. Curious readers might want to reread the description of the pivot method on page 224 and then work through the logic of how these formulas reflect the sample-to-bootsample relationship in the population-to-sample estimate.

We now move on to the BC_a bootstrap, which is almost always superior to both the pivot and percentile methods. It is similar to the percentile method just shown, in that the parameter is estimated from numerous bootstrap samples, these estimates are sorted, and bounds are extracted from the sorted array. The difference is that the chosen elements are selected from slightly adjusted locations. The calling parameter list is identical to that for the percentile method, but for clarity here it is:

```
void boot_conf_BCa (   // BCa bootstrap algorithm
  int n ,                // Number of cases in sample
  double *x ,            // Variable in sample
  double (*user_t) (int , double *) , // Compute parameter
  int nboot ,            // Number of bootstrap replications
  double *low2p5 ,       // Output of lower 2.5% bound
  double *high2p5 ,      // Output of upper 2.5% bound
  double *low5 ,         // Output of lower 5% bound
  double *high5 ,        // Output of upper 5% bound
  double *low10 ,        // Output of lower 10% bound
  double *high10 ,       // Output of upper 10% bound
  double *xwork ,        // Work area n long
  double *work2          // Work area nboot long
  )
{
  int i, rep, k, z0_count ;
  double param, theta_hat, theta_dot, z0, zlo, zhi, alo, ahi ;
  double xtemp, xlast, diff, numer, denom, accel ;
```

It begins by evaluating the parameter for the original sample. Then it computes and saves the parameter values for nboot bootstrap samples. While doing this, it counts z0 for Equation 6-10.

```
  theta_hat = user_t ( n , x ) ;        // Parameter for full set

  z0_count = 0 ;                        // Will count for computing z0 later
  for (rep=0 ; rep<nboot ; rep++) {     // Do all bootstrap reps (b from 1 to B)
    for (i=0 ; i<n ; i++) {             // Generate the bootstrap sample
      k = (int) (unifrand() * n) ;      // Select a case from the sample
      if (k >= n)                       // Should never happen, but be prepared
        k = n - 1 ;
      xwork[i] = x[k] ;                 // Put bootstrap sample in xwork
      }

    param = user_t ( n , xwork ) ;      // Param for this bootstrap rep
    work2[rep] = param ;                // Save it for CDF later
```

```
   if (param < theta_hat)              // Count how many < full set param
     ++z0_count ;                      // For computing z0 (Equation 6-10)
   }

 z0 = inverse_normal_cdf ( (double) z0_count / (double) nboot ) ; // In STATS.CPP
```

Now we do the jackknife described in step 2, in other words, Equation 6-11. The original sample is reprocessed n times, each time omitting one case. Then we evaluate Equation 6-12.

```
 xlast = x[n-1] ;
 theta_dot = 0.0 ;
 for (i=0 ; i<n ; i++) {             // Jackknife Equation 6-11
   xtemp = x[i] ;                    // Preserve case being temporarily removed
   x[i] = xlast ;                    // Swap in last case
   param = user_t ( n-1 , x ) ;      // Param for this jackknife
   theta_dot += param ;             // Cumulate mean across jackknife
   xwork[i] = param ;               // Save for computing accel later
   x[i] = xtemp ;                    // Restore original case
   }

 theta_dot /= n ;                    // This block of code evaluates Equation 6-12
 numer = denom = 0.0 ;
 for (i=0 ; i<n ; i++) {
   diff = theta_dot - xwork[i] ;
   xtemp = diff * diff ;
   denom += xtemp ;
   numer += xtemp * diff ;
   }

 denom = sqrt ( denom ) ;
 denom = denom * denom * denom ;
 accel = numer / (6.0 * denom + 1.e-60) ;
```

The hard work is done. We sort the bootstrap sample parameters, exactly as we did for the percentile method.

```
 qsortd ( 0 , nboot-1 , work2 ) ;     // Sort ascending
```

We modify the user's fractile points as described in Equation 6-13 of step 3 on page 226.

```
zlo = inverse_normal_cdf ( 0.025 ) ;
zhi = inverse_normal_cdf ( 0.975 ) ;
alo = normal_cdf ( z0 + (z0 + zlo) / (1.0 - accel * (z0 + zlo)) ) ;
ahi = normal_cdf ( z0 + (z0 + zhi) / (1.0 - accel * (z0 + zhi)) ) ;
```

The last step is identical to what we did for the percentile method, except that instead of using the given fractile points, we use the modified points, and we must do the lower and upper bounds separately. We cannot use the same k for both.

```
k = (int) (alo * (nboot + 1)) - 1 ; // Unbiased quantile estimator
if (k < 0)
  k = 0 ;
*low2p5 = work2[k] ;

k = (int) ((1.0-ahi) * (nboot + 1)) - 1 ;
if (k < 0)
  k = 0 ;
*high2p5 = work2[nboot-1-k] ;
```

We showed only the 0.025 (lower) and 0.975 (upper) bounds here. Several other bounds are done in the source code in BOOT_CONF.CPP. Feel free to use whatever fractiles you want.

The BOUND_MEAN Program and Results with SPX

The file BOUND_MEAN.CPP contains a complete program that extends the PER_WHAT program presented on page 198. The trading system is exactly the same, so please review that section as needed. One simplification is done: the optimization criterion in the BOUND_MEAN implementation is always the mean return when a position is open. Other training options available in PER_WHAT are omitted, although readers should have no trouble putting them back if desired. One other small change is that PER_WHAT computes performance based on only one return type, selected by the user, while BOUND_MEAN computes the three main return types simultaneously for easy comparison.

But the largest change is that BOUND_MEAN computes a t-score (Equation 6-3 on page 217) and associated p-value (Equation 6-4 on page 217) for a hypothesis test of the null hypothesis that the true mean return is zero (or negative) versus the alternative that the true mean is positive. It also computes a 90 percent confidence lower bound for the true mean using Equation 6-9 on page 220. Finally, it computes 90 percent confidence lower bounds using three different bootstrap algorithms: the percentile method, the pivot method (page 224) and the BC_a method (page 225). All of these results are printed in a compact table.

The program is invoked as follows:

BOUND_MEAN max_lookback n_train n_test n_boot filename

Let's break this command down:

- max_lookback: Maximum moving-average lookback tried during training (parameter optimization).

- n_train: Number of bars in the training set for each walkforward fold. It should be much greater than max_lookback to get good parameter estimates.

- n_test: Number of bars in the test set for each walkforward fold. Smaller values (even just 1) make the test more robust against nonstationarity in the market but take much longer to execute.

- n_boot: Number of bootstrap replications. This should be as large as runtime allows. A value of 10,000 is not unreasonable and should be considered a minimum for serious testing.

- filename: Name of the market file to read. It has no header. Each line in the file is for a single bar, and it has the date as YYYYMMDD and at least one price. Any numbers after the first number following the date are ignored. For example, a line in a market history file might look like the following, and only the first price (1075.48) would be read. Readers who would prefer to use the close for open/high/low/close files can easily modify this code.

    ```
    20170622 1075.48 1077.02 1073.44 1073.88
    ```

Before jumping into key parts of the source code, let's take a look at the output of this program when applied to the many decades of SPX. This is shown in Figure 6-1.

```
nprices=23557  max_lookback=100  n_train=1000  n_test=100
OOS mean return per open-trade bar (times 25200) = 9.90984
  StdDev = 309.92461  t = 1.28  p = 0.1000  lower = -0.00220
OOS mean return per complete trade (times 1000) = 7.61384
  StdDev = 49.95066  t = 1.39  p = 0.0843  lower = 0.00053
OOS mean return per 10-bar group (times 25200) = 0.70590
  StdDev = 24.97851  t = 1.34  p = 0.0898  lower = 0.03174

90 percent lower confidence bounds
            Open posn   Complete    Grouped
Student's t  -0.0022     0.0005      0.0317
Percentile   -0.0678     0.0007      0.0329
Pivot         0.2265     0.0007      0.0180
BCa           0.0197     0.0010      0.0394
```

Figure 6-1. *BOUND_MEAN for moving-average breakout in SPX*

We have 23,557 days of prices (!). The maximum moving-average lookback in training the system is 100 days; we use 1,000 training cases and do the OOS testing 100 days at a time. For the bar-based returns, we multiply by 25,200 to make the returns roughly annualized percents.

Our three primary types of return are tested. The *open-trade* or *open-posn* returns are the bar returns on which a position is open. The *complete* returns are the net returns for each completed trade (round turn). The *grouped* returns are the bar returns, whether a position is open or not, crunched into blocks of ten days. Those returns are much smaller than the open-position returns because of all the zeros (the return of a bar is zero if no position is open) included in the average. By sheer coincidence, the p-value for the t-test-based test happens to be essentially 0.1, so we should not be surprised to see that the 90 percent confidence lower bound for the true mean is essentially zero (–0.0022). If this is not clear, please refer to page 222 for the discussion about the equivalence between hypothesis tests and the lower bound of a confidence interval. Also note that the bootstrap tests give lower bounds near zero, although the pivot method, as is common, is the oddball. For all its intuitive appeal, the pivot method is usually the least reliable of the three common bootstrap algorithms.

There is an important lesson to be learned from this demonstration. The approximate annualized mean return for bars on which a position is open is 9.91 percent, a fairly impressive number when taken in isolation. But the t-test probability that a worthless system could have achieved results at least this good by sheer luck is 0.1000, which is distressingly nonsmall. Moreover, if we look at the 90 percent confidence bound on the lower limit of the true mean, that around which future returns would be centered, this lower bound is actually negative! Granted, it's barely negative, virtually zero, but still, this is not a system I would want to trade. The various bootstrap bounds for all three families of returns are equally uninspiring. Back to the drawing board.

We now take a look at a few code snippets from the BOUND_MEAN program. The trading system (opt_params() and comp_return()) was thoroughly discussed on page 198, which dealt with the PER_WHAT program. Please refer to that section as needed. We focus now on the walkforward code. A discussion follows the code listing.

```
train_start = 0 ;      // Starting index of training set
nret_open = nret_complete = nret_grouped = 0 ;

for (;;) {

  // Train

  crit = opt_params ( n_train , prices + train_start ,
              max_lookback , &lookback , &thresh , &last_pos ) ;

  n = n_test ;  // Test this many cases
  if (n > nprices - train_start - n_train) // Don't go past the end of history
    n = nprices - train_start - n_train ;

  // Test with each of the three return types

  comp_return ( 0 , nprices , prices , train_start + n_train , n , lookback ,
          thresh , last_pos , &n_returns , returns_grouped + nret_grouped ) ;
  nret_grouped += n_returns ;

  comp_return ( 1 , nprices , prices , train_start + n_train , n , lookback ,
          thresh , last_pos , &n_returns , returns_open + nret_open ) ;
  nret_open += n_returns ;

  comp_return ( 2 , nprices , prices , train_start + n_train , n , lookback ,
        thresh , last_pos , &n_returns , returns_complete + nret_complete ) ;
  nret_complete += n_returns ;
```

```
// Advance fold window; quit if done
train_start += n ;
if (train_start + n_train >= nprices)
   break ;
}
```

We initialize the start of the first training set to be the beginning of the market history. The three counters that count the number of each type of return (open position, complete, grouped) are zeroed.

The first step in the walkforward loop is to call opt_params() to find the optimal lookback and threshold. This routine also returns the position as of the end of the training set. The purpose of this is discussed in the section on PER_WHAT. We then assume that the number of test cases will be the number specified by the caller, but we make sure we do not overrun the market history.

We call comp_return(), specifying that all bars be included in the return, regardless of whether a position is open. This will be clumped for the group returns later. The other two calls to comp_return() are for open-position bars and complete returns, respectively.

After all three OOS tests are done, we advance to the next fold and break out of the walkforward loop if no OOS test cases remain.

At this point, the *grouped* returns are still ungrouped, just individual bar returns. We group them now, using an arbitrary grouping of ten bars, which the reader can easily change or even make a user parameter.

```
crunch = 10 ;   // Change this to whatever you wish
n_returns = (nret_grouped + crunch - 1) / crunch ;   // This many returns after crunching

for (i=0 ; i<n_returns ; i++) {           // Each crunched return
   n = crunch ;                           // Normally this many in group
   if (i*crunch+n > nret_grouped)         // May run short in last group
     n = nret_grouped - i*crunch ;        // This many in last group
   sum = 0.0 ;
   for (j=i*crunch ; j<i*crunch+n ; j++)  // Sum all in this gorup
     sum += returns_grouped[j] ;
   returns_grouped[i] = sum / n ;         // Compute mean per group
   }

nret_grouped = n_returns ;
```

We can now compute the t-score and associated p-value. The code for the open-position returns (all variables end in _open) is as follows:

```
mean_open = 0.0 ;
for (i=0 ; i<nret_open ; i++)
   mean_open += returns_open[i] ;
mean_open /= (nret_open + 1.e-60) ;

stddev_open = 0.0 ;
for (i=0 ; i<nret_open ; i++) {
   diff = returns_open[i] - mean_open ;
   stddev_open += diff * diff ;
   }

if (nret_open > 1) {
   stddev_open = sqrt ( stddev_open / (nret_open - 1) ) ;
   t_open = sqrt((double) nret_open) * mean_open / (stddev_open + 1.e-20) ;
   p_open = 1.0 - t_CDF ( nret_open-1 , t_open ) ;
   t_lower_open = mean_open - stddev_open / sqrt((double) nret_open) *
                  inverse_t_CDF ( nret_open-1 , 0.9 ) ;
   }
else {
   stddev_open = t_open = 0.0 ;
   p_open = 1.0 ;
   t_lower_open = 0.0 ;
   }
```

In the previous code, we cumulate the mean and standard deviation using the usual formulas. If we have fewer than two returns, the standard deviation is undefined, so we use reasonable defaults. Otherwise, we compute the t-score with Equation 6-3 and its associated p-value using Equation 6-4. Notice how we prevent division by zero when computing the t-score. Then the lower bound for the true mean at 90 percent confidence is computed using Equation 6-9.

The percentile and pivot bootstraps are computed by calling the boot_conf_pctile() subroutine described on page 228. The code for the open-position returns is shown here. The trivial routine find_mean() just adds the returns and divides by the number of them. The computed lower bound is returned in b1_lower_open. All other bounds are ignored by supplying dummy variables for the computed values.

On page 229 we saw that it is easy to obtain the pivot-method confidence bounds from the percentile bounds. We use that simple formula to compute b2_lower_open, the lower bound using the pivot method. My *Assessing and Improving Prediction and Classification* book goes into detail on the relationship between these two methods. However, because I do not generally recommend the pivot method, I won't bother going into detail here.

```
boot_conf_pctile ( nret_open , returns_open , find_mean , n_boot ,
          &sum , &sum , &sum , &sum , &b1_lower_open , &high ,
          xwork , work2 ) ;

b2_lower_open = 2.0 * mean_open - high ;
```

Finally, we call boot_conf_BCa() to compute the lower bound on the true mean using the generally good BC_a method.

```
boot_conf_BCa ( nret_open , returns_open , find_mean , n_boot ,
          &sum , &sum , &sum , &sum , &b3_lower_open , &high ,
          xwork , work2 ) ;
```

Beware of Bootstrapping Ratios

The bootstrap almost always works quite well for the mean and other well-behaved performance measures. But for ratio-based measures that can violently blow up when the denominator becomes small, the bootstrap often fails. The two classic examples of such measures are the Sharpe ratio and the profit factor. In this section, we'll present the BOOT_RATIO program (complete source code is in BOOT_RATIO.CPP), which generates random trades and explores the behavior of bootstrap confidence intervals for the Sharpe ratio and profit factor of these trades.

Before experimenting, we discuss the test philosophy of the program. The essence of a confidence interval, whether it be a closed interval (lower and upper bounds) or an open interval (just one bound), is that it be violated with specified probability. For example, suppose we want to compute a lower bound on a performance statistic and we want to be confident that the true value of the performance statistic is at or above our lower bound 95 percent of the time. Equivalently, when we compute this lower bound from a random sample, we want our computed bound to exceed the true value 5 percent of the time. If it exceeds the true value more often, we are in a dangerous situation, because our confidence bound is not as good as we thought it was. If it exceeds the true value less than 5 percent of the time, the situation is not quite so bad, because this just means that we are correct even more often than we think we are. But this situation is still bad in a way because it means that our computed bound is needlessly loose, perhaps so loose that we lose faith in our trading system. It may be that our computed lower bound is so low that we discard the potential trading system, when in fact if the lower bound had been computed correctly, we might have been happy with the trading system.

The BOOT_RATIO program is invoked as follows:

BOOT_RATIO nsamples nboot ntries prob

Let's break this command down:

- nsamples: Number of price changes in market history
- nboot: Number of bootstrap replications
- ntries: Number of trials for generating summary
- prob: Probability that a trade will be a win

It generates random market price changes, each nsamples long. Each change is considered to be a win with probability prob; otherwise, it is a loss. Given this set of returns, nboot bootstrap samples are used to compute lower and upper bounds for the profit factor using the percentile, pivot, and BC_a methods. These bounds are computed with violation probabilities of 0.025, 0.05, and 0.1.

The true profit factor of the randomly generated set of wins and losses is prob / (1 − prob). So after we compute these six bounds (three probabilities each for lower and upper), we compare each to the true profit factor and note whether the bound is violated.

This process is repeated ntries times, and for each of these six bounds and each of these three bootstrap methods we count violations so we can compare the actual number of violations to the correct number.

While the ntries trials are performed, we keep track of the Sharpe ratio of the population of random returns, a total of nsamples times ntries of them. After all profit factor trials are complete, we repeat the entire process for the Sharpe ratio. There is no simple way to compute the theoretical Sharpe ratio, so we use this population value. To ensure accuracy, we start both the profit factor trials and the Sharpe ratio trials with the same random seed, ensuring that exactly the same set of wins and losses are generated. After these trials are complete, results are printed.

Figure 6-2 shows the BOOT_RATIO results for sets of 1000 returns, and Figure 6-3 shows results for sets of 50 returns. The system being tested is worthless (prob=0.5). A very large number of bootstrap replications and trials were employed to ensure stability. Observe that in both figures, the mean and true Sharpe ratios are essentially zero, and the mean and true profit factors are essentially one, as expected. For the situation of just 50 returns, the mean profit factor is a bit above one because the denominator can sometimes be very small, resulting in a few extreme profit factors that inflate the mean. The charts are divided into three columns, corresponding to prob=0.025, 0.05, and 0.1. The left number inside each parenthesized pair is the failure rate in percent (100*prob) for the lower bound, and the right number is that for the upper bound. So, we hope that both of these numbers equal the percent for that column.

```
Final Sharpe ratio...
Mean sr = 0.00025  true = -0.00079
Pctile 2.5: (2.80 2.50)   5: (4.80 4.80)   10: (11.60 10.10)
BCa    2.5: (2.70 2.50)   5: (4.60 4.90)   10: (11.60  9.80)
Pivot  2.5: (2.60 2.40)   5: (4.60 4.80)   10: (11.40  9.70)

Final profit factor...
Mean pf = 1.00042 true = 1.00000
Pctile 2.5: (1.40 2.50)   5: (3.20 5.60)   10: ( 9.20 11.40)
BCa    2.5: (1.30 2.40)   5: (3.20 5.50)   10: ( 9.30 11.00)
Pivot  2.5: (0.60 4.50)   5: (1.80 7.70)   10: ( 6.90 12.60)
```

Figure 6-2. *BOOT_RATIO results with 1,000 returns*

```
Final Sharpe ratio...
Mean sr = 0.00548  true = 0.00494
Pctile 2.5: (3.40 2.00)   5: (6.20 5.60)   10: (10.80 11.30)
BCa    2.5: (2.70 1.60)   5: (5.20 4.90)   10: ( 9.70 10.50)
Pivot  2.5: (0.70 0.80)   5: (3.20 2.10)   10: ( 8.60  8.20)

Final profit factor...
Mean pf = 1.05289 true = 1.00000
Pctile 2.5: (2.40 2.80)   5: (4.80 4.60)   10: ( 9.80 10.10)
BCa    2.5: (1.70 2.40)   5: (4.50 4.30)   10: ( 9.10  9.10)
Pivot  2.5: (0.00 9.00)   5: (0.00 12.20)  10: ( 0.60 15.70)
```

Figure 6-3. *BOOT_RATIO results with 50 returns*

Note the following:

- Problems are most apparent in the leftmost column, which is for a 2.5 percent failure rate (97.5 percent confidence in each bound). We want all of these parenthesized numbers to be 2.5.

- The pivot method is the worst by far. For the profit factor at 2.5 percent expected failure rate and 50 trades, the lower bound *never* fails to be below the true profit factor. This means that the lower bound is so extremely low that it is worthless. Meanwhile, the upper bound fails to be above the true profit factor almost four times as often as expected, a disastrous situation.

- Profit factor is more poorly behaved than Sharpe ratio.

But all is not lost with profit factor. The problem, especially with a small number of returns, is the extremely heavy right tail, with a tiny denominator giving rise to huge profit factors. All we have to do is work with the log of the profit factor, which tames the tail. Figure 6-4 shows the result when instead of bootstrapping the profit factor we bootstrap its log. There's quite a difference, especially for the lower bound which is our main interest. The BC_a upper bound at 2.5 percent does deteriorate a little, which is troubling, but it would be rare to care about the upper bound. And for 5 percent and 10 percent failure rates, both bounds improve a lot. The lesson is that if we are bootstrapping a distribution with a heavy tail, we should transform in such a way as to tame the tail.

```
Final profit factor...
Mean log pf = 0.00342 true = 0.00000
Pctile 2.5: (2.96 2.62)  5: (5.56 5.17)  10: (10.66 10.17)
BCa     2.5: (2.40 2.15)  5: (5.00 4.58)  10: (10.06  9.57)
Pivot   2.5: (1.49 1.32)  5: (3.94 3.60)  10: ( 9.23  8.75)
```

Figure 6-4. *BOOT_RATIO log profit factor results with 50 returns*

Bounding Future Returns

In prior sections we discussed finding bounds (usually just a lower bound) for the true mean of the population from which future returns will appear. That's a fairly straightforward task, doable with relatively simple and easily understood calculations. We now tackle a much more complex task, yet one that can be quite useful in practice.

Rather than being concerned with the true mean around which future returns will cluster, we want to bound actual returns.

There is little or no point in trying to bound individual bar returns; those will have so much variation relative to their mean that bounds would be worthless. But we might well be interested in bounding returns because of complete trades. And in real life we would absolutely love to be able to bound grouped mean returns. The primary purpose of this would be to help us confirm ongoing performance. For example, suppose we perform an extended walkforward run to produce many years of OOS returns. We might group these returns by the month and compute monthly average returns. Using the technique of this section, we could find a probable lower bound on our expected future monthly returns. As we trade the system, we keep track of its actual monthly performance. If this performance falls below our previously computed lower bound, we would justifiably become suspicious that our trading system is suffering degradation.

Readers who have minimal mathematical background may be somewhat intimidated by the contents of this section. However, there is no need to skip it in terror. Please be assured that code fragments illustrating the key parts of the operation will be supplied along the way, and a complete program that puts it all together with an actual trading system and market data will close out the presentation.

The technique is divided into three sections. We will begin with a method for finding an approximate but reasonable lower bound for future returns. Then we will explore how to quantify inevitable random errors in our computation of this lower bound. Finally, for those rare instances in which we also want an upper bound on future returns, we generalize the algorithm to that situation.

Deriving a Lower Bound from Empirical Quantiles

Before commencing, we must be absolutely clear on the difference between material in this section and that in prior sections. Until this point, we were bounding the *mean* of the population from which returns were (and presumably will continue to be) drawn. This is useful because we want to be reasonably sure that the true mean of our population of returns is large enough to be worth trading. After all, future returns will tend to center around this mean.

But now we will attempt to bound the actual returns themselves. Most often these will be group returns, such as the monthly return of our system. We may want to know a probability-based lower bound on the monthly returns we can expect over the upcoming months. Occasionally we may also be interested in bounding net return of completed trades. This task is much more difficult than just bounding the mean of the population from which these returns are drawn.

We begin with a collection of OOS returns. For this task, we need a great many such returns to obtain reliable bounds, typically a bare minimum of a hundred returns, and preferably many hundreds or even thousands. Thus, if we are working with, say, monthly returns, we need an extended OOS test covering upwards of ten years. If necessary, we can shorten the return period, perhaps using weekly returns. But shorter return periods result in greater variance in the returns, which in turn results in computed lower bounds so low that they are of little value. Thus, we are caught in a difficult compromise: having more returns from shorter intervals gives us bounds that are more accurate but less useful. Just do your best.

Our fundamental assumption is that our collection of OOS returns is a fair representation of the population of returns from which future returns will be drawn. As we will see in the next section, this is not strictly true, and the implication is that our computed lower bound is subject to troubling random error, which we will quantify later. But for now, assume that it is true.

First, some intuition. Suppose we have 100 OOS returns (monthly, completed trades, or whatever) in our collection. Also suppose that 10 percent of these returns have a value of -8 or less. Then our initial technique is based on the assumption that future returns will also have a 10 percent chance of being -8 or less. The more returns we have in our collection, the more we can be confident in the validity of this critical assumption, an idea that we'll quantify in the next section.

We need a definition. The *quantile* of order p of the distribution of the random variable X is defined as the value x such that $P\{X < x\} \leq p$ and $P\{X < x\} \geq p$. We saw something similar in Equation 6-6 when we found the t-score corresponding to a specified probability. In that case we were finding the quantile of a continuous distribution, the Student's-t distribution. But here we have a discrete distribution, a collection of numbers. Thus, to be fully rigorous, we need to cover both sides of the value, and even then x may not be unique; it may be the interval between two discrete values.

It is easiest to think of quantiles in terms of continuous distributions, so with no deleterious practical implications we will do so from now on. For example, if we know that there is a 10 percent (0.1) probability that a return will be less than or equal to -8, we say that the 0.1 quantile of this distribution is -8. Our algorithm for computing a lower bound for returns computes the quantiles of the OOS returns, assumes that this collection is representative of the true population, and uses these empirical quantiles to compute whatever bounds are desired.

We can be more rigorous. A lower bound for future returns is computed from the n OOS returns as follows: suppose we want a lower bound in which we can have $1-p$ confidence (the probability of failure is some small p such as 0.05). Sort the returns in ascending order. Compute $m=np$, and if m is not an integer, truncate the fractional part. This formula provides a conservative (lower than the exact) bound. If we happen to want an unbiased but slightly less conservative lower bound, let $m=(n+1)p$. Then the mth smallest return in the sorted sample is our approximate lower bound.

Confidence in the Computed Lower Bound

This is a good time for readers to review the section "Interlude: What Does *Unbiased* Really Mean?" on page 125. That section makes the point that unbiased doesn't necessarily mean, um, unbiased. In fact, it is virtually certain that our OOS collection of returns is biased in some way. Random sampling error may have resulted in our OOS collection underestimating the future returns, meaning that our collection is pessimistically biased. Equally likely, it may overestimate future returns, making it unduly optimistic. Whatever the case, it almost certainly is *not* a good representation of future returns. If our collection of returns truly is out-of-sample, we say that it is unbiased only because it does not have a preordained prejudice toward being optimistic or pessimistic. It could go either way. This balance in the type of bias it may exhibit is what allows us to call it unbiased. But be assured, it's biased one way or the other, and we have no way of knowing which it is.

The implication is that our computed lower bound is a little bit (or perhaps a lot!) off. If our OOS collection is pessimistically biased because of bad luck in sampling, our computed lower bound will be too low. Or if our collection is optimistic, with wins over-represented, our computed lower bound will be too high. Naturally, this can have serious consequences when we put our lower bound to work keeping track of ongoing performance. What we need to do is to quantify the possible error in our lower bound. This is the topic of this section.

We saw in the prior section that we specify some small failure rate p and compute the lower bound for future returns as the $m=np$th smallest return in our OOS collection. In doing so, we smugly assume that there is only smallish probability p that future returns will be less than or equal to our computed lower bound.

But remember that our OOS set is, by random chance, optimistic or pessimistic. There are two things we must worry about. The most serious consideration is how large that true failure rate for our computed lower bound might truly be. For example, suppose we let p be 0.1, implying that we want a lower bound such that only 10 percent of the time in the future will the return be less than or equal to this lower bound. The question of the moment is, "How high (greater than our specified p) might be the *actual* probability of obtaining a return less than or equal to this lower bound?" In other words, it may be that future returns will (to our dismay) be less than or equal to this lower bound with a probability that is higher than the 0.1 we desire and expect. We would like to make a probability statements about this situation.

The most straightforward probability statement is the following: What is the probability that the m smallest OOS return, which we have chosen for our lower bound on future returns, is really the q quantile or worse of the return distribution, where we specify some q that is disturbingly larger than the p we desire? We hope that this probability is small, because this event is a serious problem in that it implies that our computed lower bound for future returns is too high and hence more likely to be violated than we believe.

For example, we may specify $p=0.1$, implying that we are willing to live with a 10 percent chance that future returns will violate our lower bound. But we may also specify $q=0.15$, a failure rate that we consider unacceptable; 10 percent of future returns violating our lower bound is okay, but 15 percent failure simply won't do. We want to compute the probability that the true failure rate of our 0.1-based lower bound is really 0.15 or worse. We hope that this probability is small.

This probability question is answered by the *incomplete beta distribution*. In a set of n cases, the probability that the mth smallest exceeds the q quantile is given by $1 - I_q(m, n-m+1)$. The subroutine orderstat_tail() in STATS.CPP computes this probability, and we will find this routine extremely useful as discussion of this topic continues.

Sometimes we would prefer to do things in the opposite order. Instead of first specifying some pessimistic $q>p$ and then asking for the probability that random sampling error gave us a lower bound with true failure rate q, we first specify a satisfactorily low probability of such deception and then compute the q that corresponds to this probability. For example, we might specify that we want very low probability (only 0.001, say) of having collected an OOS return set that provided a lower bound whose actual probability of violation is seriously greater than what we expect. Suppose we have 200 OOS returns, and we set $p=0.1$, meaning $m=20$. Thus, the 20th smallest OOS return is our lower bound on future returns. We need to find the pessimistic $q>p$ such that $1-I_q(20, 181)=0.001$. The subroutine quantile_conf() in STATS.CPP (more on that later) tells us that $q=0.18$. In other words, there is only the tiny probability of 0.001 that our lower bound, which we hope to be violated 10 percent of the time, will actually be violated 18 percent or more of the time. Looked at another way, we have the near certainty of 0.999 that our supposed $p=0.1$ lower bound will in fact fail no more than 18 percent of the time. That's not very good, but on the other hand, demanding such high certainty is asking a lot.

If our goal in computing a lower bound on future returns is only to have an idea of how bad things can be for future returns from our chosen trading system, the "pessimistic q" approach just described is all we need. Suppose that the opposite of what we have explored is true. If, in fact, our computed lower bound is too low rather than too high (the true failure rate is less than our chosen p rather than greater), the only implication is that future losses (assuming ongoing stability of our trading system) will not be as severe as we think they might be. That's good, unless our lower bound is so bad that we reject our trading system. But we should be hesitant about rejecting a system based on its projected worst returns, because these will almost always be negative and discouraging. We should more greatly value bounds on the expected mean return, as discussed earlier. Thus, the pessimistic q method is sufficient if we are simply gathering information about worst-case scenarios in the future.

However, an important use for a computed lower bound on future returns is to track ongoing performance of a trading system that has been put into use. When we design the final system, we should set a reasonable probability of failure p (perhaps 0.05 to 0.1 or so) and use the technique of this section to compute a lower bound for future returns. If, at some point in the future, we get a return below this lower bound, we should become suspicious that the system is deteriorating. If it happens again, we should seriously consider abandoning or at least revising the system.

When we use our lower bound this way, we need more than just a pessimistic $q>p$, an indication of how seriously our computed lower bound exceeds the true quantile for our desired failure rate. We should be even more fearful of the opposite error: the true failure rate for our computed lower bound is less than our desired failure rate p. This happens when our computed lower bound is too low. In this unfortunate situation, we may observe one or more returns that are somewhat above our lower bound, and hence not worrisome, when in fact these losses are exceeding the true lower bound corresponding to our desired failure rate. So we will make the worst sort of error, neglecting to flag legitimate deterioration of our trading system.

The process for computing an "optimistic" $q<p$ is almost identical to what we did earlier in this section. We could use orderstat_tail() to compute the probability that the mth smallest OOS return (which is our lower bound) exceeds some specified optimistic $q<p$,

although now we have to subtract this probability from one to get the probability of this unfortunate occurrence. This is because orderstat_tail() computes the probability that the computed bound is *above* the specified quantile $q>p$, the problem addressed earlier, at the beginning of this section. But now we are worried about the opposite problem. We want the probability that the computed bound is *below* the specified optimistic quantile $q<p$. This probability must be small if we are to avoid the mistake of failing to detect truly legitimate deterioration of our trading system.

As was the case for the pessimistic q test, we have an alternative to specifying an optimistic q and then computing its probability. Instead, we could use quantile_conf() with a *large* probability (such as 0.95 to 0.999 or so) to compute an optimistic q. We'll explore all of these possibilities later, in a high-detail quasitheoretical section, followed by a practical section.

To summarize this section, we have n OOS returns, and we want to compute a lower bound for future returns. We choose a smallish probability of failure, p, as the probability that future returns will be less than or equal to our computed bound. Let $m=np$ for a conservative bound, or $m=(n+1)p$ for an unbiased bound. To quantify the effects of random error, we have some pessimistic $q>p$, resulting from our bound being too large, and an associated probability. We may also consider some optimistic $q<p$, resulting from our bound being too small, and an associated probability. We must find the relationship between these quantities.

What About an Upper Bound on Future Returns?

At first thought, one might believe that it would be unusual to want to compute an upper bound on future returns. After all, what do we care if our returns are better than expected? Our main concern would seem to be how bad our future returns might be, so we know what to expect. We may even want (actually, we *should* want!) to keep track of ongoing performance of an existing system and raise a red flag if we start getting returns below our expected lower limit.

But careful thought reveals that if we are watching a running system, it's not just excessively poor trades that flag possible deterioration. We should also become suspicious if we are not seeing as many good trades as we expect. Remember that bounds have associated failure rates (which we specify), and in the case of an upper bound, what we call a failure (exceeding the upper bound) in reality would be considered a success!

Thus, we would be inclined to use a much larger "failure" rate for upper bounds and expect to see that degree of "failure" if the system is still performing on target. For example, we might set an upper bound failure rate of $p=0.4$, thereby expecting that 40 percent of future trades will have returns at least as large as the computed upper bound. If the rate drops significantly below 40 percent, we should become suspicious.

It should not be surprising that upper bounds and associated optimistic and pessimistic q values can be computed with exactly the same mathematics as for lower bounds. For a lower bound we use the mth smallest OOS return, and for an upper bound we use the mth largest. Probabilities are similarly reversed. Rather than pedantically stating these simple transformations now, we'll explore them with source code in the next section.

The CONFTEST Program: Overview

This section describes a "tutorial" program that has no practical use but that demonstrates in detail the ideas behind computation of bounds for future returns. In the next section we'll present a practical program that executes a real trading system with real market data and computes the quantities discussed in the last few sections. The purpose of the current section is to solidify the ideas we're dealing with and make the reader comfortable with what the computed quantities really mean.

The program is invoked as follows:

CONFTEST nsamples fail_rate low_q high_q p_of_q

Let's break this command down:

- nsamples: Number of OOS cases in each trial (at least 20). In real life it would make no sense to have fewer than 100 OOS cases and preferably at least several hundred. Otherwise, the computed bounds have too much random variation to be practical.

- fail_rate: Desired rate of failure for computed bounds. This is p in prior discussions. For lower bounds this would typically be smallish, perhaps 0.01 to 0.1. For upper bounds this would usually be larger, perhaps 0.2 to 0.5. The CONFTEST program uses fail_rate for both.

- low_q: Worrisome failure rate below desired (< fail_rate). This is the optimistic q, resulting from the computed lower bound being too low due to random sampling error in the OOS set. The program computes the probability that the true quantile is this bad or worse.

- high_q: Worrisome failure rate above desired (> fail_rate). This is the pessimistic q, resulting from the computed lower bound being too high because of random sampling error in the OOS set. The program computes the probability that the true quantile is this bad or worse.

- p_of_q: Small probability of failure; to get limits. This is the reverse formulation, in which the user specifies a small (typically 0.01 to 0.1) probability of error, and the program computes the associated low_q and high_q.

The program computes the quantities discussed earlier and then it generates a large number of random "OOS return" sets having known quantiles and confirms that the computed quantities are correct. Before exploring the code, let's take some example numbers and work through what the program does.

Suppose the user specifies nsamples=200 and fail_rate=0.1. The program computes $m=(n+1)p$ to get an unbiased quantile estimate. In this case, we see that the 20th smallest OOS return will be used as our lower bound on future returns, and the 20th largest OOS return will be the upper bound. There is no reason why the same failure rate has to be used for both bounds, and some readers may want to add the option of different rates. It was done this way for convenience.

Our expectation for this pair of parameters is that there is (hopefully!) a 10 percent chance that a future return will be less than or equal to our computed lower bound. Similarly, we expect that 10 percent of future returns will equal or exceed our computed upper bound.

Alas, life is not that simple. Our OOS set on which our bounds are based is itself a random sample, subject to error. If we were able to wave a magic wand and guarantee that our OOS sample is a perfect representation of the population of returns, our goal would be met perfectly. In other words, if the sample were perfect, our computed lower bound would be the exact fail_rate=0.1 quantile of the distribution of returns; smaller returns would occur with probability 0.1. And our computed upper bound would be the exact 0.9 quantile of the distribution of returns. But the sample is not perfect, so we need to quantify the effect of random sampling error.

One possible error is that our computed lower bound is too low. The result of this error is that the unknown true "normal operation" failure rate would be lower than the 0.1 we want, meaning that we could fail to detect deterioration in its early stages, when subpar returns do not drop down all the way to our excessively low lower bound. To quantify this, we could specify some hypothetical quantile $q<p$ that would concern us

and then find the probability that our computed lower bound is actually at the q quantile or worse (lower still).

For example, suppose we specify low_q=q=0.07, which is considerably less than the failure rate of 0.1 that we desire but probably not so small that our chance of missing early deterioration would be severely impacted. The program finds the probability that our computed lower bound is less than or equal to the q=0.07 quantile of the distribution of returns. If our computed lower bound happens to be exactly the 0.07 quantile, this means our bound would be violated just 7 percent of the time rather than the 10 percent of the time we want. By the time future returns violate our lower bound 10 percent of the time, performance would have deteriorated moderately, since under normal operation we would expect violation just 7 percent of the time. Thus, we would miss an early warning, though probably not by much. The program finds the probability that our computed lower bound is less than or equal to the q=.07 quantile of the distribution of returns, and this turns out to be 0.0692. Equivalently, we can assert 1-0.0692=0.9308 (about 93 percent confidence) that our computed lower bound is greater than the 0.07 quantile of returns. That's decent odds.

The other possible error is that our computed lower bound is too large. The result of this error is that the unknown true "normal operation" failure rate would be greater than the 0.1 we want, meaning that we would get returns at or below our lower bound more often than 10 percent of the time. This might us to conclude that our trading system is deteriorating when in fact it's just fine. We could specify some hypothetical quantile $q>p$ that would concern us and then find the probability that our computed lower bound is actually greater than the q quantile.

For example, suppose we specify high_q=q=0.12, which is somewhat more than the failure rate of 0.1 that we desire but probably not so large that our chance of falsely concluding deterioration would be wildly excessive. If our computed lower bound happened to be exactly the 0.12 quantile, this means our bound would be violated 12 percent of the time rather than the 10 percent of the time we want, not terribly serious. The program finds the probability that our computed lower bound is greater than the q=.12 quantile of the distribution of returns, and this turns out to be 0.1638. Equivalently, we can assert 1-0.1638=0.8362 (about 84 percent confidence) that our computed lower bound is less than or equal to the 0.12 quantile of returns. That's not great, but it's pretty good.

We can also approach these probability statements from the opposite direction, specifying the probability of having a bad true quantile and then computing the optimistic and pessimistic q values corresponding to this probability. For example, we could specify p_of_q=0.05. The program would then compute an optimistic q of 0.0673 and a pessimistic q of 0.1363. Recall that we specified p=0.1, meaning that we want a failure rate of 10 percent. These figures show that there is a 5 percent chance that the true failure rate is 6.73 percent or less, and another 5 percent chance that the true failure rate is greater than 13.63 percent.

The same ideas apply to the upper bound, except with directions reversed. In this case, failure is a future return equaling or exceeding the upper bound. The optimistic situation is the upper bound being too large, and the pessimistic situation is the upper bound being too small, exactly the opposite as for the lower bound. All calculations are performed the same way, as will be seen when the code is presented.

After these probabilities are all computed from the user-supplied parameters, their veracity is tested. This is done by generating a large number of test sets, each containing nsamples simulated OOS returns from a distribution whose quantiles are known in advance from theory. For each test set, the lower and upper bounds are found using $m=(n+1)p$. Then these computed lower and upper bounds are compared to the optimistic and pessimistic q values, both those supplied by the user as low_q and high_q, and those based on the user-supplied p_of_q. A count is kept of how many times the computed bound is outside the optimistic or pessimistic limits. For each possible situation, the count divided by the number of tries gives the observed probability of occurrence. This continually updated observed probability is printed to the screen along with the theoretically correct value as computed by the program, and the user can confirm that operation is correct.

The CONFTEST Program: Code

We now explore essential code snippets from the complete program CONFTEST.CPP. The user parameters are read as follows:

```
nsamps = atoi ( argv[1] ) ;
lower_fail_rate = atof ( argv[2] ) ;            // Our desired lower bound's failure rate
lower_bound_low_q = atof ( argv[3] ) ;          // Test 1 optimistic q
lower_bound_high_q = atof ( argv[4] ) ;         // Test 1 pessimistic q
p_of_q = atof ( argv[5] ) ;                     // Test 2: Want this chance of bad q
```

The next few lines are the essential computations discussed in prior sections. We use $m=(n+1)p$ to get an unbiased quantile estimate and then subtract one because C++ indexing has origin zero. This gives the index of the lower bound in the sorted array of OOS returns. If a careless user specifies a tiny fail rate, make sure we do not have a negative subscript. The subroutine orderstat_tail() in STATS.CPP computes the probability that the mth smallest item in a sample exceeds a specified quantile of the distribution. Thus, lower_bound_high_theory is the probability associated with the pessimistic q, and lower_bound_low_theory is the probability associated with the optimistic q. The former is the probability that our computed lower bound is disturbingly larger than the quantile associated with lower_bound_high_q, which is greater than lower_fail_rate, leading to excessive failure rate. The latter is the probability that our computed lower bound is disturbingly smaller than the quantile associated with lower_bound_low_q, which is lower than lower_fail_rate, leading to misleadingly low failure rate.

```
lower_bound_index = (int) (lower_fail_rate * (nsamps + 1) ) - 1 ;
if (lower_bound_index < 0)
   lower_bound_index = 0 ;

lower_bound_high_theory =
         orderstat_tail ( nsamps , lower_bound_high_q , lower_bound_index +1 ) ;
lower_bound_low_theory =
         1.0 - orderstat_tail ( nsamps , lower_bound_low_q , lower_bound_index +1 ) ;

p_of_q_high_q = quantile_conf ( nsamps , lower_bound_index+1 , p_of_q ) ;
p_of_q_low_q = quantile_conf ( nsamps , lower_bound_index+1 , 1.0 - p_of_q ) ;
```

When we compute lower_bound_low_theory, we must subtract the probability from 1.0, because orderstat_tail() computes the probability that the lower bound *exceeds* the specified quantile, while we want the probability that the lower bound is *less than or equal to* the specified quantile.

In the previous code, p_of_q_high_q reverses what we did when computing lower_bound_high_theory. Instead of specifying a pessimistic q and then computing its associated probability, we specify the probability (p_of_q) and compute the associated pessimistic q. This is done with the subroutine quantile_conf() in STATS.CPP. We compute p_of_q_low_q similarly, remembering that because we are looking at probabilities *below* the lower bound instead of shown previously, we must subtract the desired probability from 1.0.

Once we have these quantities, we compute similar values for the upper bound. The lower bound is the *m*th smallest return, and the upper bound is the *m*th largest. For convenience, this program sets the upper bound failure rate to be equal to that for the lower bound, and it reflects the pessimistic and optimistic *q* accordingly. There is no need to have this symmetry, and readers should feel free to make the upper bound parameters different from the lower bound parameters if desired. But do note that relationships reverse for the upper bound: the pessimistic *q* is *less than* the user's failure rate, while it was *greater than* the failure rate for the lower bound. The same relationship holds for the optimistic *q*.

```
upper_bound_index = nsamps-1-lower_bound_index ;
upper_fail_rate = lower_fail_rate ;  // Could be different, but c hoose symmetric here
upper_bound_low_q = 1.0 - lower_bound_high_q ;  // Note reverse symmetry
upper_bound_high_q = 1.0 - lower_bound_low_q ;  // Which is for convenience
upper_bound_low_theory = lower_bound_high_theory ;  // but not required
upper_bound_high_theory = lower_bound_low_theory ;
```

We are now ready to run the testing part of the program to verify that the calculations just done are correct. We begin by zeroing the various failure counters.

```
lower_bound_fail_above_count = lower_bound_fail_below_count = 0 ;
lower_bound_low_q_count = lower_bound_high_q_count = 0 ;
lower_p_of_q_low_count = lower_p_of_q_high_count = 0 ;
upper_bound_fail_above_count = upper_bound_fail_below_count = 0 ;
upper_bound_low_q_count = upper_bound_high_q_count = 0 ;
upper_p_of_q_low_count = upper_p_of_q_high_count = 0 ;
```

An endless loop generates sample OOS returns. The easiest distribution to use is just a uniform distribution, because this distribution has the special property that its quantile function is the identity: the quantile of any probability is that probability. This avoids the need to spend a lot of computer time finding quantiles. The scaling factor f avoids a division every time we report ongoing results to the user. We sort the data so that we can easily find the *m*th smallest and largest values of the sample.

```
for (itry=1 ; ; itry++) {
  f = 1.0 / itry ;

  for (i=0 ; i<nsamps ; i++)
    x[i] = unifrand () ;

  qsortd ( 0 , nsamps-1 , x ) ;
```

We begin with the lower bound tests, and they will be explained one at a time. In every test, remember that the quantity on the right of the inequality is not only a probability, but because the distribution is uniform, it is also the quantile associated with that probability. Thus, even though on first glance it looks like we are comparing the lower bound to probabilities, which makes no sense, we are actually comparing the lower bound to quantiles.

These first two tests are not terribly interesting.

```
lower_bound = x[lower_bound_index] ; // Our lower bound

if (lower_bound > lower_fail_rate)
  ++lower_bound_fail_above_count ;

if (lower_bound < lower_fail_rate)
  ++lower_bound_fail_below_count ;
```

The two tests just shown compare the computed lower bound to the theoretically correct quantile for the user's desired failure rate, which is the correct lower bound. Because our computed lower bound is an unbiased estimate of the correct (unknown in practice but known in this test) lower bound, we would expect the computed lower bound to hover close to the theoretically correct lower bound, overshooting and undershooting roughly equally. Thus, we would expect each of these two inequalities to be true very nearly half the time. These are not particularly useful tests, but they do serve as an easy sanity check.

The next two tests let us verify that the probabilities associated with the optimistic and pessimistic q (lower_bound_low_theory and lower_bound_high_theory) are correct.

```
if (lower_bound <= lower_bound_low_q) // Is our lower bound disturbingly low?
  ++lower_bound_low_q_count ;

if (lower_bound >= lower_bound_high_q) // Is our lower bound disturbingly high?
  ++lower_bound_high_q_count ;
```

Those tests were done with the user-supplied lower_bound_low_q and lower_bound_high_q. Once again, remember that these quantities are probabilities, but because our simulated OOS returns follow a uniform distribution, they are also the quantiles associated with these probabilities. If all is correct, these two tests should be true with probability lower_bound_low_theory and lower_bound_high_theory, respectively.

Now we perform exactly the same tests, except that instead of comparing the lower bound to the user-supplied optimistic and pessimistic q quantiles, we compare the lower bound to the values computed to have user-specified probability p_of_q. We expect each of these two tests to be true with probability p_of_q.

```
if (lower_bound <= p_of_q_low_q)  // Ditto, but lim its gotten via p of q
  ++lower_p_of_q_low_count ;

if (lower_bound >= p_of_q_high_q) // Rather than us er-specified
  ++lower_p_of_q_high_count ;
```

The next block of tests repeats the previous ones, but this time with regard to the computed upper bound. As with the lower-bound tests, in every case the quantity on the right side of the inequality is both a probability and its associated quantile, because our test distribution is uniform. Probability directions reverse at the upper bound, because a bound being outside a threshold at the low end means that it is less than the threshold, while a bound being outside a threshold at the high end means that it is above the threshold. Thus, we must subtract all probabilities from 1.0 to get the probability in the opposite direction. This was done earlier for upper_bound_low_q and upper_bound_high_q. It was not done for the other thresholds, so it must be done here.

```
upper_bound = x[upper_bound_index] ;    // For upper bound test

if (upper_bound > 1.0-upper_fail_rate)    // This should fail with about 0.5 prob
  ++upper_bound_fail_above_count ;        // Because upper_bound is unbiased

if (upper_bound < 1.0-upper_fail_rate)    // Ditto for this
  ++upper_bound_fail_below_count ;

if (upper_bound <= upper_bound_low_q)  // Is our upper bound disturbingly low?
  ++upper_bound_low_q_count ;

if (upper_bound >= upper_bound_high_q) // Is our upper bound disturbingly high?
  ++upper_bound_high_q_count ;

if (upper_bound <= 1.0-p_of_q_high_q)
  ++upper_p_of_q_low_count ;

if (upper_bound >= 1.0-p_of_q_low_q)
  ++upper_p_of_q_high_count ;
```

We periodically print results so far. Those print statements are long and omitted here; see the file CONFTEST.CPP if you want. Sample output from the program is shown on the next page.

Using the parameters in the example given on page 249, we first see these parameters echoed and the essential quantities as computed. This is shown in Figure 6-5. The user specified 200 samples, a failure rate of 0.1, optimistic q of 0.07, and pessimistic q of 0.12. The probability associated with the former was computed to be 0.0692, and that for the latter 0.1638. The user also specified a "probability of q" of 0.05, which gave an optimistic q of 0.0673 and a pessimistic q of 0.1363.

```
nsamps=200  lower_fail_rate=0.100  lower_bound_low_q=0.0700  p=0.0692  lower_bound_high_q=0.1200  p=0.1638
p_of_q=0.050  low_q=0.0673  high_q=0.1363
```

Figure 6-5. *CONFTEST parameters and essential computations*

After running several million trials, we get the results shown in Figure 6-6. We expect the "fail above" and "fail below" rates to be about 0.5, and these came out pretty close to that. Why the slight bias? This bias would rapidly vanish for very large samples, but with just 200 cases, even though we use the "unbiased" formula the act of truncation in computing m introduces slight bias. There are interpolation methods that largely correct for this bias by looking at the next further extreme case and moving in that direction per the truncation. But these methods are not worth bothering with in this application, especially since the slight bias is in the conservative direction.

```
Lower bound fail above=0.466  Lower bound fail below=0.534
Lower bound below lower limit=0.0691  theory p=0.0692  above upper limit=0.1640  theory p=0.1638
Lower p_of_q below lower limit=0.0500  theory p=0.0500  above upper limit=0.0501  theory p=0.0500

Upper bound fail above=0.535  Upper bound fail below=0.465
Upper bound below lower limit=0.1638  theory p=0.1638  above upper limit=0.0691  theory p=0.0692
Upper p_of_q below lower limit=0.0500  theory p=0.0500  above upper limit=0.0499  theory p=0.0500
```

Figure 6-6. *CONFTEST results*

Note how closely the obtained probabilities match the computed theoretical probabilities. We see, for example, 0.0691 obtained versus 0.0692 expected. And for those tests in which p_of_q=0.05, we obtain rates of 0.499 to 0.501.

This CONFTEST program was supplied and explored mainly to reinforce the concepts involved in bounding future returns. However, the reader can use it to explore the impact of pessimistic and optimistic q values for various sample sizes and failure rates.

The BND_RET Program

The file BND_RET.CPP contains source code for a program that demonstrates a practical application of the return-bounding methods described in prior sections. It reads a market file in the same format as the BOUND_MEAN program (page 232) and executes the primitive moving-average-crossover system used in the TRN_BIAS program (page 123). Please see those references if needed. Here we focus strictly on computation of bounds for future returns.

We begin with snippets of code and explanations. The mathematics is exactly the same as in the CONFTEST program already shown, but I chose to label some variables differently for the sake of approaching issues from a different direction. Variables with labels containing *high_q* and *low_q* have reverse relationships at the low and high bounds. For the sake of readers who may be confused by this, I renamed variables using the phrases *opt_q* and *pes_q* for the optimistic and pessimistic values, respectively. All computation and math are exactly the same; only the names have changed. Hopefully, by looking at the algorithms from both perspectives, the reader will better understand the process.

Normally, the user can specify the key test parameters shown next. But for the sake of the demonstration at the end of this section, here are the values that will be used in the demonstration, temporarily hard-coded into the program:

```
max_lookback = 100 ;      // Max lookback for long-term moving average
n_train = 1000 ;          // Number of training cases for optimizing trading system
n_test = 63 ;             // Group bar returns to produce quarterly returns
lower_fail_rate = 0.1 ;   // Desired failure rate for lower bound (a typical value)
upper_fail_rate = 0.4 ;   // Desired failure rate for upper bound (a ty pical value)
p_of_q = 0.05 ;           // Desired probability of bad bound limits
```

The first three parameters are described in the *TrnBias* program writeup. The last three parameters are related to bounding future returns. The number 63 arises because there are typically 63 trading days in a quarter, meaning that this study will involve bounding quarterly returns.

The walkforward code is straightforward. Here it is, and a brief description follows:

```
train_start = 0 ; // Starting index of training set
n_returns = 0 ;   // Will count returns (after grouping)
total = 0.0 ;     // Sums returns for user's edification
```

```
for (;;) {

    IS = opt_params ( n_train , max_lookback , prices + train_start ,
                        &short_lookback , &long_lookback ) ;
    IS *= 25200 ;  // Approximately annualize

    n = n_test ;     // Test this many cases
    if (n > nprices - train_start - n_train) // Don't go past the end of history
      n = nprices - train_start - n_train ;

    OOS = test_system ( n , prices + train_start + n_train - long_lookback ,
                        short_lookback , long_lookback ) ;
    OOS *= 25200 ;  // Approximately annualize

    returns[n_returns++] = OOS ;
    total += OOS ;

    // Advance fold window; quit if done
    train_start += n ;
    if (train_start + n_train >= nprices)
      break ;
    }

printf ( "\n\nAll returns are approximately annualized by multiplying by 25200" ) ;
printf ( "\nmean OOS = %.3lf with %d returns", total / n_returns, n_returns ) ;
```

At all times, train_start is the index of the first case in the training set for the current fold. Returns are computed in groups of 63 bars each, and n_returns counts how many such grouped returns are created during the walkforward. The total return is also cumulated, purely to report to the user.

The first step in the walkforward loop is to call opt_params() to find the optimal short-term and long-term moving-average lookbacks. Its in-sample performance (mean return per bar) is multiplied by 25200 to roughly annualize day-bar returns.

Normally, the OOS test period will be whatever is specified by the user, which is 63 in this demonstration. However, the last fold probably will not happen to have exactly this many test cases, so we shrink it to however many cases remain.

The address given to test_system() looks cryptic and requires a bit of thought to understand. The first OOS test case return is at train_start + n_train, which is the price immediately following the training set. The trade decision for the movement to this first OOS price must be based on the most recent prices *prior* to this OOS price. We will be looking at long_lookback historical prices to make the decision, so we must subtract this quantity from the OOS position to get the pointer to the first case of those on which the decision is based. If this is not clear, draw a little timeline of prices, marking the locations of the training and test sets, and the long-term moving-average lookback. This will make it clear. The test_system() subroutine returns the mean return per bar across the n test cases. This quantity is annualized, saved in the returns array, and cumulated.

We compute the lower and upper bounds from the sorted array of OOS returns. These are the *m*th smallest and *m*th largest, respectively.

```
qsortd ( 0 , n_returns-1 , returns ) ;
```

```
lower_bound_m = (int) (lower_fail_rate * (n_returns + 1) ) ;
if (lower_bound_m < 1)
  lower_bound_m = 1 ;
```

```
lower_bound = returns[lower_bound_m-1] ;
```

```
upper_bound_m = (int) (upper_fail_rate * (n_returns + 1) ) ;
if (upper_bound_m < 1)
  upper_bound_m = 1 ;
```

```
upper_bound = returns[n_returns-upper_bound_m] ;
```

We could let the user supply optimistic and pessimistic q values, but this program arbitrarily decides to place them 10 percent below and above the user-specified failure rates. Feel free to change these offsets to whatever you want.

```
lower_bound_opt_q = 0.9 * lower_fail_rate ;  // Arbitrary choice; could be user input
lower_bound_pes_q = 1.1 * lower_fail_rate ;
```

```
upper_bound_opt_q = 0.9 * upper_fail_rate ;
upper_bound_pes_q = 1.1 * upper_fail_rate ;
```

Now we compute the quantities that let us assess the accuracy of our computed bounds using these precomputed q values.

lower_bound_opt_prob = 1.0 - orderstat_tail (n_returns , lower_bound_opt_q ,
                                             lower_bound_m) ;
lower_bound_pes_prob = orderstat_tail (n_returns , lower_bound_pes_q ,
                                        lower_bound_m) ;

upper_bound_opt_prob = 1.0 - orders tat_tail (n_returns , upper_bound_opt_q ,
                                              upper_bound_m) ;
upper_bound_pes_prob = orderstat_tail (n_returns , upper_bound_pes_q ,
                                        upper_bound_m) ;

Finally, we use the "inverse" procedure: we use the user-specified probability p_of_q to find the optimistic and pessimistic q values.

lower_bound_p_of_q_opt_q = quantile_c onf (n_returns , lower_bound_m ,
                                          1.0 - p_of_q) ;

lower_bound_p_of_q_pes_q = quantile_conf (n_returns , lower_bound_m , p_of_q) ;

upper_bound_p_of_q_opt_q = quantile_c onf (n_returns , upper_bound_m ,
                                          1.0 - p_of_q) ;

upper_bound_p_of_q_pes_q = quantile_conf (n_returns , upper_bound_m , p_of_q) ;

Figure 6-7 shows sample output from the program when applied to decades of the OEX index, using the parameters shown on page 257. I've tried to be quite verbose so as to make the meaning of all numbers as clear as possible. At the same time, I've avoided the needless differentiation between "less than or equal to" versus "less than" and so forth. I took care to be specific in the mathematical presentation, just for correctness. But in practice we can treat the returns as essentially continuous, so the distinction is pointless and just adds complexity.

```
All returns are approximately annualized by multiplying by 25200
mean OOS = 1.021 with 124 returns

The LOWER bound on future returns is -38.942
It has an expected user-specified failure rate of 10.00 %
  (This is the percent of future returns less than the lower bound.)

We may take an optimistic view: the lower bound is too low.
  (This results in a lower failure rate.)
The probability is 0.4407 that the true failure rate is 9.00 % or less
The probability is 0.0500 that the true failure rate is 5.68 % or less

We may take a pessimistic view: the lower bound is too high.
  (This results in a higher failure rate.)
The probability is 0.2775 that the true failure rate is 11.00 % or more
The probability is 0.0500 that the true failure rate is 14.26 % or more

The UPPER bound on future returns is 9.043
It has an expected user-specified failure rate of 40.00 %
  (This is the percent of future returns greater than the upper bound.)

We may take an optimistic view: the upper bound is too high.
  (This results in a lower failure rate.)
The probability is 0.1812 that the true failure rate is 36.00 % or less
The probability is 0.0500 that the true failure rate is 32.91 % or less

We may take a pessimistic view: the upper bound is too low.
  (This results in a higher failure rate.)
The probability is 0.1802 that the true failure rate is 44.00 % or more
The probability is 0.0500 that the true failure rate is 47.27 % or more
```

Figure 6-7. *BND_RET output for moving-average crossover on OEX*

Note that the annualized return is 1.021 percent; this is a mighty poor trading system! We would expect 10 percent of future quarterly returns to be a worse loss than 38.942 percent annualized, so if we get a couple such bad quarters, we should be highly suspicious. We would expect 40 percent of future quarterly returns to be at least 9.043 percent annualized, so if we fail to be up there regularly, we should be suspicious. The remaining values in the output are self-explanatory and indicate moderate but not excellent adherence to our specified 10 percent and 40 percent bounds. This is because we have only 124 returns, dangerously few.

Bounding Drawdown

Let's review the types of performance bounding we've seen so far, all of which are based on analyzing out-of-sample returns:

- If our OOS returns do not contain any extreme values and have a reasonable bell-curve distribution shape, we can bound the mean of future returns by using the Student's-t distribution.

- If we do not want to make the assumptions required for the Student's-t distribution, we can use a bootstrap, especially the BC_a method, to bound the mean of future returns. This is probably the single most important bounding technique in our toolbox.

- We can use a bootstrap to bound the log of the profit factor of the distribution of future returns.

- With considerable caution, we can use a bootstrap to bound the Sharpe ratio of the distribution of future returns.

- With no restrictive assumptions on the nature of the distribution of returns, we can approximately bound individual future returns by sorting historical returns and looking at mth smallest or largest values. This is especially useful if the returns we bound are grouped returns, such as monthly or quarterly results, because we can then use these bounds to track ongoing performance and detect deterioration. However, unlike prior bounds in this list, these are not reliable single numbers. They are subject to random variation that we must quantify in a way that reveals how much we can trust them.

Of course, one performance measure that is of great interest to market traders is the drawdown that they might encounter in the future. We could, in theory at least, use a bootstrap to bound the *mean* drawdown over a specified time period, that value around which randomly observed future drawdowns will be centered. This is easy to do: just take numerous bootstrap samples from the set of OOS returns and compute the mean drawdown of each sample using some random sampling procedure. The percentile method (or its more advanced version, the BC_a method) provides confidence bounds for the *average* drawdown expected in the future. For example, suppose we find that in 10 percent of the bootstrap samples the mean drawdown is 34 percent or more. Then we can assert that there is a 90 percent chance that the average future drawdown is less than 34 percent.

But this figure is really of very little value. Unless the computed value at a reasonable probability is extremely large or extremely small, we don't much care what the *average* drawdown is. What we really want is a probability-based bound on what *actual* drawdown we will experience. For example, if we were able to compute that there is a 35 percent chance that we will experience a drawdown in excess of 70 percent next year, we would find this information most useful!

The bad news is that we can't do this, at least not with the degree of certainty we would like. We run into the same situation that plagued us in the prior section, where we computed probability-based bounds on individual future returns. We found that the bounds themselves were subject to random error, and so we had to qualify our assertions with additional probability statements. That's what we have to do with bounds on future drawdowns. And it's not fast or easy. Or particularly accurate, for that matter. But this would be such a useful figure to have in hand that we will pursue the subject, being sure to keep our fingers firmly crossed as we compute.

Intuition Gone Wrong

Before jumping into the relatively complex subject of correctly bounding future drawdowns, we need to be clear on the difference between bounding the *mean* drawdown and bounding *actual* drawdowns. The former is the average drawdown that we can expect in the future. The latter is an individual drawdown that we actually experience. The latter will tend to center around the former, but individual drawdowns can easily be much worse than the average (or much less worse, of course). For obvious reasons, we care mainly about how bad our *next* drawdown might be, as opposed to how bad drawdowns will be on average.

This issue presents an opportunity to show an example of how easily intuition can lead us astray. Consider the following *flawed* reasoning:

1) Our returns are out-of-sample and hence unbiased.

2) Therefore, our returns are a fair representation of the returns that we can expect in the future.

3) Drawdown is dependent on order; a long string of contiguous losses will produce a huge drawdown, while alternating wins and losses will produce only tiny drawdowns.

4) Future returns will be similar to those in our current OOS sample. Only two differences will occur. First, there will be some randomness in the appearance of wins and losses, with the possibility that we may be blessed with a few more wins than in our OOS sample, or cursed with a few more losses. Second, the order in which wins and losses appear will be different. These are the two factors that will impact future drawdown.

5) We can use a computer to simulate these two random effects. We take a random sample with replacement from our returns and evaluate its drawdown. Then do it again and again, several thousand times. The distribution of drawdowns we obtain is representative of the distribution of possible future drawdowns. For example, suppose we find that 5 percent of these bootstrap trials had a drawdown of 60 percent or more. Then we assert that in the future we have a 5 percent chance of suffering a drawdown of 60 percent or more.

The fatal flaw in this otherwise solid reasoning lies in step 2. Please review the section "Interlude: What Does *Unbiased* Really Mean?" on page 125. The problem is that the term *unbiased* in the statistical sense does not mean unbiased in the practical sense that most people understand. In fact, our OOS sample almost certainly *is* biased. It is unduly pessimistic. Or optimistic. We don't know, but whichever is the case, it is *not* a fair representation of future returns. We call it unbiased only because undue optimism and pessimism are balanced, with neither favored.

The computer simulation in step 5 does not take into account the fact that our OOS returns are themselves a random sample and hence optimistic or pessimistic, perhaps greatly so. This is a huge source of variation not taken into account by this algorithm. As a result, extreme drawdowns are far more likely than the computer simulation implies. When we discuss the DRAWDOWN program on page 267, we'll see that for catastrophic drawdowns, this algorithm can underestimate their probability by more than a factor of 10. Even for modest drawdowns, the probability can be low by a factor of 2. This is an error of the worst sort, because it is anti-conservative. Overestimating the probability of a severe drawdown would be troubling, but underestimating this probability can be disastrous.

Bootstrapping Drawdown Bounds

First the bad news: computing probabilistic bounds for future drawdowns is very slow, typically involving on the order of a hundred million iterations of a slow computation. A single such computation for an established trading system can usually be done in a few seconds to a minute at most, a manageable time. But if you want to use drawdown bounds inside a training algorithm for optimizing parameters of a trading system, you could easily be looking at hours or even days of computer time. This can be a deal-killer. Our one out is that the tremendously faster algorithm shown on page 264 in step 5 can be used in a training algorithm provided that two essential and often reasonable conditions are met. This will be discussed in more detail in conjunction with the DRAWDOWN program presented on page 267.

And now yet another bit of bad news: the results of these computations may not be all that accurate. Like raw profit factors and Sharpe ratios, drawdown-based statistics aren't terribly bootstrap-friendly. Still, we can usually get results that are a lot better than nothing. The algorithm about to be shown deserves a place in every market trader's toolbox.

Let's briefly review the three factors that determine the relationship between computations done with an observed set of OOS returns and future drawdowns. Understand that we have an unknown distribution of returns from which our historical OOS data and future trades are drawn. These are the three factors that concern us:

1) The set of OOS returns on which our computations are based is a random sample from the population of possible returns.

2) The drawdown in a future time period depends on the size and relative quantity of wins and losses drawn from that population.

3) This future drawdown depends on the order in which wins and losses are appear.

The algorithm shown on page 264 in step 5 takes into account Factors 2 and 3 but ignores Factor 1. We must take care of that.

Conceptually, the solution is simple: we just embed the page 264 step 5 algorithm inside an outer bootstrap that addresses Factor 1. The outer algorithm would use the percentile bootstrap (or perhaps the BC_a method, which is probably not worth the extra effort) to compute confidence bounds for the drawdown bounds. Here is the complete double-bootstrap algorithm, stated here for computation of the drawdown bound at a user-specified large (perhaps 0.9–0.99) drawdown confidence DD_conf, and a user-specified largish (perhaps 0.6–.9) confidence in the drawdown bound, Bound_conf.

For 'outer' replications
    Draw an 'outer' bootstrap sample from the OOS returns
    For 'inner' replications
        Draw an 'inner' bootstrap sample from the outer bootstrap sample
        DD_inner [inner] = drawdown of this inner sample
    Sort DD_inner ascending
    m = DD_conf * inner
    DD_outer [outer] = DD_inner [m]
Sort DD_outer ascending
m = Bound_conf * outer
Bound = DD_outer [m]

We should be clear on the meaning of the two user-specified confidence levels, DD_conf and Bound_conf. The former is the probability that our future drawdown will not exceed the computed value. For example, we might want to compute the drawdown that we can be DD_conf confident will never be exceeded. We might, for instance, specify DD_conf=0.9 and receive from the algorithm a drawdown of, say, 65 percent. Then we can be 90 percent certain that individual future drawdowns will not exceed 65 percent.

Unfortunately, it's not that simple. The computed bound, such as the 65 percent just cited, is itself a random quantity because our OOS sample is itself a random sample. So we need to compute a probability-based bound on the drawdown bound. In this example, we might specify Bound_conf=0.7, in which case the algorithm will compute a larger bound that has a 70 percent chance of equaling or exceeding the actual DD_conf=0.9 bound. In this example, we might find that the final bound is 69 percent, rather than the less conservative 65 percent. In other words, for this example, there is a 70 percent chance that the actual (but unknown) drawdown bound in which we can have 90 percent confidence does not exceed 69 percent.

That might take a while to sink in. It's a bound on a bound. There is some true but unknown drawdown bound for which there is probability DD_conf of being the upper limit for future drawdowns. Stated more rigorously, and perhaps more clearly, there is user-specified probability DD_conf that future drawdowns will not exceed this unknown upper bound. If we could be absolutely certain that our OOS sample *exactly* replicates the distribution of possible future returns, we could use the page 264 step 5 algorithm to compute this bound and be justifiably happy.

Unfortunately, our OOS set does not replicate the distribution of possible returns. Making things worse is the fact that random sampling errors have an asymmetric effect on bound computation; the effect on drawdown bounds is not balanced for optimistic and pessimistic OOS samples, so we cannot just say that everything will balance out in the end. Optimistic OOS samples work against us far more strongly than pessimistic samples work for us.

For this reason, we have to compute a drawdown upper bound that is *larger* than that computed by the page 264 step 5 algorithm. We specify a probability that this larger bound is *at least as large* as the true but unknown upper bound that corresponds to the specified DD_conf. We usually don't have to go overboard on this confidence, unless we are looking at catastrophic values. But suppose we do want to go out into the region of ruin, perhaps setting DD_conf=0.999. The associated drawdown is an important number, because if we see that the drawdown at this very high confidence level is, say, 12 percent we will be ecstatic, while if we see that it is 98 percent, we should rightly tremble. After all, 99.9 percent is a high probability, near certainty, but definitely not certain. Failure can still happen. Since this is such a crucial figure, we should be extra-confident in its computed value. Thus, we would be inclined to set Bound_conf=0.9 or maybe even more when DD_conf is huge. Conversely, if we are just looking for routine drawdowns, perhaps setting DD_conf=0.9, then most people would be comfortable setting Bound_conf=0.7 or so. This gives us a 70 percent chance that our computed bound equals or exceeds the unknown true bound, which will be exceeded just 10 percent of the time.

The DRAWDOWN Program

The file DRAWDOWN.CPP contains source code for a program that lets the user experiment with computation of drawdown bounds for various hypothetical trading systems. It demonstrates how to implement the drawdown bounding algorithm shown on page 266 in a way that lets it compute several bounds simultaneously. It also shows how badly the page 264 step 5 algorithm underestimates the probability of catastrophic drawdowns under many common conditions, as well as demonstrating the conditions under which this algorithm, which is orders of magnitude faster than the "correct" algorithm, is reasonably accurate.

The program is invoked as follows:

DRAWDOWN Nchanges Ntrades WinProb BoundConf BootstrapReps QuantileReps TestReps

Let's break down this command:

- Nchanges: Number of price changes

- Ntrades: Number of trades, less than or equal to Nchanges

- WinProb: Probability of winning, typically near 0.5

- BoundConf: Confidence (typically .5–.999) in correct DD bound

- BootstrapReps: Number of bootstrap reps

- QuantileReps: Number of bootstrap reps for finding drawdown quantiles

- TestReps: Number of trial reps for this study

The DRAWDOWN program generates Nchanges price changes, which represent the (log) OOS returns on which bound computation will be based. This may encompass a time period longer than the time period over which you want to consider drawdowns. For example, you might have 10 years of OOS data but want to consider drawdowns over a single year, or perhaps even just a quarter. So, you specify an equal or lesser quantity, Ntrades, which spans the desired time period.

The price changes follow a normal distribution, and they will be positive with probability WinProb, which we would normally set to 0.5 or some value slightly above 0.5 if we want to stay in the realm of realistic systems.

The user cannot set DD_conf, but four useful value are hard-coded into the program and computed simultaneously. These are 0.999 for catastrophic drawdowns, 0.99 for serious drawdowns, 0.95 for fairly bad drawdowns, and 0.9 for drawdowns that could be expected occasionally. Multiple DD_conf values can be computed in essentially the same amount of time as a single value, so it is most efficient to compute them together in a single run.

The user specifies Bound_conf, and this value is used for the two largest (0.9 and 0.95) values of DD_conf. However, $1.0 - (1.0 - Bound\_conf) / 2.0$ is used for the two smallest values. This increase above the user-specified value is in deference to the fact that for smaller values of DD_conf we typically would want increased confidence in the computed bounds. This is where the most serious drawdowns occur, so we'd better be sure of ourselves.

BootstrapReps is the number of replications used in the page 264 step 5 algorithm, and it is also the number of outer replications used in the "correct" algorithm on page 266.

QuantileReps is the number of inner replications used in the "correct" algorithm on page 266.

These two algorithms are used to compute upper bounds for future drawdowns. In case any readers are interested, a lower bound for the mean return is also computed but then incorrectly used as if it were a bound for future returns. This provides additional demonstration of the difference between bounding future means and future values. I won't discuss this test further, but some readers may be interested in studying that aspect of the source code.

After we have eight drawdown bounds computed (four values of DD_conf for the incorrect and correct methods), a large number of trade returns are generated from the same distribution as was used for generating the OOS data on which the bound computation depended. The program counts how often each of the eight bounds are violated. If the bound computation is correct, the violation rates should equal one minus the corresponding values of DD_conf. If the violation rate exceeds the corresponding DD_conf, we have the extremely serious error of the algorithm underestimating the probability of a drawdown exceeding the bound. If the violation rate is less than DD_conf, we have the much less serious error of the algorithm overestimating the bound. This is still a problem, because we are being too conservative and perhaps rejecting a trading system unfairly. But unfairly rejecting a trading system is a lot better than putting a system to work trading real money and then discovering too late that its true probability of serious drawdown is much worse than we thought.

This whole process of generating hypothetical OOS returns, computing drawdown bounds, and seeing how these bounds actually perform is repeated TestReps times and the results averaged. These average performances, along with the ratio of the attained failure probability to the correct failure probability, are printed to the screen and to a file called DRAWDOWN.LOG.

Before examining key code fragments that illustrate this algorithm, let's devote one paragraph to more mathematically inclined readers who have bootstrap experience and who may be questioning the rationale behind the algorithm on page 266. A central idea is that although the inner loop has been called a bootstrap, it really is not. It just looks like one and calling it a bootstrap is not a huge crime if one is not being too strict. However, there is really only one bootstrap at work here, the outer loop. This bootstrap is using the percentile method to estimate confidence intervals for a particular statistic.

This statistic is the user's desired quantile, that corresponding to DD_conf. For every outer-loop bootstrap sample, this statistic is estimated by repeated sampling in the inner loop. This, of course, makes computation of this statistic independent of the order in which the outer-loop sample is generated; it is dependent only on the empirical distribution. So, the bottom line is that the inner loop is simply computing an estimate of the sample statistic derived from the empirical distribution of the outer-loop bootstrap sample. If you do not understand this paragraph, don't worry; you don't need to do so.

First, we examine the code that generates our bootstrap sample data for both the incorrect and correct drawdown bounding algorithms. All calling parameters are self-explanatory except make_changes. This would be set to *True* the first time it is called in a replication loop, which causes a set of prices changes, representing the log of our OOS returns, to be generated and saved. For remaining replications, make_changes is false, which retains the originally generated sample. Regardless, a random sample is collected from the saved changes.

```
void get_trades (
   int n_changes ,        // Number of price changes (available history)
   int n_trades ,         // Number of these changes defining drawdown period
   double win_prob ,      // Probability 0-1 of a winning trade
   int make_changes ,     // Draw a new random sample from which bootstraps are drawn?
   double *changes ,      // Work area for storing n_changes changes
   double *trades         // n_trades are returned here
   )
{
   int i, k, itrade ;

   if (make_changes) {   // Generate the sample?
     for (i=0 ; i<n_changes ; i++) {
       changes[i] = normal () ;
       if (unifrand() < win_prob)
         changes[i] = fabs ( changes[i] ) ;
       else
         changes[i] = -fabs ( changes[i] ) ;
       }
     }
```

```
// Get the trades from a standard bootstrap
for (itrade=0 ; itrade<n_trades ; itrade++) {
  k = (int) (unifrand() * n_changes) ;
  if (k >= n_changes)
    k = n_changes - 1 ;
  trades[itrade] = changes[k] ;
  }
}
```

Just to be clear on how drawdown is computed, here is the code for that routine. Some methods report drawdown as a percent of maximum equity. However, this requires specification of an initial equity that has a significant effect on reported values. A frequently better way is to compute drawdown as an absolute number, which removes the ambiguity of initial equity and also makes the impact of drawdown uniform across the time interval. This is ideal for trading scenarios in which negative equity is possible, such as leveraged futures trading. Also, if the trades are the log of equity changes, this method gives results that are monotonically related to percent drawdown, with the translation easy to implement, as is shown on page 280.

```
double drawdown (
  int n ,        // Number of trades
  double *trades    // They are here
  )
{
  int icase ;
  double cumulative, max_price, loss, dd ;

  cumulative = max_price = trades[0] ;
  dd = 0.0 ;

  for (icase=1 ; icase<n ; icase++) {
    cumulative += trades[icase] ;
    if (cumulative > max_price)
      max_price = cumulative ;
```

```
    else {
      loss = max_price - cumulative ;
      if (loss > dd)
        dd = loss ;
      }
    } // For all cases

  return dd ;
}
```

This routine cumulates equity as a running sum of returns and keeps track of the maximum equity. As each return is processed, the current equity is compared to the maximum, and the largest difference to date is the drawdown.

The correct bounding algorithm requires that, for each bootstrap sample, we do a large number of samples to estimate the desired DD_conf quantile. But the sampling and sorting in this process is extremely time-consuming, so this routine computes four different quantiles simultaneously at essentially no additional expense.

```
void drawdown_quantiles (
  int n_changes ,          // Number of price changes (available history)
  int n_trades ,           // Number of trades
  double *b_changes ,      // n_changes changes bootstrap sample supplied here
  int nboot ,              // Number of bootstraps used to compute quantiles
  double *bootsample ,     // Work area n_trades long
  double *work ,           // Work area nboot long
  double *q001 ,           // Computed quantiles
  double *q01 ,
  double *q05 ,
  double *q10
  )
{
  int i, k, iboot ;

  for (iboot=0 ; iboot<nboot ; iboot++) {
    for (i=0 ; i<n_trades ; i++) {
      k = (int) (unifrand() * n_changes) ;
```

```
      if (k >= n_changes)
        k = n_changes - 1 ;
      bootsample[i] = b_changes[k] ;
      }
    work[iboot] = drawdown ( n_trades , bootsample ) ;
    }

  qsortd ( 0 , nboot-1 , work ) ;

  k = (int) (0.999 * (nboot+1) ) - 1 ;
  if (k < 0)
    k = 0 ;
  *q001 = work[k] ;

  k = (int) (0.99 * (nboot+1) ) - 1 ;
  if (k < 0)
    k = 0 ;
  *q01 = work[k] ;

  k = (int) (0.95 * (nboot+1) ) - 1 ;
  if (k < 0)
    k = 0 ;
  *q05 = work[k] ;

  k = (int) (0.90 * (nboot+1) ) - 1 ;
  if (k < 0)
    k = 0 ;
  *q10 = work[k] ;
}
```

This code does bootstrap sampling (although as discussed earlier, it's not really a bootstrap) a great many times. These samples are taken from the outer-loop bootstrap sample, making all n_changes of them available. In practice, because the statistics computed by this routine are estimates subject to random error, it is important that nboot here be very large. I typically use 10,000, and larger values would not be unreasonable.

For each of these samples it computes and saves the drawdown for the specified n_trades size interval. After all sampling is complete, it sorts the saved drawdowns and uses the unbiased quantile formula to estimate the four desired quantiles.

Note that the if(k<0) checks are not needed in this because they will always be false. But this check is a good habit to get into, because in general it can happen that k will equal –1.

For both tests, we have a trivial routine to find a quantile. It assumes that the data is sorted ascending.

```
static double find_quantile ( int n , double *data , double frac )
{
  int k ;

  k = (int) (frac * (n+1) ) - 1 ;
  if (k < 0)
    k = 0 ;
  return data[k] ;
}
```

The page 264 step 5 algorithm, which I call the "incorrect" method here (though its results can be acceptable under some circumstances) is as follows:

```
for (iboot=0 ; iboot<bootstrap_reps ; iboot++) {
  make_changes = (iboot == 0)  ?  1 : 0 ; // Generate sample on first pass only
  get_trades ( n_changes , n_trades , win_prob , make_changes , changes , trades ) ;
  incorrect_drawdowns[iboot] = drawdown ( n_trades , trades ) ;
  } // End of incorrect method bootstrap loop

qsortd ( 0 , bootstrap_reps-1 , incorrect_drawdowns ) ;

incorrect_dd_001 = find_quantile ( bootstrap_reps , incorrect_drawdowns , 0.999 ) ;
incorrect_dd_01 =  find_quantile ( bootstrap_reps , incorrect_drawdowns , 0.99 ) ;
incorrect_dd_05 =  find_quantile ( bootstrap_reps , incorrect_drawdowns , 0.95 ) ;
incorrect_dd_10 =  find_quantile ( bootstrap_reps , incorrect_drawdowns , 0.9 ) ;
```

The outer loop draws many bootstrap samples. The first time, get_trades() is called with make_changes true so that a set of simulated OOS returns is generated prior to bootstrap sampling. For subsequent passes through this loop, sampling is done from the original collection. For each sample, the drawdown is computed and saved.

After all replications are complete, the drawdowns are sorted into ascending order. The find_quantile() routine is called for each desired quantile.

The correct routine is a little more complex. We have to distinguish between the bootstrap sample size (n_changes) and the size of the sample (n_trades) for the test statistic (a specified quantile). The actual bootstrap (the outer loop) is sampling from the complete set of available OOS returns, because this is our presumed population. But our test statistic is a quantile of the distribution of drawdowns experienced during *a specified time period*, which may be shorter than the length encompassed by the entire OOS set.

```
for (iboot=0 ; iboot<bootstrap_reps ; iboot++) {
  make_changes = (iboot == 0)  ?  1 : 0 ; // Generate sample on first pass only
  get_trades ( n_changes , n_changes , win_prob , make_changes , changes , trades ) ;
  drawdown_quantiles (
         n_changes , n_trades , trades , quantile_reps , bootsample , work ,
         &correct_q001[iboot] , &correct_q01[iboot] ,
         &correct_q05[iboot],&correct_q10[iboot] ) ;
  } // End of incorrect method bootstrap loop

qsortd ( 0 , bootstrap_reps-1 , correct_q001 ) ;
qsortd ( 0 , bootstrap_reps-1 , correct_q01 ) ;
qsortd ( 0 , bootstrap_reps-1 , correct_q05 ) ;
qsortd ( 0 , bootstrap_reps-1 , correct_q10 ) ;
correct_q001_bound = find_quantile (
                      bootstrap_reps , correct_q001 , 1.0 - (1.0 - bound_conf) / 2.0 ) ;
correct_q01_bound = find_quantile (
                      bootstrap_reps , correct_q01 , 1.0 - (1.0 - bound_conf) / 2.0 ) ;
correct_q05_bound = find_quantile ( boots trap_reps , correct_q05 , bound_conf ) ;
correct_q10_bound = find_quantile ( boots trap_reps , correct_q10 , bound_conf ) ;
```

After we have a collection of bootstrapped quantiles at each of the four specified levels, we use the simple percentile algorithm to find confidence bounds for the quantiles. For the two larger fractiles (0.1 and 0.05) we choose the user-specified confidence level, typically something moderately larger than 0.5. But for the two more extreme fractiles (0.01 and 0.001) we push the confidence level further, under the arbitrary but reasonable assumption that when we are dealing with more extreme (serious!) drawdowns, we had better be more sure of our computed bound. Note that we could use the frequently superior BC_a bootstrap here, but the added complexity is probably not worthwhile. Feel free to try it.

The last step in this test program is to generate "future" returns and compare their drawdowns to the previously computed bounds. A good method for bound computation will provide bounds whose actual failure rate is close to their desired failure rate. Here are some snippets from that code:

```
for (ipop=0 ; ipop<POP_MULT ; ipop++) {

  for (i=0 ; i<n_trades ; i++) {
    trades[i] = normal () ;
    if (unifrand() < win_prob)
      trades[i] = fabs ( trades[i] ) ;
    else
      trades[i] = -fabs ( trades[i] ) ;
    }

  crit = drawdown ( n_trades , trades ) ;

  if (crit > incorrect_drawdown_001)
    ++count_incorrect_drawdown_001 ;

  if (crit > correct_q001_bound)
    ++count_correct_001 ;

  ...Test other bounds similarly...

  } // For ipop
```

We generate a large number of trial return sets, each containing n_trades trade returns. Naturally, this trade set is generated in the same way as the trade sets used for computing the bounds.

For each trade set, we compute the drawdown and compare it to the computed bounds, counting how many times the bound is violated (the actual drawdown exceeds the computed bound). After we have completed a large number of compute-bound-test-bound trials, we divide the failure counts by the number of trials and print each bound's failure rate along with the correct rate, knowing that these rates will be equal if the bound computation is correct.

Experiments with the DRAWDOWN Program

I ran a series of experiments with the DRAWDOWN program; readers can feel free to run their own experiments. For all of these tests, the probability of a win was set to 0.6, which would be fairly typical of a real-life trading system with balanced wins and losses. There were 5,000 bootstrap replications; 10,000 samples were used for computing the quantile bounds; and the process was repeated for 2,000 trials. These numbers are large enough to provide reliable results.

Three different configurations were used. First, I used 63 returns for both the OOS and the drawdown periods. This corresponds to using a quarter of daily data to bound drawdown in the next quarter. Then I expanded this to 252 returns each, corresponding to using one year of OOS returns to bound drawdown in the next year. Finally, I used 2,520 returns with a drawdown period of 252 returns. This corresponds to using 10 years of OOS data to bound drawdown in the next year.

Prob	OOS	DD	Incorrect	0.5	0.6	0.8
0.001	63	63	13.65	4.49	3.42	1.64
0.01	63	63	4.29	1.74	1.37	0.71
0.05	63	63	2.16	2.15	1.65	0.85
0.10	63	63	1.66	1.66	1.31	0.72
0.001	252	252	5.84	1.81	1.35	0.59
0.01	252	252	2.55	1.02	0.80	0.41
0.05	252	252	1.62	1.62	1.26	0.64
0.10	252	252	1.36	1.37	1.10	0.61
0.001	2520	252	1.54	0.79	0.68	0.45
0.01	2520	252	1.16	0.76	0.68	0.51
0.05	2520	252	1.06	1.06	0.95	0.72
0.10	2520	252	1.04	1.03	0.94	0.75

In the previous table, each entry is the factor by which the *actual* rate of violating the drawdown bound exceeds the presumed rate. Ideally they should be equal; values greater than 1.0 are much worse than values under 1.0 because a ratio above 1.0 means that the drawdown violates the supposed bound more frequently than it should (and that you think it will!).

The first column is the failure-to-bound rate whose corresponding bound we want to compute. The second column is the number of OOS returns made available to compute the bounds. The third column is the number of returns that define the upcoming drawdown period. The fourth column is the excess failure ratio for the "incorrect" page 264 step 5 algorithm. The remaining three columns are the excess failure ratio for the "correct" algorithm using confidence levels of 0.5, 0.6, and 0.8. (But note how these confidences are extended for the two smallest probabilities, as explained on page 269.) The following results should be noted:

- The quality of the incorrect method depends tremendously on the size of the OOS sample. This makes sense, because larger OOS samples more accurately represent the underlying population of returns. Small OOS samples are more subject to the random variation that makes the incorrect method incorrect.

- The quality of the incorrect method depends tremendously on the specified failure rate. For modest failure rates, such as 0.10 (a 10 percent chance that the upcoming drawdown will exceed the computed bound), the incorrect method performs reasonably well, though even then in every test it still underestimates the true failure rate, a dangerous property.

- When the OOS sample is small (63) *and* we are looking at rare catastrophic events (p=0.001), the incorrect method underestimates the probability of catastrophic drawdown by a factor of 13.65, a huge problem. But this is a difficult situation, as evidenced by the fact that even the correct method at a confidence level of 0.8 underestimates this probability by a factor of 1.64.

- If we use the correct method with a confidence level of 0.8 (extended for small probabilities as explained on page 269), then other than this extreme combination of small sample and tiny probability, the computed bounds are always conservative (they overestimate the violation rate). Yet they do not do so to an extreme degree. The worst case is a ratio of 0.41, not a serious penalty considering the confidence that we get in return. This trade-off is a no-brainer for me.

The CHOOSER_DD Program

On page 179 we saw the CHOOSER program, which selects equities to purchase and hold for one day, based on the evolving performance of multiple selection criteria. This program was used to demonstrate nested walkforward. Now we take this same trading system and show how to compute confidence bounds for future drawdown. This is implemented in the program whose source code is in CHOOSER_DD.CPP. Readers interested in the trading system should refer to the section beginning on page 179. Here we will focus on the drawdown aspects of this program.

Recall that the out-of-sample returns for this trading system are in the array OOS2 at indices OOS2_start up to but not including OOS2_end. Thus, we have n OOS cases, as shown in the first line of the following code. We do a large number of bootstrap replications, at least several thousand if we want good accuracy. For each bootstrap sample we call drawdown_quantiles() to compute the four predefined quantiles in which we are interested.

It is vital to notice that each bootstrap sample is the size of the complete OOS set, because this is the presumed population from which we are sampling. On the other hand, we specify n_trades to be the number of trades in the drawdown period, and it may be less than n. This is 252, a year of daily returns, in the program, but it can be easily changed by the reader. This quantity defines the statistic we are bounding.

```
n = OOS2_end - OOS2_start ;

for (iboot=0 ; iboot<bootstrap_reps ; iboot++) {
   for (i=0 ; i<n ; i++) {          // Collect a bootstrap sample from the entire OOS set
      k = (int) (unifrand() * n) ;
      if (k >= n)
        k = n - 1 ;
      bootsample[i] = OOS2[k+OOS2_start] ;
      }

   drawdown_quantiles ( n , n_trades , bootsample , quantile_reps , quantile_sample ,
                     work ,  &q001[iboot] , &q01[iboot] ,&q05[iboot] ,&q10[iboot] ) ;
   } // End of bootstrap loop
```

The drawdown_quantiles() routine is identical to that we have already seen on page 272, and the drawdown computed by drawdown() shown on page 271 is also identical, with one crucial exception. We change the last line like this:

```
return 100.0 * (1.0 - exp ( -dd )) ; // Convert log change to percent
```

Recall that all OOS returns are the log of the price change ratio (the difference of log prices). Also recall the basic mathematical principle that the log of a product is the sum of the logs of the items being multiplied. Thus, the computed drawdown is the log of the ratio of the peak equity to the trough equity. The simple formula in the previous line of code computes the percent equity loss, which is the most common way to express drawdown. For example, suppose we start at an equity of 1, reach a peak equity of 3, and have a subsequent trough of 2. We will have dd=log(3)–log(2). That final line of code will return $100*(1-\exp(\log(2)-\log(3))) = 100*(1-2/3) = 33.3$ percent, which is what most users would expect.

After all bootstrap_reps samples have been processed, we sort each of the four statistic collections ascending so that we can easily find any specified quantile using the find_quantile() routine shown on page 274. Code for the 0.001 bound is shown here; the code for the other three bounds is similar:

```
qsortd ( 0 , bootstrap_reps-1 , q001 ) ;
fprintf ( fpReport, "\n        0.5      0.6      0.7      0.8      0.9      0.95" ) ;
fprintf ( fpReport, "\n0.001 %8.3lf   %8.3lf   %8.3lf   %8.3lf   %8.3lf   %8.3lf",
        find_quantile ( bootstrap_reps , q001 , 0.5 ),
        find_quantile ( bootstrap_reps , q001 , 0.6 ),
        find_quantile ( bootstrap_reps , q001 , 0.7 ),
        find_quantile ( bootstrap_reps , q001 , 0.8 ),
        find_quantile ( bootstrap_reps , q001 , 0.9 ),
        find_quantile ( bootstrap_reps , q001 , 0.95 ) ) ;
```

It's important to understand the meaning of the computed bounds. These refer to the bounds for a *particular time interval specified in advance*, and also to equity changes *only within that interval.* Prior equity is ignored, even though drawdown may be a continuation of an existing drawdown in progress. Also, this is not the probability that we will *ever* see such an extreme drawdown. It applies to a single specified time period only. Typically, we would let this be the upcoming year.

As a demonstration, I ran the CHOOSER_DD program on the same data that was employed on page 179. The output is shown in Figure 6-8. Each row corresponds to the probability that the drawdown within a specified single future time period (such as the next year, and ignoring equity prior to that time period) will exceed the tabled value. The columns correspond to confidence that the shown bound is at least equal to the unknown correct bound. Note that we pay surprisingly low penalty for greatly increased confidence in our bound.

```
Mean =      8.7473

25200 * mean log return of each criterion, and pct times chosen
    Total return    17.8898   Chosen 67.8 pct
    Sharpe ratio    12.9834   Chosen 21.1 pct
    Profit factor   12.2799   Chosen 11.1 pct

25200 * mean return of final system = 19.1151

Drawdown approximate bounds.

Rows are drawdown probability, columns are confidence in bounds.
          0.5       0.6       0.7       0.8       0.9       0.95
0.001    63.042    63.636    64.312    65.115    66.211    67.081
0.01     54.046    54.744    55.361    56.111    57.228    58.057
0.05     45.147    45.839    46.500    47.191    48.345    49.192
0.10     40.336    40.999    41.614    42.277    43.361    44.276
```

Figure 6-8. *Output of the CHOOSER_DD program*

CHAPTER 7

Permutation Tests

Overview of Permutation Testing

We begin with a general overview of the concept behind permutation testing. Of necessity, many theoretical details are omitted; see my book *Data Mining Algorithms in C++* for more in-depth treatment. Suppose we are training or testing some system and its performance depends on the order in which data is presented to it. Here are some examples:

1) We have a completely defined trading system, and we want to measure its performance out-of-sample. The order of price changes in its market price history is of great consequence.

2) We have a proposed a market trading system, and we must optimize one or more of its parameters to maximize a measure of its performance. The order of price changes in its market price history is of great consequence.

3) We have a model that, on a regular basis, examines indicators and uses the values of these variables to predict near-term changes in market volatility. We want to train (optimize) this model, or test it on OOS data. We will then measure the in-sample (if training) or out-of- sample (if testing) error of this model. The order of the predicted variable, future volatility, with respect to the order of the indicators is (of course!) of great consequence.

Although the precise details of how permutation testing would be employed in each of these examples is somewhat different, the underlying idea is the same. We perform whatever task we want (training or testing a trading system or predictive model) using the original data in its correct order. Then we randomly permute the data and repeat our training or testing activity, and we record the result. Then we permute again, and again, many (hundreds or even thousands) times. We compare the performance figure

© Timothy Masters 2018
T. Masters, *Testing and Tuning Market Trading Systems*, https://doi.org/10.1007/978-1-4842-4173-8_7

obtained from the original data with the distribution of performance figures from the permutation results and thereby may reach a conclusion.

How do we do this comparison? We are testing some measure of performance, whether it be the net return of a trading system, the mean error of a predictive model, or any other performance measure appropriate to our operation. Our operation may or may not be useful: our trading system may or may not be able to legitimately capitalize on market patterns to make money. Our predictive model and the indicators on which it bases its decisions may or may not have true predictive power. But there's one thing we can usually be quite sure of: if we permute the data on which our operation is based, any legitimate ability will vanish because predictive patterns are destroyed. If we randomly permute the price changes in a market history, the market will become unpredictable, and hence any trading system will be hobbled. If we randomly change the pairing between indicators and a target variable for a predictive model, the model will not have any authentic relationships to learn or make use of.

This leads to our method for using permutation testing. Suppose for the moment that we repeat the training or testing with nine different permutations. Including the original, unpermuted data, we have ten performance measures. If we sort these, the original performance can occupy any of the ten possible ordered positions, from best to worst, or any position in between. If our operation is truly worthless (the trading system has no ability to detect profitable market patterns or the model has no predictive power), then the original order will have no advantage. Thus, the original performance has an equal probability of occupying any of the positions. Conversely, if our operation has legitimate power, we would expect that its original performance would come in at or near the best. So, the position of our original performance in the sorted performances provides useful information about the ability of our operation.

We can be more rigorous. Continue to suppose that we have performed nine permutations. Also suppose we find, to our great joy, that the original unpermuted data has the best performance of the ten values. This, of course, is great news and very encouraging. It is evidence that our operation is finding useful patterns in the data when the data is not permuted. But how meaningful is this finding? What we can say is that if our operation is truly worthless there would be a 0.1 probability that we would have obtained this result by sheer luck. In other words, we have obtained a p-value of 0.1. If this conclusion and terminology are not perfectly clear, please review the material on hypothesis tests that begins on page 210.

What if our original performance is the second best of the ten performers? Under the null hypothesis that our operation is worthless, there is a 0.1 probability of it landing in that second slot, and also a 0.1 probability that it would have done better, landing in the top slot. Thus, there is probability (p-value) of 0.2 that a worthless operation would have obtained the performance we observed, or better.

In general, suppose we perform m random permutations, and also suppose that the performance of k of these permutations equals or exceeds the performance of the original data. Then, under the null hypothesis that our operation is worthless, there is probability $(k+1)/(m+1)$ that we would have obtained this result or better by luck.

If we want to be scrupulously rigorous in our experimental design, we would choose a p-value *in advance* of doing the permutation test. In particular, we would choose a small probability (typically 0.01 to 0.1) that we find to be an acceptable likelihood of falsely concluding that our operation has legitimate ability when it does not. We would choose a large m (over 1,000 is not unusual or excessive) such that $m+1$ times our p-value is an integer, and solve for k. Then perform the permutation test and conclude that our operation is worthy if and only if k or fewer of the permuted values equal or exceed the original value. If our operation is truly worthless, there is our chosen probability that we will falsely conclude that it is worthy.

Testing a Fully Specified Trading System

Suppose we have developed a trading system and we want to test its performance on a set of market history that we held out from the development process. This will give us an unbiased performance figure. We have already explored some important uses for returns obtained in this out-of-sample time period. If none of the returns is extreme and the shape of their distribution is roughly bell-curve-shaped, we can cross our fingers and use the parametric tests described on page 216. If we want to be more conservative, we can use the bootstrap test described on page 222. But as we'll see soon, a permutation test provides a potentially valuable piece of information not provided by either of the tests just mentioned.

Moreover, permutation tests have none of the distribution assumptions that limit utility of parametric tests, and they are even more robust against distribution problems than bootstrap tests. Thus, permutation tests are a vital component of a well-equipped toolbox.

When we permute market price changes to perform this test, we must permute *only* the changes in the OOS time period. It is tempting to start the permutation earlier, with the price changes that drive the trade decisions. For example, suppose we look back 100 bars to make a trade decision. The data for our test will start 100 bars before the beginning of the OOS test period so that we can begin making trade decisions immediately, on the first bar of the OOS period. But these 100 early bars must *not* be included in the permutation. Why? Because their returns will not be included in the original, unpermuted performance figure. What if these early bars are unusual in some way, such as having a strong trend? When these unusual bars get permuted into the OOS segment, they would impact results relative to the original result which does not include their influence. So, they must not be allowed to invade the OOS test area.

Testing the Training Process

Perhaps the single most important use of permutation testing is evaluation of the process by which your trading system is optimized. There are primarily two very different ways in which a trading system can fail. The most obvious failure mode is that the system is not able to detect and capitalize on predictive patterns in market prices; it's weak or unintelligent. It should be apparent that permutation testing will easily detect this situation, because the performance of your system on unpermuted data, as well as on permuted data, will be poor. Your system's performance will not stand out above the permuted competition.

However, this is not the situation we are most interested in, because we would almost certainly never get this far. The weakness of a trading system will be apparent long before we reach the point of expending precious computer resources; we'll see the dismal performance quickly.

The problem in which permutation testing is valuable is the opposite of weakness: your system is too powerful at detecting predictive patterns. The term commonly employed for this situation is *overfitting*. When your system has too many optimizable parameters, it will tend to see random noise as predictive patterns and learn these patterns along with any legitimate patterns that might be present. But because noise does not repeat (by definition), these learned patterns will be useless, even destructive, when the system is put to use trading real money. I have often seen people develop systems that look back optimizable distances for several moving averages, optimizable distances for volatility, and optimizable thresholds for changes in the quantities. Such systems produce astonishing performance in the training period and yet produce completely random trades out-of-sample.

This is where permutation testing comes to the rescue. An overfitted trading system will perform well not only on the original data but on permuted data as well. This is because an overfitted system is so powerful that it can learn "predictive" patterns even on permuted data. As a result, *all* in-sample performances, permuted and unpermuted, will be excellent, and the original performance will not stand out from its permuted competitors. So, all you need to do is repeat the training process on many sets (at least 100) of permuted data and compute the p-value as described earlier, $(k+1)/(m+1)$. This may require a lot of computer time, but it is almost always worthwhile. In my own personal experience working with trading system developers over the years, I have found this technique to be one of the most valuable tools in my toolbox. Unless you get a small (0.05 or less) p-value, you should be suspicious of your system specification and optimization process.

Walkforward Testing a Trading System Factory

In many or most development situations, we have an idea for a trading system, but our idea is not fully specified; there are one or more aspects of it, such as optimizable parameters, that are left unspecified. As a simplistic example, we may have a moving-average crossover system that has two optimizable parameters, the long-term and short-term lookbacks. The system definition, along with a rigorously defined method for optimizing its parameters, and verified by OOS testing of the system, make up what we might call a *model factory*. In other words, prior to optimization we do not have an actual trading model; it's just an idea along with a way of converting the idea into something concrete. The actual trading system we end up with will depend on the market data on which it is trained. Our goal now is to assess the quality of our model factory, as opposed to assessing the quality of a completely defined trading system. If we are able to conclude that our model factory is probably effective at producing good trading systems, then when we use up-to-date data to create a trading system from the model factory, we can be confident that our system will have respectable performance. This, of course, is the whole idea behind walkforward testing that we have explored from numerous different angles in prior chapters. But the distinction between testing *complete systems* versus testing our *training process* versus testing our *model factory* is especially pertinent to permutation testing. This is the reason for emphasizing this distinction here.

When we mate permutation testing with walkforward testing, we have to be careful about what is permuted, just as we did when testing a fully specified system. In particular, consider the fact that when we walk the original unpermuted system forward, the training data in the first fold will never appear in any OOS area. Since this section of historical data may contain unusual prices changes such as large trends, we must make sure it never appears in the OOS area of permuted runs. Thus, the first training fold *must* be omitted from permutation.

Do we also permute the first training fold that is omitted from the OOS permutation? I've never seen any convincing argument for or against this, and my gut instinct is that it makes little difference. However, my own practice is to also permute the first training fold, in isolation, of course. This would likely provide more variety in trade decisions. For example, it may be that the original data leads to a large preponderance of, say, long positions in the first OOS fold. If the market overall has a strong upward bias, this would inflate permuted performance. But if permuting the first training fold often reduces the number of long positions, this would give more variety of trade outcomes, which is our ultimate goal in a permutation test. On the other hand, I do not consider this to be an overwhelming argument, so if you chose to avoid permuting the first training fold, I don't think you will be committing a grave sin.

Another decision concerns if and how to permute walkforward folds. There are two choices. You can do a single permutation of all market changes after the first training fold and then just do the walkforward on this permuted data. Alternatively, you can do a separate, isolated permutation with each fold. You could even break this second alternative into several subalternatives, pooling the IS and OOS data in each fold into a single permutation group or separating the IS and OOS sets of each fold into separately permuted groups.

What is the difference between these alternatives? Honestly, not enough research has been done to provide rigorous guidance in this choice. It seems that the dominant factor involves stationarity in market behavior. If you want to assume that the characteristics (especially trend and volatility) of the market are constantly changing and you want your testing method to adapt to these ever-changing conditions, then you would likely want to permute each fold separately to preserve local behavior. Personally, I prefer to focus on market patterns that are universal, as opposed to trying to track perceived changes and be vulnerable to whipsaws. For this reason, my own habit is to permute all market changes after the first fold's training set as a single large group. But I claim no special knowledge or expertise in this matter. All I can say is that this is what makes the most sense to me, and it is what I do in my own work. Feel free to disagree.

Regardless of how you choose to permute, you will have an OOS performance figure for the original, unpermuted data, as well as a similar figure for each permutation. As in the other tests, all you have to do is count how many of those permuted performances equal or exceed that of the original data. Use the p-value = $(k+1)/(m+1)$ formula, which gives the probability that your original OOS performance could have been as good as or better than what you obtained by sheer luck from a truly worthless model factory. Unless this p-value is small (0.05, or even 0.01 or less) you should doubt the quality of your factory and hence mistrust any trading system produced by it.

Permutation Testing of Predictive Models

Everything so far has concerned trading systems. But financial market traders may use predictive models to do things such as predict upcoming changes in volatility. It is often the case that variables other than market price histories are involved, things such as economic indicators or concurrent forecasts of other quantities. These are typically called *predictors* because they are the quantities used by the model to make predictions. We also have a "truth" variable, usually called the *target* variable. This is the quantity that we are trying to predict, and to train the predictive model we need to know the true value of the target that corresponds to each set of predictors. In the volatility example, the target would be the near-term future change in volatility.

In discussing trading systems, we identified three situations: 1) testing a fully specified system on out-of-sample data; 2) testing our training process, with a special eye on detecting overfitting; and 3) testing our model factory. Permutation testing of predictive models falls into the same three categories in what should be an obvious manner, so we will not distinguish between them in this discussion. Rather, we will focus on special aspects of permutation.

Understand that in the context of pairing targets with predictor sets, for the vast majority of models the order in which training data appears is irrelevant. It is only the *pairing* of predictor sets with targets that impacts training. We want them to be concurrent: we pair the correct value of the target at a given time with the current values of the predictors. We permute by disrupting this pairing, randomly reordering the targets so that they become paired with different predictor sets. When we do this, there are two vital issues, both of which will be described in more detail soon.

1) Indicator sets must not permute with respect to one another, only with respect to the target. This preserves intraset correlation, which is critical to correct testing.

2) There must not be any serial correlation in *both* one or more predictors *and* the target. Serial correlation in one or the other is fine, even common, but it must not be present in both.

For the first issue, consider this toy example. Suppose we have two predictors: recent trend of the S&P 100 index and recent trend of the S&P 500 index. These two quantities are used to predict the volatility of S&P 100 next week relative to its volatility in the week just ended. At the close of trading every Friday we compute these two recent trends as well as the volatility during the week that just ended. When we train our predictive model on historical data, we also know the volatility during the upcoming week, so we subtract the prior week's volatility from the upcoming week's volatility to get the change, which is our target variable. When we put the trained model to use, we will predict the upcoming change in volatility.

The correct way to permute this data is to randomly reorder the targets so that targets get attached to pairs of predictors that are from different weeks, thus destroying any relationship that could be predictive. What if we also permuted the predictors? If we did that, we would often get nonsensical predictor pairs. We might end up with a predictor pair in which S&P 100 has a strong uptrend while S&P 500 has a strong downtrend. In real life, this sort of pairing would be extremely unlikely, if not impossible. One key idea behind permutation testing is that we must create permutations that could have occurred in real life with equal probability under the null hypothesis that the model is worthless. If we generate nonsensical or highly unlikely permutations, the method fails.

For the second issue, consider that one or more of the predictors may have serial correlation (the value of a variable at a given time is related to its value at nearby times). In fact, this is extremely common, almost universal. For example, suppose a predictor is the trend over the prior 20 bars. When we advance by one bar, we still have 19 of the prior 20 bars going into the calculation, so the trend is unlikely to change much.

If we are not careful, the target variable may have serial correlation as well. For example, in the volatility example I defined the target as the *change* in volatility, not the actual volatility. If we use volatility as the target, we will find significant serial correlation, because volatility usually changes slowly; the volatility next week will be close to the volatility this week. But changes in volatility are much less likely to have serial correlation. Of course, it may still exist, but certainly it will be greatly reduced, if not totally eliminated.

Even change in volatility will have serious serial correlation if we have overlapping time periods. For example, suppose that on each day of the week, five days a week, we compute the change in volatility over the upcoming five days and compare it to the prior five days. Each time we advance the window, most days will be in common, so successive values of volatility change will be highly correlated.

The key point is that serial correlation in just one or more predictor variables, or in just the target, is harmless. This is because we can then view permutation as permuting whichever is not serially correlated and avoid destroying the serial correlation in the other. But if both are serially correlated, permutation will destroy this property, and we will be in the situation of processing pairings that could not occur in real life, a major sin.

Recall once more that a key tenet of permutation testing is that our permutations must have equal probability in real life if our model is worthless.

It's worth noting that this serial correlation restriction is not unique to permutation tests. This restriction is shared by virtually all standard statistical tests. The fact that some observations are dependent on other observations effectively reduces the degrees of freedom in the data, making tests behave as if there are fewer observations than there really are. This leads to an increased probability of rejecting the null hypothesis, the worst sort of error.

The Permutation Testing Algorithm

Most readers should be fairly clear by now on how a permutation test, often called a *Monte Carlo permutation test* (MCPT), is performed. However, we will now ensure the clarity of the informal presentation by stating the algorithm explicitly. In the following pseudocode, nreps is the total number of evaluations, including the original, unpermuted trial. Each trial results in a performance figure being found, with larger values implying better performance. If we are testing a fully specified trading system or predictive model, this is the performance obtained on an out-of-sample set. If we are testing our training process, this is the final (optimal) in-sample performance. If we are testing a model factory, this is the performance obtained by pooling all OOS folds. To be compatible with C++, zero origin is used for all array addressing.

```
for irep from 0 through nreps-1
    if (irep > 0)
        shuffle

    compute performance

    if (irep == 0)
        original_performance = performance
        count = 1
    else
        if (performance >= original_performance)
            count = count + 1

p-value = count / nreps
```

We compute the performance on the unshuffled data first and save this performance in original_performance. We also initialize our counter of the number of times a computed performance equals or exceeds the original performance. From then on we shuffle and evaluate the performance on shuffled data, incrementing the counter as indicated. The p-value is computed using the formula already seen several times, $(k+1)/(m+1)$, where k is the number of times a permuted value equals or exceeds the original value, and m is the number of permutations. We'll explore several programs demonstrating this algorithm at the end of this chapter.

Extending the Algorithm for Selection Bias

On page 124 we began an extended discussion of selection bias. If necessary, please review all of that material. Here we show how Monte Carlo permutation testing) can be extended to handle selection bias. To put this topic in context, here is a common scenario. We have several competing trading systems, say two or maybe hundreds. Perhaps they have been submitted by different developers for our consideration, or perhaps they are all the same basic model but with different trial parameter sets. In any event, we choose the best from among the competitors. There are two questions that this algorithm will answer.

1) The less important but still interesting question concerns the competitors taken individually. For each competitor (ignoring other competitors), what is the probability that we would have obtained performance as least as good as what we observed if that competitor were actually worthless? This is exactly the same question answered by the basic algorithm shown in the prior section, answered separately for each competitor.

2) The really important question concerns the best (highest performing) competitor. Suppose all of the competitors are worthless. If we test a large number of them, it is likely that at least one will be lucky and do well by sheer random chance. Thus, we cannot just determine which one is the best performer and then use what might be called its *solo* p-value, the probability that if it were worthless it would have done as well as it did by sheer luck.

CHAPTER 7   PERMUTATION TESTS

This is the p-value computed by the algorithm in the prior section. Such a test would be strongly prejudiced by the fact that we picked the best system. Of course, it's going to do well on a solo test! So, we have to answer a different question: if all the competitors are worthless, what is the probability that the *best* of them would have performed at least as well as what we observed? We might call this the *unbiased* p-value because it takes into account the bias induced by selecting the best competitor.

The algorithm for answering these two questions is shown here.

```
for irep from 0 through nreps-1

    if (irep > 0)
        shuffle

    for each competitor
        compute performance of this competitor
        if (irep == 0)
            original_performance[competitor] = performance
            solo_count[competitor] = 1 ;
            unbiased_count[competitor] = 1 ;
        else
            if (performance >= original_performance[competitor])
                solo_count[competitor] = solo_count[competitor] + 1

    if (irep > 0)
        best_performance = MAX ( performance of all competitors )
        for each competitor
            if (best_performance >= original_performance[competitor)
                unbiased_count[competitor] = unbiased_count[competitor] + 1

for all competitors
    solo_pval[competitor] = solo_count[competitor] / nreps
    unbiased_pval[competitor] = unbiased_count[competitor] / nreps
```

Readers should examine this algorithm and confirm that for each individual competitor, the solo_pval computed here is exactly the same as would be computed by the algorithm in the prior section for any individual competitor.

Note that this algorithm computes an unbiased_pval for every competitor. For each permutation, it finds the best performer and compares this to the score for each competitor, incrementing the corresponding counter accordingly. For whichever competitor had the best original performance, this is a perfect apples-to-apples comparison, best-to-best, and hence this is a correct p-value for the best performer. For all other competitors, this p-value is conservative; it is an upper bound for the true p-value. Thus, *any* competitor that has a small unbiased_pval is worthy of serious consideration.

Partitioning Total Return of a Trading System

Suppose you have just trained a market trading system, optimizing its parameters in such a way as to maximize a measure of performance. On page 286 we saw how a Monte Carlo permutation test could be used to gather information about whether the model is too weak (unable to find predictive patterns) or too strong (overfitting by mistaking noise for authentic patterns). We also saw ways to employ permutation testing to evaluate a completely specified model using OOS data and also a way to evaluate the quality of a trading-system factory. Now we look at one more interesting way to use permutation testing to gather information about the quality of a trading system. This method is not quite as rigorous as the prior tests, and its results should usually be taken with a liberal grain of salt. But its development reveals much about how seemingly good performance is obtained from a trading system, and the technique also provides one more indication of possible future performance.

Suppose we have just trained a trading system by adjusting its parameters so as to maximize a performance measure. We can roughly divide its total in-sample return into three components.

1) Our model (hopefully!) has learned legitimate *Skill* at detecting predictive patterns in the market history and thereby making intelligent trade decisions. This component of performance will likely continue into the future.

2) Our model has also mistaken some noise patterns as legitimate and thereby learned responses to patterns that, by definition, will not repeat. This component of performance, called *TrainingBias*, will not continue into the future.

3) If the market has an overall long-term trend (like most equity markets, which trend upward over the long term), most training algorithms will favor a position that takes advantage of the trend. In particular, it will favor long positions for up-trending markets and short positions for down-trending. This *Trend* component of performance will continue into the future for only as long as the trend continues.

This last component deserves more discussion, especially since it is the subject of controversy among some trading system developers. Imagine that you have trained a trading system (optimized its parameters) on two equity markets, individually. Market *A* has a strong uptrend over its training-set history, while market *B* ends its history at about the same price level as where it began. You find that the optimal parameters of your Market *A* trading system provide a great preponderance of long trades, while the optimal parameters for the system trained on Market *B* give about an equal number of long and short trades. It doesn't take Sherlock Holmes to deduce that the reason for the abundance of long trades in the system developed on Market *A* might have something to do with the fact that Market *A* enjoyed steady gains, while the long/short balance in the other system is due to the fact that Market *B* had no appreciable trend.

The big philosophical question is this: should we let the underlying long-term trend of a market exert that much influence on the long/short trade balance of a system we are designing? In my own experience, I have found that most trading system developers do so without even thinking about the issue. And I tend to agree with this philosophy; if a market has an obvious long-term trend, we might as well go with the flow instead of fighting a current by rowing upstream.

On the other hand, it is definitely worthwhile pondering the alternative. After all, who's to say that a long-term trend will continue, and what happens to a strongly unbalanced system if the trend reverses? This is one argument against letting a strongly trending market strongly influence our trade balance.

There's an even deeper way of looking at the issue. Suppose, for example, that we have a strongly uptrending market and that we have developed a long-only day-bar system that is in this market half of all trading days. Consider the fact that if we just flip a coin every day and take a long position when it comes up heads, we would also, on average, make a lot of money just from the trend. So one could easily argue that a trading system's "intelligence" should be measured by the degree to which it beats a hypothetical random trading system that has the same number of long and short positions.

It all boils down to a simple but fraught question. If your system makes a lot of money from a trend but can't beat a coin toss, is it really any good? One school of thought says that if it ties a profitable coin-toss system, it has no intelligence. Another school of thought says that the very fact that it was able to capitalize on a long-term trend is a sign of intelligence. Then the sage in the corner points out that the second argument falls apart if the trend reverses, while the first argument is more likely to hold up. Yet another voice pipes up from the shadows, pointing out that long-term trends generally persist over the, well, long term. And the argument goes on.

Regardless of your opinion, it's worthwhile to explore this issue further. As usual throughout this book, we regard returns as the log of changes. Let *MarketChange* be the total change over the extent of the market history in our training set. Under our definition of change, this is the log of the ratio of the final price to the first price. Let n be the number of individual price change returns (one less than the number of prices). Then we can define *TrendPerReturn* = *MarketChange* / n.

Some developers subtract this quantity from the return of every bar during optimization to remove the effect of trend on computed performance. (Of course, when computing indicators or anything else involved in making trade decisions, one would use the original prices. This correction is used only for computing performance measures such as return, profit factor, or Sharpe ratio.) This option can be applied to any of the trading systems used as examples in this book, and indeed virtually every trading system anyone could imagine. However, other than this brief mention, we will not pursue this idea further. At this time, we have a different use for trend.

What would be the expected total return of a random trading system having the same number of long and short positions as our trained system? For every individual price-change return during which we hold a long position, on average the trend will boost our return by *TrendPerReturn*. Conversely, for every one in which we hold a short position, our return will be decreased by *TrendPerReturn*. So, the net effect will be the difference in these position quantities.

In keeping with the nomenclature presented in the beginning of this section, we define the *Trend* component of the system's total return as shown in Equation 7-1.

$$Trend = (NumLong - NumShort) * TrendPerReturn \qquad (7\text{-}1)$$

Because we can compute *TrendPerReturn* from the market price history and because we know the position counts from the trained system, the *Trend* component of the system's total return can be explicitly computed.

Recall that the underlying premise for the material in this section is that the total return of our trained trading system is the sum of three components: legitimate skill, long/short imbalance that capitalizes on trend, and training bias (learning random noise as if it were real patterns). This is expressed in Equation 7-2.

$$TotalReturn = Skill + Trend + TrainingBias \qquad (7\text{-}2)$$

Suppose we were to randomly permute the market changes and retrain the system. The *TrendPerReturn* will remain the same because we're just mixing up the order of price changes, and we still have the same number of individual returns. But the number of long and short positions will likely change, so we have to use Equation 7-1 to compute the *Trend* component of the total return for this permuted run. Because the permutation is random, we have destroyed predictable patterns, so the *Skill* component is zero. Any total return over and above the *Trend* component is *TrainingBias*. In other words, we can compute the *TrainingBias* for this permuted run using Equation 7-3.

$$TrainingBias = PermutedTotalReturn - Trend \qquad (7\text{-}3)$$

Too much randomness is involved for a single such test to provide a useful estimate of the *TrainingBias* inherent in your proposed trading system and its training algorithm. But if we perform hundreds, or even thousands, of permutations and average the value computed by Equation 7-3, we can arrive at a generally respectable estimate for *TrainingBias*.

This lets us compute two extremely useful performance figures. First, we can compute an unbiased estimate of future return by subtracting the training bias from the total return of our system. This figure includes the *Trend* component of total return, appropriate if we hold to the philosophy that taking advantage of long-term trend is good. This is expressed in Equation 7-4.

$$UnbiasedReturn = TotalReturn - TrainingBias \qquad (7\text{-}4)$$

If we are also interested in the more restrictive definition of trading system intelligence, the degree to which our system can outperform a random system having the same number of long and short trades, we can estimate its *Skill* using Equation 7-5.

$$Skill = UnbiasedReturn - Trend \qquad (7\text{-}5)$$

We will explore a program that demonstrates this technique on page 310.

Essential Permutation Algorithms and Code

Before presenting complete programs that demonstrate the techniques discussed in this chapter, we'll focus on several of the key permutation algorithms that will be essential tools for this family of tests.

Simple Permutation

We begin with the basic permutation algorithm. This is the standard method for correctly permuting a vector, doing it in such a way that every possible permutation is equally likely. It requires a source of uniformly distributed random number in the range 0.0 <= unifrand() < 1.0. It is important to make sure that the random generator can never return exactly 1.0; if you cannot be sure of this, you must take appropriate action to ensure that an out-of-bound subscript is not generated. In the following code, the random j must be strictly less than i.

```
i = n ;              // Number remaining to be shuffled
while (i > 1) {      // While at least 2 left to shuffle
   j = (int) (unifrand () * i) ;
   --i ;
   itemp = indices[i] ;          // Swap elements i and j
   indices[i] = indices[j] ;
   indices[j] = itemp ;
   }
```

In this code, we initialize i to be the number of elements in the vector, and at each pass through the while() test, it will be the number remaining to be shuffled. We randomly select an index j that is equally likely to point to any of the elements yet to be shuffled. Decrement i so that it points to the last element in the aray that remains to be shuffled and swap elements j and i. Note that it is possible that j==i so that no swap takes place. We work backwards from the end of the array to the front, stopping only when we no longer have anything to swap.

Permuting Simple Market Prices

We jump to a slightly higher level of difficulty when we permute market prices. Obviously we can't just swap prices around. Imagine what would happen if we permuted decades of equity prices whose market history begins at 20 and ends at 800. So we have to deconstruct the price history into changes, permute the changes, and then reconstruct the permuted price history. Moreover, we can't permute simple *differences* in price, because differences at large price times are greater than differences at small price times. So, we compute the changes as ratios. Equivalently, we take the log of prices and permute the changes in logs.

Another complication is that we must exactly preserve the trend in the price history so that position imbalances are handled correctly. This is easy to do; we just keep the starting price the same. Since the reconstructed price series applies the same changes, just in a different order, we end up at the same price in the end. Only the ups and downs in the interior are changed.

The first step is to deconstruct the price history into changes. The following simple code assumes that the supplied prices are actually the log of the original prices. We must supply the work area changes, which is nc long. Note that the last element of changes is unused.

```
void prepare_permute (
   int nc ,               // Number of cases
   double *data ,         // Input of nc log prices
   double *changes        // Work area; returns computed changes
   )
{
   int icase ;

   for (icase=1 ; icase<nc ; icase++)
      changes[icase-1] = data[icase] - data[icase-1] ;
}
```

That preparation code needs to be done only once. From then on, any time we want to permute the (log) price history, we call the following routine:

```
void do_permute (
   int nc ,                    // Number of cases
   double *data ,              // Returns nc shuffled prices
   double *changes             // Work area; computed changes from prepare_permute
   )
{
   int i, j, icase ;
   double dtemp ;

   // Shuffle the changes. We do not include the first case in the shuffling,
   // as it is the starting price, so there are only nc-1 changes.

   i = nc-1 ;                  // Number remaining to be shuffled
   while (i > 1) {             // While at least 2 left to shuffle
     j = (int) (unifrand() * i) ;
     if (j >= i)              // Must not happen, be safe
       j = i - 1 ;
     --i ;
     dtemp = changes[i] ;
     changes[i] = changes[j] ;
     changes[j] = dtemp ;
     } // Shuffle the changes

   // Now rebuild the prices, using the shuffled changes

   for (icase=1 ; icase<nc ; icase++)
     data[icase] = data[icase-1] + changes[icase-1] ;
}
```

Recall that prepare_permute() left the last element in changes unused, so we have nc–1 changes to shuffle. We assume that the caller has not changed the first element in data, and we rebuild from there.

Permuting Multiple Markets with an Offset

As was pointed out earlier, if our trading system references multiple markets, we must permute them all the same way so that inter-market correlation is kept intact. Otherwise, we might end up with market changes that would be nonsensical in the real world, with some markets going up strongly while other markets with which they are highly correlated going down strongly. This lack of real-world conformity would be devastating, because a key tenet of Monte Carlo permutation testing is that all permutations must be equally likely if the null hypothesis is true.

To be able to do this, we must make sure that every market has a price on every date; any dates for which one or more markets have no price must be removed. In practice, if we stick with broadly traded markets, we generally lose few or no dates because they all trade on normal trading days. If markets are closed for a holiday, nothing trades, and if they are open for normal business, everything trades. Still, we must make sure that there is no missing data for any date, which would make simultaneous permutation impossible. A fast algorithm for doing this is as follows:

```
Initialize each market's current index to 0
Initialize the grand (compressed) index to 0
Loop
    Find the latest (largest) date at each market's current index across all markets
    Advance all markets' current index until the date reaches or passes this date
    If all markets have the same current date:
        Keep this date by copying market records to the grand index spot
        Advance each market's current index as well as the grand index
```

In the code that follows, we have the following:

- market_n[]: For each market, the number of prices present

- market_price[][]: For each market (first index) the prices (second index)

- market_date[][]: For each market (first index) the date of each price (second index)

- market_index[]: For each market, the index of the record currently being examined

- grand_index: The index of the current record in the compressed data

```
for (i=0 ; i<n_markets ; i++)        // Source markets all start at the first price
   market_index[i] = 0 ;
grand_index = 0 ;                     // Compressed data starts at first record

for (;;) {

   // Find max date at current index of each market

   max_date = 0 ;
   for (i=0 ; i<n_markets ; i++) {
      date = market_date[i][market_index[i]] ;
      if (date > max_date)
         max_date = date ;
      }

   // Advance all markets until they reach or pass max date
   // Keep track of whether they all equal max_date

   all_same_date = 1 ;                        // Flags if all markets are at the same date

   for (i=0 ; i<n_markets ; i++) {
      while (market_index[i] < market_n[i]) {  // Must not over-run a market!
         date = market_date[i][market_index[i]] ;
         if (date >= max_date)
            break ;
         ++market_index[i] ;
         }

      if (date != max_date)                   // Did some market jump over max?
         all_same_date = 0 ;

      if (market_index[i] >= market_n[i])     // If even one market runs out
         break ;                              // We are done
      }

   if (i < n_markets)                         // If even one market runs out
      break ;                                 // We are done

   // If we have a complete set for this date, grab it
```

```
if (all_same_date) {
  for (i=0 ; i<n_markets ; i++) {
    market_date[i][grand_index] = max_date ;  // Redundant, but clear
    market_price[i][grand_index] = market_price[i][market_index[i]] ;
    ++market_index[i] ;
    }
  ++grand_index ;
  }
}
```

n_cases = grand_index ;

We are now ready to consider the permutation of multiple markets. It will often be the case that we want to permute different sections of the market history separately. If we are permuting a single market, this is easily done by just offsetting the price in the calling parameter for the permutation routine. But when we have an entire array of markets, we can't do this, so we have to explicitly specify an offset distance.

Here is how the permutation will be done. We have nc cases from price index 0 through nc–1. Case offset is the first case that will change, and offset must be positive because the case at offset–1 is the "basis" case and remains unchanged. The last case examined is at nc–1, but it, too, will remain unchanged. Thus, the shuffled array starts and ends at the original prices. Only the interior prices change.

If a dataset is permuted in separate sections, the sections must not overlap. The "basis" case at offset–1 is included in the region that cannot overlap. For example, we could permute with offset=1 and nc=5. Cases 1 through 3 would then change, with the end cases (0 and 4) remaining unchanged. A subsequent permute must then begin at offset=5 or more. Case 4 is not changed by either permute operation.

Here is the preparation routine that must be called first and only once if multiple permutations are done:

```
void prepare_permute (
  int nc ,              // Number of cases total (not just starting at offset)
  int nmkt ,            // Number of markets
  int offset ,          // Index of first case to be permuted (>0)
  double **data ,       // Input of nmkt by nc price matrix
  double **changes      // Work area; returns computed changes
  )
```

```
{
  int icase, imarket ;

  for (imarket=0 ; imarket<nmkt ; imarket++) {
    for (icase=offset ; icase<nc ; icase++)
      changes[imarket][icase] = data[imarket][icase] - data[imarket][icase-1] ;
    }
}
```

The permutation is just a simple generalization of the single-market method shown in the prior section.

```
void do_permute (
  int nc ,              // Number of cases total (not just starting at offset)
  int nmkt ,            // Number of markets
  int offset ,          // Index of first case to be permuted (>0)\
  double **data ,       // Returns nmkt by nc shuffled price matrix
  double **changes      // Work area; computed changes from prepare_permute
  )
{
  int i, j, icase, imarket ;
  double dtemp ;

  // Shuffle the changes, permuting each market the same to preserve correlations

  i = nc-offset ;         // Number remaining to be shuffled
  while (i > 1) {         // While at least 2 left to shuffle
    j = (int) (unifrand() * i) ;
    if (j >= i)           // Should not happen, but be safe
      j = i - 1 ;
    --i ;

    for (imarket=0 ; imarket<nmkt ; imarket++) {
      dtemp = changes[imarket][i+offset] ;
      changes[imarket][i+offset] = changes[imarket][j+offset] ;
      changes[imarket][j+offset] = dtemp ;
      }
    } // Shuffle the changes

  // Now rebuild the prices, using the shuffled changes
```

```
for (imarket=0 ; imarket<nmkt ; imarket++) {
  for (icase=offset ; icase<nc ; icase++)
    data[imarket][icase] = data[imarket][icase-1] + changes[imarket][icase] ;
  }
}
```

Permuting Price Bars

Permuting price bars is considerably more involved than permuting a simple array of prices. There are four major issues to consider, and perhaps a few other more minor issues that may be relevant in some circumstances. These are important:

- We must never let the open or close be outside the range defined by the high and low of the bar. Even if our trading system ignores the high and low, violating this basic tent is bad karma.

- If our trading system examines the high and low of bars, we must not damage the statistical distribution of these quantities, either in regard to their relationship to the open and close or in regard to their spread. These quantities must have the same statistical properties after permutation as before.

- We must not damage the statistical distribution of the price change as we move from the open of the bar to the close. The distribution of open-to-close changes must be the same after permutation as before permutation.

- We must not damage the statistical distribution of the inter-bar gaps, the price change between the close of one bar and the open of the next bar. This is much more important than you might realize and easy to get wrong if you are not careful.

Satisfying the first three conditions is easy. We just define the high, low, and close in terms of the open. If we are (as usual) dealing with the log of prices, for each bar we compute and save the high minus the open, the low minus the open, and the close minus the open. Then, when we have a new opening price, we add these differentials to it to get the new high, low, and close, respectively. As long as we keep these trios of differences together (do not swap a high difference in one bar with a low difference in another bar), it should be obvious that the first condition is satisfied. And as long as our

305

permutation algorithm does not alter the statistical distribution of the open, it should be clear that the second and third conditions are satisfied. The fourth condition is the monkey wrench.

The intuitive way to permute bars is severely incorrect. Suppose we just permute the opens in the same way that we have been permuting single price arrays: compute the open-to-open changes, permute these changes, rebuild the array of opens, and use the "three differences" method just discussed to complete each bar. As already pointed out, the first three conditions are satisfied by this algorithm.

But here's the problem. Remember that most of the time, a bar opens very close to where the prior bar closed, often at exactly the same price. However, under this incorrect permutation algorithm, it will often happen that we will have an unfortunate combination of two common events: we have a large increase in the permuted open-to-open change, and the first bar has a large open-to-close drop in price. The result is a gigantic, completely unrealistic gap in the close-to-open change.

For example, we might have a bar that opens at 100 and closes at 98, not unrealistic. The next bar *should* open very near 98. But at the same time, the next permuted open might be 102, also not unrealistic. The result is a move from 98 to 102 just going from the close of one bar to the open of the next bar. The chance of this happening in real life is nearly zero. And of course, the opposite could happen as well: we have a bar with large upward movement open-to-close, while the permuted open-to-open move to the next bar is a large drop. The problems induced by this are not just theoretical; they will utterly destroy permutation testing of many trading systems. Real markets do not behave this way.

The solution to this problem is easy, though a bit messy. We split the (relatively large) intra-bar changes and the (mostly tiny) inter-bar changes into two separate series and permute each separately. When we rebuild the permuted series, we get each new bar in two steps. First, we use the permuted inter-bar change to move from the close of one bar to the open of the next. Then we use the permuted intra-bar change to move from the open to the close, picking up the high and low along the way.

In the code that appears soon, understand that the permutation routines will be called with the first bar on which a trade decision is possible. If there is a lookback, we assume that this has been taken into account.

The code that prepares for permutation is straightforward. As usual, we assume that all prices are actually log prices. If they are the real prices, we must use ratios rather than differences; otherwise, the algorithm is the same.

The first bar is the "base" bar, and it does not change at all. Subsequent bars will be generated from its close. As we will see when we examine the code, the close of the last bar will also remain unchanged. For each bar, rel_open is the gap between the prior close and the current open. The high, low, and close of the current bar are all relative to the open of the bar.

```
void prepare_permute (
   int nc ,                // Number of bars
   double *open ,          // Input of nc log prices
   double *high ,
   double *low ,
   double *close ,
   double *rel_open ,      // Work area; returns computed changes
   double *rel_high ,
   double *rel_low ,
   double *rel_close
   )
{
   int icase ;

   for (icase=1 ; icase<nc ; icase++) {
      rel_open[icase-1] = open[icase] - close[icase-1] ;
      rel_high[icase-1] = high[icase] - open[icase] ;
      rel_low[icase-1] = low[icase] - open[icase] ;
      rel_close[icase-1] = close[icase] - open[icase] ;
      }
}
```

The permutation routine has a parameter, preserve_OO, that needs special explanation. The vast majority of example trading systems in this book are based on a single price series, with trades being executed as market-on-close to the close of the next bar (possibly continuing on to the close of a subsequent bar). This can sometimes give slightly optimistic results, not to mention that it is tinged with a hint of being unrealistic and unobtainable in real life. A more conservative approach is to open a trade on the open of the bar following the trade decision. If we are partitioning the total return of the trading system as described beginning on page 294 and we want to be squeaky clean about how we define the total trend across the test period, we must define the trend by

the change from the first open after the earliest possible decision to the last open, and
we need this change to be the same for all permutations. (This is probably excessively
cautious, but it's easy to do, so we might as well.) For this difference to remain the same
for all permutations, we must not allow the first close-to-open change or the last open-
to-close change to take part in the permutation. Setting preserve_OO to any nonzero
number does this. With this in mind, here is the permutation code. First we shuffle the
close- to-open changes.

```
void do_permute (
   int nc ,                   // Number of cases
   int preserve_OO ,          // Preserve next open-to-open (vs first open to last close)
   double *open ,             // Returns nc shuffled log prices
   double *high ,
   double *low ,
   double *close ,
   double *rel_open ,         // Work area; input of computed changes
   double *rel_high ,
   double *rel_low ,
   double *rel_close
   )
{
   int i, j, icase ;
   double dtemp ;

   if (preserve_OO)
      preserve_OO = 1 ;

   i = nc-1-preserve_OO ;   // Number remaining to be shuffled
   while (i > 1) {           // While at least 2 left to shuffle
      j = (int) (unifrand() * i) ;
      if (j >= i)            // Should not happen, but be safe
         j = i - 1 ;
      --i ;
      dtemp = rel_open[i+preserve_OO] ;
      rel_open[i+preserve_OO] = rel_open[j+preserve_OO] ;
      rel_open[j+preserve_OO] = dtemp ;
      } // Shuffle the close-to-open changes
```

In the previous code, we note the effect of preserve_OO. If it is input zero, we shuffle all nc–1 close-to-open inter-bar changes. But if it is one, we have one less change to shuffle, and we offset all shuffling by one. This preserves the first inter-bar close-to-open change, meaning that the open of the second bar, which is the opening price of the first possible "next bar" trade, remains unchanged for all permutations.

Next we shuffle the intra-bar changes. We must shuffle the high, low, and close identically to preserve the high and low bounding the open and close. The effect of preserve_OO is slightly different here. Instead of preserving the first close-to-open change, it preserves the last open-to-close change. Because the last close is always preserved, allowing the last bar's open-to-close difference to change would change the open of the last bar.

```
i = nc-1-preserve_OO ; // Number remaining to be shuffled
while (i > 1) {      // While at least 2 left to shuffle
  j = (int) (unifrand() * i) ;
  if (j >= i)        // Should never happen, but be safe
    j = i - 1 ;
  --i ;
  dtemp = rel_high[i] ;
  rel_high[i] = rel_high[j] ;
  rel_high[j] = dtemp ;
  dtemp = rel_low[i] ;
  rel_low[i] = rel_low[j] ;
  rel_low[j] = dtemp ;
  dtemp = rel_close[i] ;
  rel_close[i] = rel_close[j] ;
  rel_close[j] = dtemp ;
  } // Shuffle the open-to-close changes
```

Rebuilding the price history using the shuffled changes is trivial.

```
for (icase=1 ; icase<nc ; icase++) {
  open[icase] = close[icase-1] + rel_open[icase-1] ;
  high[icase] = open[icase] + rel_high[icase-1] ;
  low[icase] = open[icase] + rel_low[icase-1] ;
  close[icase] = open[icase] + rel_close[icase-1] ;
  }
}
```

Example: P-Value and Partitioning

The file MCPT_TRN.CPP contains an example of computing a training p-value (pages 286 and 291) and total return partitioning (page 294) for a primitive moving-average crossover system trained on OEX. The program is executed with the following command:

MCPT_TRN MaxLookback Nreps FileName

Let's break this command down:

- MaxLookback: Maximum moving-average lookback

- Nreps: Number of MCPT replications (hundreds or thousands)

- FileName: Name of market file (YYYYMMDD Price)

The following Figures 7-1 and 7-2 is the output of this program when executed with the S&P 100 and S&P 500 indexes. It's fascinating what extremely different results are obtained. Please refer to the previously cited pages for detailed explanations of the computed quantities. An overview of the program's code begins on the next page.

```
8800 prices were read, 1000 MCP replications with max lookback = 300

p-value for null hypothesis that system is worthless = 0.1940
Total trend = 2.5517
Original nshort = 2160
Original nlong = 6340
Original return = 3.4073
Trend component = 1.2549
Training bias = 2.3851
Skill = -0.2326
Unbiased return = 1.0222
```

Figure 7-1. *Output of the MCPT_TRN program for OEX*

```
13963 prices were read, 1000 MCP replications with max lookback = 300

p-value for null hypothesis that system is worthless = 0.0010
Total trend = 3.6165
Original nshort = 6393
Original nlong = 7267
Original return = 8.8095
Trend component = 0.2313
Training bias = 2.6148
Skill = 5.9633
Unbiased return = 6.1946
```

Figure 7-2. *Output of the MCPT_TRN program with SPX*

The moving-average crossover system is the same as we have seen in prior examples. It computes short-term and long-term moving averages (where the lookbacks are optimizable) and takes a long position when the short term MA is above the long-term MA, and it takes a short position when the reverse is true. We focus here on computation of the performance figures.

First, we compute the total trend and divide it by the number of individual returns to get the trend per individual return. Remember that the first price on which a valid trade decision can be made is the "basis" price, with permutation beginning on the change from it to the next bar. By starting at this point, we ensure that all possible individual trade returns are subject to permutation, and we also guarantee that no change prior to a possible trade can be permuted into the mix, which could change the total trend. Then we call the preparation routine listed on page 299 to compute and save the price changes.

```
trend_per_return=(prices[nprices-1]-prices[max_lookback-1]) / (nprices-max_lookback) ;
prepare_permute ( nprices-max_lookback+1 , prices+max_lookback-1 , changes ) ;
```

In the MCP loop, we permute on all but the first pass. We will need the number of long and short returns from the optimized system to compute the trend component. For the first, unpermuted trial save all "original" results.

```
for (irep=0 ; irep<nreps ; irep++) {
  if (irep)   // Shuffle
    do_permute ( nprices-max_lookback+1 , prices+max_lookback-1 , changes ) ;

  opt_return = opt_params ( nprices , max_lookback , prices ,
                        &short_lookback , &long_lookback , &nshort , &nlong ) ;
  trend_component = (nlong - nshort) * trend_per_return ;  // Equation 7-1 on page 297

  if (irep == 0) {        // This is the original, unpermuted trial
    original = opt_return ;
    original_trend_component = trend_component ;
    original_nshort = nshort ;
    original_nlong = nlong ;
    count = 1 ;   // Algorithm on Page 291
    mean_training_bias = 0.0 ;
    }
```

```
  else {        // This is a permuted trial
    training_bias = opt_return - trend_component ;        // Equation 7-3 on page 297
    mean_training_bias += training_bias ;                 // Average across permutations
    if (opt_return >= original)                           // Algorithm on Page 291
      ++count ;
    }
  }    // For all replications

mean_training_bias /= (nreps - 1) ;                       // First trial was unpermuted
unbiased_return = original - mean_training_bias ;         // Equation 7-4 on page 297
skill = unbiased_return - original_trend_component ;      // Equation 7-5 on page 297
```

Example: Training with Next Bar Returns

The file MCPT_BARS.CPP contains a demonstration program that does the same p-value computation and total return partitioning as the prior example. However, instead of using a single price series, the price data is day bars (although it could be bars of any length). Moreover, it uses a more conservative method for computing returns. The return of each trade decision is the (log) price change from the open of the next bar to the open of the following bar. Finally, it is a different trading system, a simple mean-reversion strategy rather than moving-average crossover. The program is invoked with the following command:

MCPT_BARS MaxLookback Nreps FileName

Let's break this command down:

- MaxLookback: Maximum moving-average lookback

- Nreps: Number of MCPT replications (hundreds or thousands)

- FileName: Name of market file (YYYYMMDD Open High Low Close)

Figure 7-3 shows the output of this program for the S&P 100 index, and Figure 7-4 shows it for S&P 500.

```
8800 prices were read, 2000 MCP replications with lookback = 3000

p-value for null hypothesis that system is worthless = 0.0565
Total trend = 1.6227
Original nlong = 2053
Original return = 1.4830
Trend component = 0.5746
Training bias = 0.2846
Skill = 0.6238
Unbiased return = 1.1984
```

Figure 7-3. Output of the MCPT_BARS program for OEX

```
13963 prices were read, 2000 MCP replications with lookback = 3000

p-value for null hypothesis that system is worthless = 0.9935
Total trend = 3.2406
Original nlong = 443
Original return = 0.3023
Trend component = 0.1310
Training bias = 0.3083
Skill = -0.1369
Unbiased return = -0.0060
```

Figure 7-4. Output of the MCPT_BARS program for SPX

As with the prior example, we see a profound difference in performance in these two markets. It's not at all surprising that, in any market, a primitive trend-following system such as MA XOVER would perform very differently from a mean reversion system. But what is surprising is how incredibly differently they perform in these two markets that would seem to be similar in composition. In fact, the p-value for SPX is almost 1.0, a stunning value. Clearly, this market is *anti*-mean-reversion! This would certainly square with this market's trend-following p-value of 0.001, the minimum possible with 1000 replications, an equally stunning value. But wow. I mean, wow. The only other consideration is that the SPX market used in this example starts its history several decades earlier(1962) than the OEX market (1982), so earlier data may play a role. Plotting an equity curve of each system in each market would be most revealing. If you beat me to it, send me an email.

Because this trading system uses a slightly different method for computing returns, it's worth examining both the system itself and the associated MCPT code. We begin with the trading system. It computes a simplistic long-term trend as the current close minus the close a user-specified fixed number of bars earlier. This is typically a large number, a thousand or several thousand bars. It also looks at the current price drop, the (log) price of the prior bar minus that of the current bar. If the long-term trend is above an optimizable threshold and the price drop is also above its own optimizable threshold, a long position is taken for the next bar. The philosophy behind this system is that a sudden sharp drop in the price of an uptrending market is a temporary aberration that will be corrected on the next bar. Here is the calling convention for this subroutine:

```
double opt_params (      // Returns total log profit starting at lookback
  int ncases ,           // Number of log prices
  int lookback ,         // Lookback for long-term rise
  double *open ,         // Log of open prices
  double *close ,        // Log of close prices
  double *opt_rise ,     // Returns optimal long-term rise threshold
  double *opt_drop ,     // Returns optimal short-term drop threshold
  int *nlong             // Number of long returns
  )
```

We will use best_perf to keep track of the best total return. The outermost pair of loops try a large variety of thresholds for the long-term uptrend and the immediate price drop.

```
best_perf = -1.e60 ;                // Will be best performance across all trials
for (irise=1 ; irise<=50 ; irise++) {      // Trial long-term rise
  rise_thresh = irise * 0.005 ;
  for (idrop=1 ; idrop<=50 ; idrop++) {   // Trial short-term drop
    drop_thresh = idrop * .0005 ;
```

Given this pair of trial thresholds, we pass through the valid market history and cumulate the total return. We also count the number of long positions taken, because we will need this to compute the trend component. We begin this cumulation at the lookback distance, as we will need this much history to compute the long-term trend. We must stop two bars before the end of the dataset because the conservatively computed return for a trade is the (log) price change from the open of the bar *after* the decision is made, to the open of the following bar.

```
total_return = 0.0 ;   // Cumulate total return for this trial
nl = 0 ;               // Will count long positions

for (i=lookback ; i<ncases-2 ; i++) {    // Compute performance across history

  rise = close[i] - close[i-lookback] ;   // Long-term trend
  drop = close[i-1] - close[i] ;          // Immediate price drop
```

```
    if (rise >= rise_thresh  &&  drop >= drop_thresh) {
      ret = open[i+2] - open[i+1] ;          // Conservative return
      ++nl ;
      }
    else
      ret = 0.0 ;

    total_return += ret ;
    } // For i, summing performance for this trial
```

All that remains is the trivial bookkeeping task of keeping track of the optimal parameters and their associated results.

```
    if (total_return > best_perf) {  // Did this trial param set break a record?
      best_perf = total_return ;
      *opt_rise = rise_thresh ;
      *opt_drop = drop_thresh ;
      *nlong = nl ;
      }

    } // For idrop
  } // For irise

  return best_perf ;
}
```

The general actions of the permutation tests are identical to those in the prior section. However, because we are computing returns using the open of the next two bars, offsets are a little different. The definition of lookback in this system is also slightly different from the max_lookback of the prior system, so that also introduces some differences. Consider the trend per return and the preparation routine. The first trade decision can be made at the bar with index lookback, so we call prepare_permute() with this offset to all four price arrays. This bar will remain fixed; permutation starts at the next bar, which is also where trade returns start. A total of nprices–lookback bars are available to the permutation routine. The first possible trade can open at bar lookback+1 and close at the open of the last bar, nprices–1.

```
trend_per_return = (open[nprices-1] - open[lookback+1]) / (nprices - lookback - 2) ;

prepare_permute ( nprices-lookback , open+lookback , high+lookback ,
          low+lookback , close+lookback , rel_open , rel_high , rel_low , rel_c lose ) ;
```

All remaining computations are identical to what we saw in the prior section, so there is no point in repeating them here. And of course, the complete source code is available in MCPT_BARS.CPP.

Example: Permuting Multiple Markets

On page 179 we examined the program whose code is available in CHOOSER.CPP. In that section we focused on how to use nested walkforward to get out-of-sample returns in a selection-bias situation. Permutation was ignored then. Now we return to that program, focusing this time on the permutation test that evaluates the probability that OOS results at least as good as those obtained could have been obtained by random good luck. Note that this is *not* the selection-bias-permutation algorithm shown on page 292. No example of that algorithm is given in this book, as it is a straightforward extension of the simpler algorithm and well documented in the flow chart. Numerous source code examples of this algorithm can be found in my book *Data Mining Algorithms in C++*. The real purpose of this section is to provide an example of permuting multiple markets simultaneously to evaluate a multiple-market trading system, as well as demonstrating how permutation should be split into segments in a walkforward situation that contains selection.

The multiple-market permutation routines were discussed in detail starting on page 301, and it wouldn't hurt to review that section. For convenience, here is the calling list for prepare_permute(); that for do_permute() is identical:

```
void prepare_permute (
   int nc ,              // Number of cases total (not just starting at offset)
   int nmkt ,            // Number of markets
   int offset ,          // Index of first case to be permuted (>0)
   double **data ,       // Input of nmkt by nc price matrix
   double **changes      // Work area; returns computed changes
   )
```

We already saw an example of splitting market history into permutation groups using a simple walkforward situation. Our motivation was the fact that the initial training fold does not appear in any OOS fold in the original, unpermuted run. Thus, we must ensure that this is also the case for the permuted trials, in case that initial period contains data that is unusual in trend, volatility, or some other important property. We must not allow any unusual data to leak into a permuted OOS fold.

The situation is more complex when we are doing nested walkforward, as in the CHOOSER program. Now we have *two* OOS folds to deal with. These are the two quantities we will have to consider:

> IS_n: Although no actual training occurs at the outer level of walkforward nesting in CHOOSER, this is the number of cases that play the role of "training set" in the program. Of particular importance in the context of permutation is the fact that in the original, unpermuted trial, none of these cases will ever appear in either level of OOS fold results. Thus, these cases must never be allowed to permute into future OOS folds and potentially contaminate them with unusual changes.

> OOS1_n: This is the number of cases in the inner level of walkforward OOS folds. The outer OOS folds, those in which we are ultimately interested because they are fully OOS, begin after IS_n+OOS1_n cases. The cases in the first inner walkforward OOS fold, those from IS_n up to (but not including) IS_n+OOS1_n, must not permute into the outer folds, because they are not there in the unpermuted trial.

With these thoughts in mind, we split the market history into three separate segments and permute each separately. It is an open question as to the wisdom (or lack thereof) of permuting the first "training" fold in general. I choose to do so here, primarily for pedagogical purposes, though I am not aware of any pros or cons. My own opinion, unsupported by any facts, is that on average it makes no difference one way or the other.

The first line of the following code prepares to permute this first "training" fold, perhaps unnecessarily. The second line handles the first inner OOS fold, and the last line handles the outer OOS fold area, which is our area of ultimate interest. For permutation, the do_permute() routine is called with the same parameters. All other operation is identical to what we have seen before.

```
prepare_permute( IS_n, n_markets, 1 , market_close , permute_work ) ;
prepare_permute( IS_n+OOS1_n, n_markets , IS_n, market_close , permute_work ) ;
prepare_permute( n_cases, n_markets , IS_n+OOS1_n, market_close, permute_work);
```

We now reproduce the output of this program that was presented earlier, before permutation tests had been discussed. The meanings of the computed p-values should now be clear.

```
Mean =    8.7473
```

```
25200 * mean return of each criterion, p-value, and percent of times
chosen...
```

```
    Total return    17.8898    p=0.076    Chosen 67.8 pct
    Sharpe ratio    12.9834    p=0.138    Chosen 21.1 pct
    Profit factor   12.2799    p=0.180    Chosen 11.1 pct
```

```
25200 * mean return of final system = 19.1151 p=0.027
```

Observe that the p-values for the three individual performance criteria are only moderately significant, with *Total return* being the best at 0.076. But for the final algorithm that uses nested walkforward to test not only market selection but performance criterion selection as well, the p-value of 0.027 is quite impressive.

Index

Printed in the United States
By Bookmasters